Yé-Yé Girls
of '60s FRENCH POP

Feral House
1240 W. Sims Way
Suite 124
Port Townsend, WA 98368
feralhouse.com

Book design by Gregg Einhorn

ISBN 978-1936239719

Printed in China

10 9 8 7 6 5 4 3 2 1

Yé-Yé Girls
of '60s FRENCH POP

BY
JEAN-EMMANUEL
DELUXE

FERAL HOUSE

For Vanda, Fifi, Helene and Véronique,
Les Filles de la Pop!
(Yé-yé girls, freakbeat goddesses,
and classy chanteuses in 1960s France and beyond)

Contents

162.079 MCE

JE NE SAIS RIEN

ELSA

IL SE FAIT TARD

DIS POURQUOI MOI, DIS-MOI POURQUOI MOI, DIS

RENDEZ-VOUS CHEZ POPOFF

Mercury RECORDS

BACH YEN

A BAS LA RENTREE
MOI JE T'AIME * * *
TE FACH' PAS *
METS TON BLUE·JEAN
JOHNNY * * * * * *

Polydor
27 061 Médium

211128 M

patricia carli

accompagnée par
JEAN BOUCHÉTY
et son orchestre

NOUS ON S'AIME
VIRGINIA
JE NE VOUDRAIS PAS PLEURER
JE TE PRÉVIENS

bel air

GEORGIA

moi j'en ai marre

disques vogue
MONO STEREO
V. 45. 1793

LILIANE SAINT PIERRE

nous resterons unis

dieu seul sait

DISQUES FLECHE
CF 14

MEDIUM 152.038 MCE

2C008-14850M

ANNE VANDERLOVE

Ballade en novembre
Les petits cafés

EMI
PATHE
ALBUM DOUBLE 284

agnès loti

C'EST TOI MON IDOLE
JE PARS SANS REGRET
ET
MAIS PEUT-ÊTRE

AZ
EP 954

FAIS COMME TU VOUDRAS
EST-CE QUE TU ME VOIS, DIS?
TU ES ROMANTIQUE . CETTE FOIS

annie markan

Mercury RECORDS

CATHERINE RIBEIRO

La Solitude

Poème non épique

JACQUELINE
taïeb

7 heures du matin
Bienvenue au pays
Ce soir je m'en vais
La plus belle chanson du monde

impact
IMP 200008 M

tiny yong

- TINY
- LA NUIT EST A NOUS
- LE SAUVAGE
- ADIEU BONNE CHANCE

BELTER

FOREWORD

THESE GIRLS ARE THE MOST LEGITIMATE OF THE POP children. Before stealing the world's stages they were the muses, the inspirations without whom none of the unstoppable songs that our male idols offered us would have had the same gourmet flavor. If the Beatles had offered us *Sgt. Pepper* without the "She loves you, yeah…" from the beginning, we wouldn't have had as much fun. The joyous hysteria, the tsunami of girls at every appearance, this wind of freedom would have been unthinkable without the sexy songs of the French girls. Lightness, grace in most the trivial things, and a dramatic oomph are the girls' privilege and pop's quintessence. These girls ARE pop. They invite the boys into their candy world, offer themselves before extracting themselves, playfully, from their suspenders to their bra straps, which they use as their swing.

Lio

sophie daumier

27 239 Medium

Polydor

ISABELLE AUBRET
LES AMANTS DE VERONE
NO MAN'S LAND
POUR AIMER IL FAUT ETRE TROIS

Polydor
27 172 Médium

70 345

DALIDA

accompagnée par
RAYMOND LEFÈVRE
et son orchestre

ITSI BITSI, PETIT BIKINI
(Itsy bitsy teenie weenie
yellow polkadot bikini)

BRAS DESSUS, BRAS DESSOUS
(Why)

O SOLE MIO

NI CHAUD, NI FROID
(Johnny kissed a girl)

France Gall

INTRODUCTION

In spite of its light-as-a-bubble appearance, pop music can tell us more than many a sociological essay.

Take, for instance, one of the songs Serge Gainsbourg penned for France Gall, "Baby Pop" (1966):

Sur l'amour tu te fais des idées
  (You get ideas about love)
Un jour ou l'autre c'est obligé
  (One of these days you'll end up)
Tu seras une pauvre gosse
  (As one poor kid)
Seule et abandonnée
  (Alone and forsaken)
Tu finiras par te marier
  (You'll have to get married)

Peut-être même contre ton gré
  (Maybe even against your will)
À la nuit de tes noces
  (On your wedding night)
Il sera trop tard pour
  (It'll be too late)
Le regretter
  (For you to regret)
Chante, danse Baby pop
  (Sing and dance, Baby pop)
Comme si demain Baby pop
  (As if tomorrow, Baby pop)
Ne devais jamais Baby pop
  (Would never, Baby pop)
Jamais revenir
  (Never have to come back)
Chante, danse Baby pop
  (Sing and dance, Baby pop)
Comme si demain Baby pop
  (As if tomorrow, Baby pop)
Au petit matin Baby pop
  (In the early morning)
Tu devais mourir
  (You just had to die)

The disastrous fate of thousands of carefree teeny-boppers was never better exposed than it is here, on the A-side of a successful single. The lyrics provide a cruel inside view of the ephemerality of youth: many youngsters of that time would very soon embrace the sadness of adult life and leave the lights of the Bus Palladium (*the* club in the mid-sixties) behind for good. We're talking pre-May '68 here, and despite the steps (albeit small) women had achieved toward equality, most female teenagers knew what they were expected to do: conform, as their own mothers did, to the views of a (still) very patriarchal society indeed.

The evolution of the status of youth, its subcultures, and its rites of passage are all reflected in the music industry. The condition of women has evolved, decade after decade, as clothes and music have evolved. More to the point: the latter can be seen as structures that allow us to analyze the evolution of morals and the place of women in society. Let's take two examples: first, in 1965, when France Gall sang the infamous "Sucettes (À L'Anis)," a hymn to oral sex in the guise of innocent praise for lollipops:

Annie aime les sucettes
    (Annie loves lollipops)
Les sucettes à l'anis
    (Anise-flavored lollipops)
Les sucettes à l'anis
    (Annie's anise lollipops)
D'Annie
Donnent à ses baisers
    (Give her kisses)
Un goût ani-
    (A real taste of Ani-)
sé lorsque le sucre d'orge
    (-se as the barley sugar)
Parfumé à l'anis
    (Anise-flavored)

Coule dans la gorge d'Annie
    (Pours into Annie's throat)
Elle est au paradis
    (She's in heaven)

Fifteen years later, Lio sang more or less the same thing on "Banana Split," with music by Jay Alanski and lyrics by Jacques Duvall:

Baisers givrés sur les
    (Frozen kisses on)
Montagnes blanches
    (Snowy mountains)
Na na na
On dirait que les choses
    (Seems things)
Se déclenchent
    (Are going to start)
Na na na
La chantilly s'écroule
    (Whipped cream is falling down)
En avalanche
    (In an avalanche)
Na na na

And in between these two huge hits by two icons of French pop music? May '68, the first oil crisis, the women's lib movement, the abortion laws, coming of age at eighteen, gay and lesbian activists (the FAHR, the Gazolines). Glam, punk, new wave. The end of the Vietnam war, the Six-Day War, General de Gaulle's and Pompidou's deaths, the second TV channel (in color!), then the third. Scorsese and Coppola's New Hollywood, then a return to the serials of yesteryear, such as *Star Wars*.

If I've gone through such a long list, it's to insist on the fact that the two smash hits I'm mentioning serve as a good introduction to the zeitgeist of the periods in which they were written. Both tried, odd as it may seem, to match the mood and preoccupations at the time. One has to have intuition (or be completely unconscious of the consequences, which is often the same thing) to write a song that will help define its time and become a standard. And of course, one needs a singer who corresponds to an archetype of the era itself. France Gall in 1965 and Lio in 1980 were indeed miles apart: Gall gentle and naïve, and Lio a Girl Power pop-feminist singer.

Studying what the girls in pop music have achieved since the 1960s, it's shocking to discover how the ways women express themselves have changed. However, it'd be a huge misunderstanding to think that the female pop singers of fifty years ago were mere puppets, prompt to follow the orders they were given without questioning. Jacqueline Taïeb was a true songwriter, as was Françoise Hardy—and Stella's humor was as sharp as Jacques Dutronc's. Contrary to popular belief, girl bands didn't start with Les Calamités in the mid-eighties. In the 1960s, groups such as OP4, Les Fizz, Les Gam's, or Les Milady's had no reason to envy their male counterparts.

Nonetheless, female artistic directors, sound engineers, and arrangers are pretty scarce in music companies, even today. Although the number of female songwriters has become more and more important as the years go by, it's still risky for a woman to be fully independent in the pop music business. This has been confirmed to me by all the artists I talked with for this book, whatever their age, whatever period their career was at its peak. Starting with cute little songs for teenage daydreams, you can arrive at the same conclusion as essayists and philosophers: it is definitely, as Pierre Bourdieu (and James Brown) said, "a man's, man's world"!

This book does not aim to be an exhaustive treatment of women in French pop music. It is mainly intended to provide insight into what Gallic artists have to offer the genre, especially as such artists are fairly unknown outside French territory, with the noticeable exception of the usual suspects: Brigitte Bardot, France Gall, Françoise Hardy, Jane Birkin, or, some years later, Vanessa Paradis. However, taking a walk on the less-trodden paths and discovering the likes of Stella, Lio, Jil Caplan, Helena Noguerra, or Fifi Chachnil can be just as gratifying.

April March, whose "Chick Habit," a cover of Gall's "Laisse Tomber Les Filles" gained her a wider audience through its inclusion in Quentin Tarantino's *Death Proof*, Laetitia Sadier (Stereolab), Françoise Cactus (ex-Lolitas and Stereo Total), Fabienne Delsol, Yasuharu Konishi, and Maki Nomiya of Pizzicato Five: for fifteen years or so, from New York to London, Tokyo to Berlin, punk, indie rock, and electro artists have been rediscovering this Francophile heritage and adapting it to the tastes of the day.

Already in the 1960s, Petula Clark, Sandie Shaw, and Marianne Faithfull released songs especially for the French market. Françoise Hardy was known in Britain and the States as "the yé-yé girl from Paris," got her picture taken with Mick Jagger, and had Bob Dylan totally smitten with her. Zouzou from Montmartre was dating Brian Jones and hanging out in trendy clubs with the Beatles or the Byrds. Nancy Sinatra (and many others) adapted Gilbert Bécaud's

Françoise Hardy

"Je T'Appartiens (Let It Be Me)" and had hits. Our *filles de la pop* were clearly more exportable than male French rockers such as Johnny Hallyday.

In the 1980s, Lio was very close to working with the Human League, and recorded *Suite Sixteen* with Sparks. Her "Banana Split" was adapted into English and became the irresistibly kitsch "Marie-Antoinette":

It's the economy, it's really bad, na na na.
What do they want of me?
I'm really mad, na na na.
Let them eat pizza, let them eat cake.
Na na na na na na na na na...

A French woman in exile in New York's no-wave 1980s, Lizzy Mercier Descloux, created new wave world music before the term was even coined (she's the songwriter on "Mais Où Sont Passées Les Gazelles?", recorded in Soweto). In 1987, a fourteen-year-old Lolita, Vanessa Paradis, had a worldwide number-one hit single with "Joe Le Taxi" (even the Reid brothers from Jesus & Mary Chain, seemingly light years away from this kind of music, proclaimed their love for the song). Paradis went on to release a Motown-influenced record sung entirely in English in 1992, then married Johnny Depp, and appeared on the front pages of cheap newspapers and gossip magazines throughout the world.

Let's not forget Elli and Jacno's Stinky Toys, the first French punk band who played the 100 Club in London in 1976, and ended up on the cover of *Melody Maker*. The duet eventually moved on to minimalist but classy electropop in the early '80s, composing the soundtrack for Eric Rohmer's best-known film, *Les Nuits De La Pleine Lune (Full Moon In Paris)*.

This is all to show the subterranean influence of French *filles de la pop* on some of the strongest currents of international pop music. According to April March, such flavor is due to its unique blend of Anglo-Saxon rhythms and continental sensitivity. The subjects French women dared to sing about in the 1960s were much more adventurous than those chosen by their English or American counterparts: the pleasures of fellatio, stories of bad LSD trips (Gall's "Teeny Weeny Boppy"), or more generally speaking, sheer enjoyment of the most sullen moments of existence (nearly all of Hardy's stuff).

Today, because of the changes in production and distribution, female French singers tend to think more globally: Helena Noguerra (who's half French and half Belgian) is probably going to sing exclusively in English on her next album, while the American Francophile April March is currently working with French band Aquaserge. The differences are being blurred, identity is becoming multiple, and the choices are much wider after more than forty years of struggle in a sexist business.

But let's not be unfair: there were (and still are) men who mentor and encourage female artists. To name but a few: Jacques Dutronc, Étienne Daho, Jacno, Jacques Duvall, Jay Alanski, Bertrand Burgalat, Olivier Libaux, and Marc Collin. And, of course, Serge Gainsbourg.

And now I'll leave you to explore this panorama of Gallic girly pop. I hope that through this book you'll come to share my passion for these extraordinary women!

Annie Philippe in
Mademoiselle Age Tendre

1
THE 1960s

Panorama

IN FRANCE, THE GENERATION OF BABY BOOMERS born after World War II was the first not to have known war. Like most European nations at the time, France was totally focused on reconstruction. The United States was endowed with the prestige of liberators, and French youth fantasized about the American way of life. Coca-Cola, chocolate bars, nylon stockings, flaming automobiles, chewing gum, Hollywood films, comics, and jazz were like promises of a better world, far from the hardships of everyday life. American military bases all around French territory had a real influence too: rock 'n' roll, imported thanks to American soldiers, stormed a nation dominated by rural traditions and the overwhelming presence of French *chanson*.

As for the intellectuals of the elite, they were only interested in jazz, and despised these new binary rhythms, which sounded too simplistic to their ears.

See, for instance, how Boris Vian and his accomplice Henri Salvador recorded dozens of parodies of rock songs under the *noms de plume* Vernon Sinclair and Henry Cording. Quincy Jones himself was hired later on to play the trumpet on their "Blouse Du Dentiste." In the land of Edith Piaf and Charles Trenet, rock was then only envisioned as a caricature of more serious things.

In the States, it was a means for teenagers to rebel against the authority of their parents. But in France, adults were keeping a watchful eye on things, at least at first. As early as 1956, orchestras led by mature professionals were diluting rock into a mish-mash of light, exotic music, as Rockin' Harry & His Bros did with "Faut Pas M' Enerver" or Dick Rasurel & Ses Berlurons did on "Tu M'As Laissé Tomber." Alfred de Ferry's "Rock," and Barendse's "T'as L' Bonjour d'Alfred" wallowed in the lowest form of Gallic humor just to have a good laugh at rock 'n' rollers. Rock was looked down upon, and more often than not mixed with Bastille Day accordions, cha-cha-cha, and paso doble.

Magali Noël is the first woman to have sung rock 'n' roll in France. She was discovered playing archetypal pinup types for directors Jules Dassin (*Rififi*), Henri Decoin (*The Case Of Poisons*), and Fellini (La *Dolce Vita*). Her rendition of Vian's "Fais-Moi Mal Johnny" played a major part in the song's success. The lyrics, very daring for the time, advocated *l'amour vache*, that is, sado-masochistic relationships:

> *Fais-moi mal, Johnny, Johnny, Johnny*
>   *(Hurt me badly, Johnny, Johnny, Johnny)*
> *Envole-moi au ciel...zoum!*
>   *(Send me to the heavens...zoom!)*
> *Fais-moi mal, Johnny, Johnny, Johnny*
>   *(Hurt me badly, Johnny, Johnny, Johnny)*
> *Moi j'aim' l'amour qui fait boum!*
>   *(I'm one who loves the love that*
>   *goes "boom!")*

Looking like a student in a business school, singer Richard Anthony was one of the first youngsters (supposedly; he was in fact much older than he pretended) to have Paul Anka, rather than Elvis Presley, as a role model. His cover version of "Three Cool Cats" by Leiber and Stoller, called "Nouvelle Vague" (new wave) was very influential. Meanwhile, Johnny Hallyday had gained status as the *"idole des jeunes"* (the kids' idol) since the very early sixties, at the expense of Vince Taylor, who was more of a purist.

June 22, 1963 marked a milestone in rock assimilation for French youth. On that day, a concert at the Nation (a square in Paris), initiated by the radio show and magazine *Salut Les Copains*, gathered no less than 150,000 teenagers, screaming their heads off to the sounds of Danyel Gérard, Mike Shannon, Les Chats Sauvages, Les Gam's, Richard Anthony, and the trendy young couple of the day, Johnny Hallyday and Sylvie Vartan. About five hundred *"blousons noirs"* (teds in leather jackets) crashed the party, and caused chaos that the police were unable to end for hours. Chairs were broken, shop windows smashed, innocent girls chased around.

The media, of course, were as stunned as the general public: France was discovering its young people existed and wanted to have their say! Here are a few quotes from the time:

> Pierre Charpy (*Paris-Presse*):
> "It's now time for the yobs!"

> Philippe Bouvard (*Le Figaro*):
> "What is the difference between the twist in Vincennes and Hitler's speeches at the Reichstag?"

> General de Gaulle:
> "These youngsters seem to have so much energy to spend. Let's have them build roads!"

Back in 1961, Vince Taylor's concert at the Palais des Sports had also ended in total confusion. The venue looked like a hurricane had struck, the *blousons noirs* having smashed to pieces all of the chairs and anything else they could break. At the time, the presenter of the state TV (ORTF) finished his diatribe against rock 'n' roll aficionados with the words: "Why should you complain, monsieur Vince Taylor, you must have a responsibility in all this, mustn't you?"

Vince Taylor's destiny is typical of France's approach to rock music. Born Brian Maurice Holden in England, he would have been one of the many contestants of the rock game had he stayed in Britain or moved to the States. In France, being a kind of rock 'n'roll purist who sang in English with suggestive attitudes, clad in black leather with motorbike chains around his neck and waist, he was an object of passion who triggered his audience's fantasies. His radical behavior (which was quite new at the time) earned him cult status among young rebels, and made the conservative majority see him as an enemy.

French showbiz types and the media preferred to support one Johnny Hallyday, who sang comprehendible French lyrics, wore clean-cut suits, and was willing to soften his repertoire whenever he was asked to do so. In the mid-sixties, Vince Taylor's downfall was mainly due to his strong LSD habit, leading him on mystical trips from which he never returned. David Bowie, who met him during the Swinging London years, drew inspiration from this dark angel with kohl under his eyes to create Ziggy Stardust.

Adults had thus won the first leg: French rock had to obey the strict rules of censorship, which were clearly influenced by both the Communist Party, who saw rock music as a pretext for a further Yankee invasion encouraged by the bourgeoisie, and the Catholic lobby, who believed that such music led to moral depravity.

Let's go back to that night of June 22, 1963, and the consequences it had. Some days later, in the well-respected daily *Le Monde*, sociologist Edgar Morin evoked the importance of *Salut Les Copains* and its boss Daniel Filipacchi, who had become the youth press tycoon overnight. Unexpectedly, Morin was in no way mocking the sweet madness that had revealed the youngsters to themselves. Better, he was trying to explain how it would be a huge mistake to neglect such passion and appeal. He coined the term "yé-yé" to depict this new music, which was replacing the rock of the pioneers, pushing to the front "nice fellows and gals" such as Hallyday, Vartan, Hardy, Sheila, and Petula Clark.

Serge Gainsbourg would later sneer at this movement by calling these musicians "original versions without originality—mere O [zeros, nothings] without the V." Besides the play on words, Gainsbourg contributed to installing in both the purists' and the general public's opinions the idea that the work of the yé-yés had no worth at all. Following Morin's article, "yé-yé" replaced both "rock" and "pop" in people's minds and vocabularies. The yé-yé wave can be seen as a kind of allegory for the era known as the *Trente Glorieuses* (the postwar economic boom), during which people believed in modernity, in plastic things, in fashion and the vigor of youth. An era filled to the brim with optimism and faith in the future. A future that looked more like *Star Trek*'s very first episodes than like a gloomy *Blade Runner*. Carefree and candy-colored, yé-yé music became, in hindsight, an oasis of exotic freshness designed to cheer people up.

Demographics were changing, and the boomers born after 1945 were becoming a majority. Young adults who were underage (meaning under twenty-one then) represented 33% of the total population of France in 1962. By 1968, they accounted for closer to 34% and spent 122.5 francs a month, according to the SOFRES survey institute. The musical industry had a new economic target, and it chose to catch the bandwagon.

As noted previously, men were exclusively in charge of the situation. They included the label heads

Jacques Wolfsohn (Vogue) and Eddie Barclay (Barclay); arrangers Bouchety, Petit, Goraguer, Colombier, and Vannier; stylists Courrèges, Cardin, and Rabanne; press mogul Daniel Filipacchi; and photographer Jean-Marie Périer. In spite of it all, women were determined to unite and take over, to at last impose their views. *Mademoiselle Age Tendre* was a magazine entirely written by and devoted to young women: next to fashion pages, the usual gossip column, and beauty advice, one could find Q&As about sexuality, societal issues, and the status of teenagers. Women's lib movements were already blooming there. As Pussy Cat sang, times were indeed changing:

> *Ils oublient que les temps ont changés.*
>   *(They're forgetting that times*
>   *have changed)*
> *Aujourd'hui c'est aux filles de décider.*
>   *(Today it's up to women to make up*
>   *their minds)*
> *Si les garçons portent les cheveux longs*
>   *(If boys wear long hair)*
> *En pantalon on peut bien s'amuser.*
>   *(We should be allowed to wear trousers and*
>   *have fun)*
> *Si les garçons portent les cheveux long*
>   *(If boys wear long hair)*
> *C'est nous qui les invitons pour danser*
>   *(We for once are inviting them for a dance)*
>
> *Le sexe fort ça ne veut plus rien dire.*
>   *(Stronger sex doesn't mean a*
>   *thing anymore)*
> *Fini le temps de la femme au foyer.*
>   *(The time of the housewife is over)*

> *Le sexe fort ça ne veut plus rien dire.*
>   *(Stronger sex doesn't mean a*
>   *thing anymore)*
> *Je dirai même que c'est bien démodé.*
>   *(I'd say it's very old-fashioned indeed)*

The energy and youth of Sylvie Vartan, Françoise Hardy, and France Gall led female artists from the previous generation to follow the trend and adopt Anglo-Saxon rhythms. Brigitte Bardot, Petula Clark, and Dalida had a go at pop and beat styles.

Besides big names, French labels signed many new artists. It is amazing how easily very young girls could gain a contract. A cute face, some outspokenness, the ability to play two or three simple chords, a certain know-how in dressing habits or just the luck

Sheila

to be noticed at the right time in the right club—be it the Drugstore, the Golf Drouot, the Bus Palladium, or Chez Castel—that was enough to launch a career. Tons of 45s and EPs were sent to influential DJs, like Hubert or Rosko (called *le plus beau, celui qui marche sur l'eau*," or "the cutest one, who can walk on water"). Some girls only lasted for one single, others became quite well-known—and most totally disappeared after May 1968!

Four names stand out at the head of the flock: Hardy, Vartan, Gall and Sheila. There are thousands behind them, yet they are not a homogeneous army. See for yourself:

The "second division": Annie Philippe, Stone, Michèle Torr, Patricia Carli, Agnès Loti, Eileen, Bernadette Grimm, Liliane Saint-Pierre, Danielle Denim, Annie Markan.

The pioneers: Gelou, Hédika, Louise Cordet, Cris Carol, Nicole Paquin.

The actresses-turned-singers: Anna Karina, Michèle Mercier, Gillian Hills, Christine Delaroche, Isabelle (De Funès), Chantal Goya, Sophie Daumier, Catherine Spaak.

Funny girls: Stella, Cléo, Violaine, Christine Pilzer, Christie Laume, Jacqueline Taïeb, Berthe, Monique Thubert, Vetty, Cozette, Natacha Snitkine, Clotilde.

The trendy ones, the icons: Dani, Zouzou, Valérie Lagrange.

The high school girls: Chantal Kelly, Alice Dona, Sophie Darel, Laura Ulmer, and Les Twins.

The gloomy ones: Marie Laforêt, Anne Vanderlove, Karine, Victoire Scott, Catherine Ribeiro.

The rocking ones: Pussy Cat, Liz Brady, Ria Bartok.

The exotic ones: Nancy Holloway, Tiny Yong, Bach Yen.

The bands: Les O, Les Petites Souris, Les Gam's, Ariane & Les 10/20, Les Roche Martin, Les Fléchettes, Les Fizz, Les Parisiennes.

The international artists with hits in French: Sandie Shaw, Petula Clark, Arlette Zola, Gigliola Cinquetti.

Gainsbourg's interpreters: Gall, Bardot, Karina, of course, plus Juliette Greco, Michèle Mercier, Minouche Barelli, Isabelle Aubret.

The "full-lung, ear-scorching singers": Patricia, Nicoletta, Esther Galil.

The girls from Quebec: Les Miladys, Trio Sourire, Les Coquettes, Michèle Richard, Louise Forestier, Claire Lepage.

The ones signed because labels wanted to quickly capitalize on other forms of success: Elsa Leroy (winner of the *Mademoiselle Age Tendre* beauty contest) and Kiki Caron (a swimmer who earned a silver medal at the Olympic Games).

More traditional singers desperate to catch the wave: Nana Mouskouri, Dalida, Annie Cordy, Line Renaud.

And, of course, **the one-hit-wonders**: Catherine Desmarets, Elizabeth, Elsa, Virginie, Jocelyne, Audrey, Olivia, Adele, Céline, Evy, Géraldine, Camille, Gaynael, Françoise Deldick, Aline, Marisa, Arielle, Jacqueline Néro, Marthe Hinny, Mary Christine, Delphine, Hélène April, Jocy, Anna St. Clair, Catherine Alfa, Christine Lebail, Zoé, Madeleine Pascal, Annie Duparc, Katia, Christie Jones.

Of course, I'm (deliberately) forgetting some names, and a few of the ones who made the list could easily change categories. It doesn't matter. My purpose is to demonstrate how numerous they were, and how logical it was for these girls to then revolutionize the social and sexual landscapes of the time.

Françoise Hardy

Age : 23 ans. **Cheveux** : châtain clair. **Yeux** : gris vert. **N°** de patron : 40. **Taille** : 1 m 72. **Poids** 53 kilos. **Largeur d'épaules** : 42 cm. **Tour de poitrine** 84 cm. **Tour de taille** : 60 cm. **Tour de hanches** : 87 cm **Pointure** : 39 1/2.

Sylvie Vartan

Age : 22 ans. **Cheveux** : blonds. **Yeux** : marron. **N°** de patron : 38. **Taille** : 1 m 68. **Poids** : 50 kilos. **Largeur d'épaules** : 40 cm. **Tour de poitrine** : 85 cm. **Tour de taille** : 59 cm. **Tour de hanches** : 85 cm. **Pointure** : 37.

From *Belles, Belles, Belles* by Anne-Marie Périer, 1967

Sheila

Age : 21 ans. **Cheveux** : châtains. **Yeux** : bleu-vert.
N° **de patron** : 40. **Taille** : 1 m 71. **Poids** : 56 kilos.
Largeur d'épaules : 40 cm. **Tour de poitrine** : 90 cm.
Tour de taille : 61 cm. **Tour de hanches** : 95 cm.
Pointure : 37.

Mireille Mathieu

Age : 21 ans. **Cheveux** : châtains. **Yeux** : noisette.
N° **de patron** : 38. **Taille** : 1 m 53. **Poids** : 43 kilos.
Largeur d'épaules : 38 cm. **Tour de poitrine** : 85 cm.
Tour de taille : 58 cm. **Tour de hanches** : 87 cm.
Pointure : 34 1/2.

2
SOCIAL AFFAIRS

Yé-Yé Girls & Marriage

IN JANUARY '68 *MADEMOISELLE AGE TENDRE* published an astonishing article called "Les Mariés Extraordinaires" (extraordinary newlyweds) which, though not directly confronting such a venerable institution as marriage, took a humorous look at it.

"Which male star would you like to wed, just for an afternoon photo shoot?" was the question asked of Sheila, Hardy, Gall, Annie Philippe, and Nicoletta, who were "very quick in making up their minds," the magazine said. "Here are these improvised weddings, introduced to you by Danièle Abitan, which will of course never happen for real and that we had the pleasure to witness anyway."

Such an idea may be viewed as a kind of comment on the phony reports of so-called "love affairs" between young stars. Since everything is fake, why not be upfront about it? Sheila chose Salvatore Adamo, France Gall said yes to Jacques Dutronc's

blue eyes, Annie Philippe agreed to become Mrs. Herbert Léonard (a sort of French Gene Pitney), Nicoletta became Mrs. Frank Alamo (a poor man's Frankie Avalon), and Françoise Hardy celebrated her union with Claude François in exhilarating 1930s style. All of this was another good example of famous people's "good will" at the time—in deep contrast with the press junkets and narrow-minded interviews of today.

In the carefree 1960s, the rise of consumption seemed to parallel the emancipation of women and young people. Plastic things were everywhere: from transistor radios to hair dryers to women's white boots. *Mademoiselle Age Tendre* held a "Teenage Miss" contest every year: readers chose their best representative, who was lucky enough to then hang out with her favorite singers and was awarded many presents, including a scooter or an automobile (!), not to mention a plethora of fashion accessories.

elles ont la grosse cote

Rita Segard **Elsa** Leroy **Françoise** Alonso **Monique** Palanque **Marianne** Seidel

REGION 4

1. Monique Fagot, 17 ans, sténodact. Pont-Ste-Maxence. Timide et volontaire.

2. Chantal Mallet, 14 ans et demi, Chartres. Déjà présente au n° 4.

REGION 5

1. Annie Jacq, 15 ans et demi, Brest. Déjà présente au n° 4.

2. Danielle Candela, 14 ans, lycéenne, Rennes. Est très gaie.

REGION 6

1. Monique Padoy, 16 ans et demi, coiffeuse, Montluçon. Fantaisiste.

2. Brigitte Rebourg, 15 ans et demi, Rochecorbon. Déjà présente au n° 4.

REGION 10

1. Christiane Farant, 16 ans et demi, étudiante, Nice. Spontanée.

2. Denise Dahan, 17 ans, Marseille. Déjà présente au n° 4.

REGION 11

1. Marianne Seidel, 15 ans et demi. Bâle. Déjà présente au n° 4.

2. Dolores Juvet, 14 ans, collégienne, Château-d'Oex. Très sportive.

REGION 12

1. Lut Vermeiren, 16 ans et demi. Lele. Déjà présente au n° 4.

2. Brigitte Knipfer, 19 ans, étudiante, Gand. Gaie et gourmande.

"First Election, Semi-Finalists," *Mademoiselle Age Tendre*, No. 5, March 1965

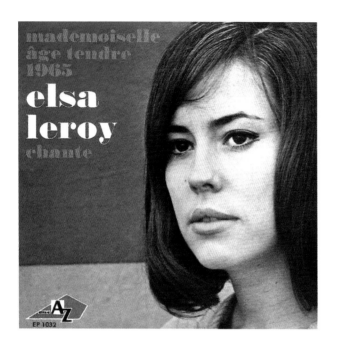

Just like the winners of today's reality shows, these young girls soon launched their own career in show business: 1965 winner Elsa Leroy released an EP in 1966 featuring "Comment Fais-Tu?" (a cover of Ian Whitcomb's "You Turn Me On"), "Mieux Vaut Tard Que Jamais" (a.k.a. "Just A Little Bit" by the Beau Brummels), "Quelle Foule, Quelle Foule!", an original by Gilles Thibaut and Micky Jones, and "Où Va Le Vent?" by Skeeter Davis.

Leroy was later seen answering Jean-Pierre Léaud's tricky questions in Jean-Luc Godard's *Masculin Féminin*, which aimed at deconstructing the myth of "this generation fed on Marx and Coca-Cola," as the film's tagline went. Léaud/Godard cruelly asked the nineteen-year-old to react to such concepts as socialism, being reactionary, the Front Populaire, and birth control. Despite his genius, Godard didn't gain in stature after such a vain exercise, and ended up looking haughty. Anyway, Leroy's EP is a gem of primal psychedelic pop describing boys literally "stepping on their long hair at some Antoine's packed gig."

Mademoiselle Age Tendre's readership couldn't care less about the critics, even prestigious ones such as Godard. France Gall, Chantal Goya, Annie Philippe, Françoise Hardy, Sheila, and countless others talked freely about their private lives, with a candy-colored perspective. They focused on themes as important as being for or against Jacques Dutronc wearing a moustache, with profound analyses such as Hardy's confession that she "wouldn't fancy Jacques this way" and "hoped he'd never wear one, because he'd look too much older!" or Sylvie Vartan's fear that "it might sting." Such serious matters were not all they had in mind, to the point that many a French citizen thought that these young people were real ignoramuses.

And so what?

Why not have fun and reject the cynicism of their parents? Why not try to bring a kaleidoscope of bright colors to a black-and-white world? The young generation would have plenty of time to wallow in regrets, as happened after May 1968. For now, the most important thing was to try and avoid being censored by the law made on July 16, 1949, which was supposed to protect the young from inappropriate publications.

Facing page: *Mademoiselle Age Tendre*: No. 6, April 1965
Photos by André Berg

J'aime beaucoup aussi cet ensemble beige. Il est en gabardine de coton ; le blouson se ferme par des boutons de métal doré (le blouson, 60 F ; le pantalon, 45 F à la Boutique Yop des Galeries Lafayette). Ma chemise est en coton bordeaux (Prisunic, 20 F) et ma ceinture en agneau vert (Gal. Lafayette, 29 F).

Voici un pantalon de coton rouge, qui porte une fermeture à glissière géante sur le devant et dont les deux poches sont taillées à la verticale (Gal. Lafayette, 45 F). Le tee-shirt est en coton rayé, à encolure « bateau » (Gal. Lafayette, 9 F).

Enfin, ceci est la tenue que je me promets de porter le plus souvent : un pantalon de toile rouille à revers (Gal. Lafayette, 45 F), un cardigan en Léacril, « ras du cou » et à manches courtes (Gal., 35 F), une ceinture en grosgrain, avec un empiècement de cuir noir (Gal., 14,50 F), et des sneakers en madras (Prisunic, 11,50 F).

MICHELE TORR : LE 'STYLE GARÇON'

3
THE MEDIA

A General View

"About three years ago Europe No. 1 [a leading French radio station] *decided to create a program especially designed for young people. It was totally new in France. At the time, rock was not popular at all. The beginnings of* Salut Les Copains *were met with general indifference, but after some understandable confusion, a huge amount of mail started to arrive at the station's HQ, proving that not only in France, but also in Belgium and Switzerland, there were thousands of young girls and boys happy to listen to a show that was truly theirs."*

> —Daniel Filipacchi, from the editorial in the first issue of *Salut Les Copains*

IN 1959, RADIO WAS STILL THE MOST IMPORTANT medium, TV sets being rather rare. Europe No. 1 and Radio Luxembourg started a revolution by bringing in an American influence, favoring live reports and a massive amount of music broadcast on the air.

Daniel Filipacchi played a major role in establishing these changes. The son of intellectual parents with friends like Prévert, Cocteau, Robert Desnos, and Django Reinhardt, he began a career as a printer and publisher, then invented the "bibliobus" system (the library van) for French holidaymakers. He was also the first to publish paperbacks. At the end of the 1940s, he became a photographer for *Paris Match* (the French version of *Life* magazine), a member of *Marie-Claire*'s editorial committee, the head of jazz label Mood, and eventually a jazz DJ for Europe n°1, aided by Frank Ténot on the *Pour Ceux Qui Aiment le Jazz* program. He was also a fan of the soul and rock music played by the black musicians he had discovered in one of his numerous stays in the U.S.

mademoiselle age tendre

pour les filles dans le vent

"Mon meilleur ami" par Sheila ! ♥♥ Sylvie : des cheveux d'ange ★★★ Catherine Deneuve ♦♦♦♦ Alain Delon ■■ Une mode-bricolage passionnante ♥♦♥♥ Quatre lectrices et l'amour, etc ●

Sylvie

Septembre 1966. N° 23. 1,50 F
Belgique : 18 FB
Suisse : 1,80 FS. Canada : 35 cents
Espagne : 23 pesetas

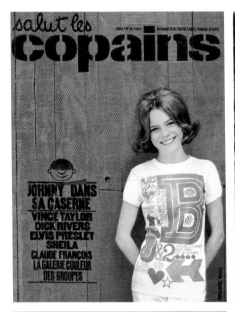

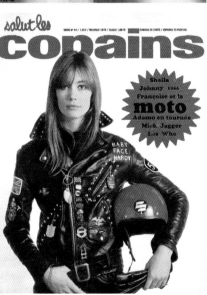

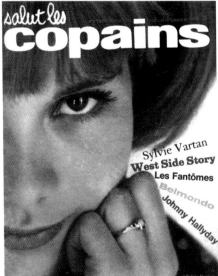

On October 19, 1963, though, when the *Salut Les Copains* radio show was launched, Filipacchi was far from imagining that it was going to have such a deep influence and help establish pop culture in France. He was given full autonomy and the final say on the entirety of *SLC*, being its sole producer—which had never before happened for any radio program. The first episodes focused on Ray Charles and Elvis (France had always been five years behind in terms of youth culture), but soon fully embraced the yé-yé movement. Filipacchi had to hire an entire staff simply to answer the letters addressed to "Françoise," "Sylvie," "France," or "Chantal" and the rest of them: all these artists were now seen by teenage fans as members of their own families. In talk shows or messages recorded for broadcast, they used the more familiar "tu" instead of the "vous" that was *de rigueur* with adults or strangers. Posters were won in quizzes that acted as mock commercials, which may seem mundane today but was totally unusual then. In many ways, by giving the youth a voice, a means to speak their minds without being controlled by their parents and the institutions, this predated May '68 by five years.

And then there was the *Salut Les Copains* magazine! In its very first issue, Sylvie Vartan herself explained how to dress well for a small sum at Prisunic, a popular chain of stores: pop singers were turning into salesmen, just like in the States. Ténot and Filipacchi, who expected *SLC* to sell 150,000 copies, were stunned when 800,000 fans bought their new bible. Even though male singers also appeared on the front page (Hallyday was a recurrent figure), the *filles de la pop* received the lion's share of the iconography. The tone of articles and interviews was rather lightweight, most of them probably motivated by solely commercial purposes and strictly directed by press attachés. Nevertheless, it was part of what gave the magazine its charm.

It's impossible not to mention here the work of photographer Jean-Marie Périer, Françoise Hardy's boyfriend before she met Jacques Dutronc. Périer was a kind of Pygmalion for her, and a creative genius in his domain. His imagination had no limits, and since he was good friends with nearly all the people he took pictures of, he was able to materialize his brilliant ideas.

In countless photos taken all over the world, he had Vartan, Hardy, Sheila, *et al.* dress up as a Middle Ages princess, Tarzan's Jane, a not-so-innocent schoolgirl, a peasant, a vaudeville dancer, an astronaut, a queen of the depths of the ocean, and so on. Périer took advantage of the good humor of his numerous connections (he was singer Henri Salvador's biological son, and famous actor François Périer's adoptive one), as well as the fact that there was no control-freak manager to act as a dictator on the sets.

The period was one of charming naiveté and openness to discoveries: the young girl who bought *SLC* in her tiny little town in France's most remote corner did so because she was sure to read something about Sylvie or Françoise. But she could also discover the likes of Marianne Faithfull, the Kinks, Julie Driscoll, and even early Pink Floyd. Such a mixing of genres has become totally impossible today: the marketing world has condemned the press to be divided into niche markets.

With at least half of the readers of *SLC* being female, Filipacchi, inspired by *Seventeen*, launched a second magazine, called *Mademoiselle Age Tendre*, in November 1964. As mentioned earlier, it was made by young girls for young girls: most of the readership was between fifteen and twenty years old, and the genius idea was to have an editorial staff of roughly the same age. Anne-Marie Périer, Jean-Marie's sister, became the first editor-in-chief, at nineteen. No shyer than editors-in-chief of more "serious" publications, she asked writers such as Didier Decoin and Jacques Serguine, or versatile artists such as Roland Topor, to give her novellas and short stories. Her general idea was that a woman could have both *"une tête bien faite et une tête bien pleine,"* or "her hair done and her head full," (in other words, being a pretty

girl should not prevent one from wanting to educate oneself). Later, she occupied the same job for twenty years at *Elle*.

With a light touch and delicate humor, little by little *Mademoiselle Age Tendre* changed the notions attached to beauty, helping readers become trendier, keeping them in touch with the important cultural movements of the time, and all of this with a good idea of the kind of background pop aesthetics should bring.

André Berg was the in-house photographer. Then a young man looking like a true beatnik, he

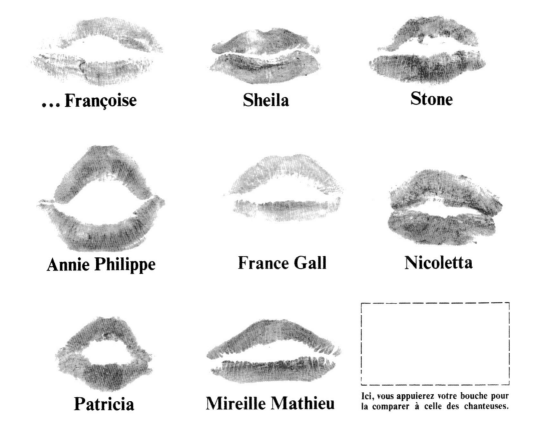

... Françoise

Sheila

Stone

Annie Philippe

France Gall

Nicoletta

Patricia

Mireille Mathieu

Ici, vous appuierez votre bouche pour la comparer à celle des chanteuses.

...us la choisirez en tenant compte de celle de vos cheveux, de votre toilette et, bien sûr, de ...jourd'hui. Ils sont roses, orangés, bruns, beiges, brillants, incolores ou blancs. Lequel préférez-vous ?

BRUN	INCOLORE	ROUGE FONCÉ	BLANC
Dément n° 10, Prisu : 3 F. Perle d'or, Orlane : 8 F. Bruncolor, Guitare : 2,50 F.	Brillant à lèvres, Twenty : 5 F. Hydra rouge, Guerlain : 8 F. Pommade rose, Elizabeth Arden : 8,50 F. Super brillant, H.H. Ayer : 7,50 F.	N° 34 Carita : 7 F.	
Garance n° 10, Ann Michaël : 5 F. Sunny nacré, Twenty : 5 F.		N° 45 Baiser : 3,40 F.	Peach Frostie n° 55, Prisunic : 3 F.

now remembers "a period when we were all living together, in a way. We all ended the day [at] Chez Castel, as there was no separation between journalists and artists: our interviews were like everyday conversations, as the latter very often dropped by to say hello at the mag's offices. They were friends, we went on holidays with them: I regularly spent time with Chantal Goya and her husband Jean-Jacques Debout, icons such as Catherine Deneuve could try different hairdos for hours just to please us during a shooting session, it was incredible, really. We also worked in England a lot, we never had to book a hotel room, we just spent the night with the people we had come to interview. There was no equivalent to *MAT*, and the stars were more than happy to take part. It was a good way of meeting different individuals: I photographed Marianne Faithfull so many times that she eventually became a friend. Twiggy, for instance, would often accept a session with us: she had already been on the covers of all of the world's magazines, but she'd be keen to oblige because she liked *MAT*. I couldn't believe I was able to work with a supermodel like her."

Mademoiselle Age Tendre accompanied young girls on the path to adulthood, even if some things had to be dealt with more carefully than others. The sex column, for instance, only appeared after May '68. Before then, it was a more common "letters to the editor" page called "Chère Anne" (Anne Braillard was the woman in charge of it), with very prudish questions and subtle innuendoes.

The Rock Papers

Disco Revue, Rockers

More serious than papers aimed at teens, rock magazines owe a lot to Jean-Claude Berthon. Clearly focused on rock pioneers (Eddie Cochran, Gene Vincent, Little Richard), his *Disco Revue* dealt with everything from Johnny Hallyday to Vince Taylor, and of course, Sylvie, Françoise, and lesser-knowns such as Gillian Hills, Stella, Hedika, *et al*. The work of a boy in his late teens based in the eastern province of Lorraine, *Disco Revue* was an antithesis to Filipacchi's publications. Berthon's idea of his job was to do a kind of amateur fanzine full of enthusiasm and keen to remain uncompromising. In no way would he publish something about the square Sheila or the deeply uncool Mireille Mathieu!

He created, as a by-product of his revue, the Club Des Rockers, whose goal was to unite fans of the same Anglo-Saxon-influenced music in those pre-Internet days. The idea was to organize "rock afternoons" at Henri Leproux's famed club Le Golf Drouot, where all things rock were played by DJs and bands could perform. In 1966, Berthon launched the *Rockers* mag before closing things down one year later. In the 1970s, he was a collaborator for *Extra* and *Rock 'n' Roll Musique* before opening a record shop and eventually vanishing into thin air. Too much of a provincial, with not enough connections, Berthon was more of a fan than a critic, torn between *SLC* and the newly-created *Rock & Folk*.

Rock & Folk

Still active after all these years, and with considerable success, *Rock & Folk* is an institution, which had its origins in the magazine *Jazz Hot*, led by Philippe Koechlin. In fact the first issue, in July 1966 (featuring Bob Dylan on its cover) was a one-shot added to *Jazz Hot*. The first true issue of *Rock & Folk* included Michel Polnareff, the king of French baroque pop, on its cover. Under Philippe Paringaux's editorial guidance, *Rock & Folk* soon developed complex, deeply intellectual analyses so characteristic of French rock critics then. Miles away from *SLC* or *MAT* in terms of sociological and literary ambitions, the magazine was not sectarian at all, and offered exciting interviews with or portraits of some of the most interesting *filles de la pop*. Where *SLC* sometimes couldn't avoid giving in to advertorial, *Rock & Folk* could more easily resist the temptation, its readership being totally different. The portraits drawn of Stone, Cléo, Sylvie Vartan, Nicoletta, Stella, Marie Laforêt, Patricia, Françoise Hardy, or France Gall were indeed more iconoclastic, though always respectful. There was also much useful information and the odd good review for Stella or Annie Philippe.

Television

Dim Dam Dom

Created for the ORTF, the official state TV channel, *Dim Dam Dom* shook up the establishment. It was a program broadcast on *Dim(anches)–Sundays*–for les Dam(es)–*ladies*–and D(h)om(mes)–*men*. Produced by Daisy de Galard (who later became head of Gaumont), it was a UFO in the very small world of television, due to its treatment of fashion, pop culture, and society. Modern, fresh, and witty, it was a must-see for men as well as women. Up-and-coming

Dim Dam Dom

film directors like Philippe Garrel, William Klein, Jean-Christophe Averty, and Agnès Varda, renowned photographers like Peter Knapp and Elia Fouli (from *Elle*), brilliant scriptwriters (Roland Topor): they all were part of this unique adventure. With each show, famous (or soon-to-become famous) actresses introduced the different segments. It's now become a real "who's who" of the 1960s.

To name but a few of those who contributed: Marie-France Pisier, Joanna Shimkus, Romy Schneider, Michèle Mercier, Alexandra Stewart, Bernadette Lafont, Nicole Calfan, Geneviève Bujold, Geraldine Chaplin, Françoise Fabian, Marlène Jobert, Annie Girardot. The *filles de la pop* were often asked to do the same by Mrs. de Gallard: Chantal Goya, Sheila, Françoise Hardy, Sylvie Vartan, France Gall, Marie Laforêt, Jane Birkin, Christine Delaroche, and so on—a dream cast, indeed! Even trendy pop bands were invited to perform: where else could you see (and listen to) the Electric Prunes or Daevid Allen (of Soft Machine, then Gong) live on TV? Unfortunately (and stupidly enough), no videotaped or DVD edition of *Dim Dam Dom* has ever been available anywhere (but I'm sure you know where to go and find those marvels I've just mentioned!).

Pop Age: An Insight Into the Filles de la Pop Era

On February 9, 1966, *Pop Age*, directed by Guy Gilles and written by Patrick Thévenon, invited its spectators to enter the universe of the *filles de la pop*. The documentary started with an old-style anchorman announcing a study of "that societal revolution of the youth," then showed a pair of young lovers entwined in front of the Western House boutique, which belonged to Maurice Chorenslup, a huge fan of Far West things—and, of course, the writer of his niece Stella's songs. A voice-over summed up the adults' opinion on the "American pop culture invasion": "freedom, cherished freedom that was ours when we escaped from the German occupiers' four years of yoke—and that we lost again when we started twenty years of this cultural stranglehold!"

A vain lament: teenagers' dreams were full of drugstores, candy bars, Marilyn Monroe, cartoons, James Dean, and Elvis. The presenter sighed that all French girls of '66 wanted to become "vamps" and "cover girls." He then commented on England, where adolescents were "no more docile, now offhand and insolent enough to let their hair grow long." The Beatles and British Invasion bands were to blame, of course.

Pop Age went on to introduce the fashionable couple formed by actress Catherine Deneuve and photograph David Bailey, then made a list of people to follow: Jean Shrimpton, Samantha Eggar, Terence Stamp, Peter O'Toole, Rita Tushingham, Albert Finney. Rather honestly, Gilles insisted on the fact that the Beatles' first Parisian gig in 1964 at the Olympia was trashed by journalists (and largely ignored by French pop music fans): according to him, it showed how square France had been (and still was), even in its everyday way of life. The idea that "some adventurers are now buying modern furniture, what madmen they are!", heard in a street survey, was revelatory and arguably funny. But all this apparent inertia wasn't preventing some upper-class young women from adopting miniskirts instead of mink and pearl necklaces.

Macha Méril, who had starred in Godard's *Une Femme Mariée* in 1964, was interviewed saying: "we shall not try and look like Brigitte Bardot any longer. The idea is not to attract men but to be their equal, to state where we women are, to use our own language to start a real dialogue with men." Such a profession of faith echoed the *filles de la pop* ethos very much (Macha's words rightfully had a song by Annie Philippe in the background).

The voice-over carried on with an allusion to suburban women themselves abandoning traditional looks for trendier boots and sculpted haircuts. The dresses and skirts were more colorful, their shapes more simple and geometric. A young stylist working for Snob boutique in Paris who had designed clothes for the movie *What's New Pussycat* claimed that she'd like to have "more of American simplicity put into French all-but-too-complex fashion." She defined this new pop age as "shocking, strange, new, free and lively." Actor Pierre Clémenti was then seen rehearsing Marc'O's *Les Idoles*, an anti-yé-yé play that was made into a film two years later. The attitude was deadpan and the mood ironic, the whole documentary closer to ethnology than pop ideology.

Stars of the moments were also discussed: people were asked about Nureyev, Ursula Andress, Tina Marquand (a.k.a. Tina Aumont), Anna Karina, Jean-Paul Belmondo, El Cordobès, Françoise Dorléac, and Françoise Hardy. A high school boy explained how Godard's *Pierrot le Fou* had touched him. The Bus Palladium, founded by James Arch in the Pigalle district in 1965, was introduced as the epicenter of modern youth, as opposed to more chic places like Chez Castel or Régine's. Proof enough of its popularity, le Bus had already been evoked in songs such as Gainsbourg's "Qui Est In, Qui Est Out," Antoine's

"Elucubrations," Michel Delpech's "Inventaire 66," or *fille de la pop* Liz Brady's simply-titled "Palladium":

Le Palladium
C'est la nouvelle boîte
    (Is the new club)
Et tout Paris en parle
    (It's the talk of Paris)
Car le jerk
    (Because jerk music)
Le shake
    (The shake)
Oh, oh, oh, oh Monkiss
Yé yé yé yé Letkiss
C'est au Palladium que l'on peut danser
ce qu'on veut
    (At the Palladium everyone can dance
    how they want)

Allez au Palladium, y'a rien de mieux.
    (Go to the Palladium, nothing's better)

C'est là-bas que chaque soir, on voit rentrer
tous les copains
    (Each night friends are going there)
Pour crier, danser, chahuter,
taper des pieds, claquer des mains
    (To shout, dance, make a racket,
    stamp their feet, and clap their hands)
Yé Yé Yé Yé Yé
Et quand ils entendent la musique
qui commence
    (And when they hear the music start)

→

*Ils ne se font jamais prier pour rentrer
dans la danse*
  *(They don't need any coaxing to enter
  the dance)*
Oh yé, yé yé yé
*Mais comment vous dire, mais comment
vous expliquer*
  (But how to say it, how to explain?)
Allez au Palladium et vous verrez
  (Go to the Palladium and see for yourself)

Jerk music ("jerk" was the name of the dance) was presented as a "sacred dance" and the Palladium as its temple.

The end of *Pop Age* came as a surprise: *Hiroshima Mon Amour* author Marguerite Duras was trying to advocate for young people, reminding of their "right to make mistakes." Next to her, a young fan of André Breton's specified that to wear long hair was a form of constant provocation. Duras added that people needed to have a source of hatred in their lives, and that the young had replaced the war in Algeria in that role for the adults. She encouraged teenagers in their laid-back attitudes, and their need for establishing strong groups of friends. Her conclusion was less positive, however: she feared that the clothes worn by her seventeen-year-old son (and many youngsters) might become like a uniform, though, according to her, individual freedom was making huge progress.

Despite its mosaic structure, sometimes fairly easy oppositions, and haughty tone, *Pop Age* was a good means of getting information about what was going on, especially as far as young women were concerned. A clear view of the mood of the day is not something commonly found in essays about the period. Critical distance enables better analysis, but lacks sentiment. The documentaries of the INA (National Audiovisual Institute) are precious for this. They set up a comprehensive portrait: on one side the pill, feminism, long hair, miniskirts, sexual freedom, and pop music; on the other, a heavy reaction from adults determined to fight childish gesticulations threatening the patriarchal structures of society, a menace coming essentially from the consumer-oriented American way of life.

Where else but in INA's archives could Stella be seen on the television show *Discorama*, answering the presenter's questions with such mockery? Saying that she only had "a little laugh" at people, that all of this was "my lovely uncle's fault," that she "truly liked horror films such as going to high school"? Or that she wouldn't be too disappointed if everything stopped for her, that she didn't know what tomorrow would bring and didn't care? She finished the interview adding that the money she had earned with her records was "locked up in a bank account until I come of age, anyway," and that her song "Si Je Chante" had flopped because it was "too bitterly ironic" (she sang "if I'm singing now, it's not for you, not for the Queen, not for the King, it's for the cash").

Stone in
Gérard Pasquier
advertisement

4
THE FOUR ACES OF HEARTS

France Gall

One day, Serge Gainsbourg was asked if he could think of someone under thirty worthy of being made into a statue, and he said something that was really overwhelming: "It'd be a huge statue of France [Gall] in barley sugar whose fingers would be licked by all children around."
—France Gall in *Rock & Folk*, February 1968

MORE THAN ANY OTHER *FILLE DE LA POP,* Isabelle "France" Gall was the one who enabled Gainsbourg to go over to the other side of pop superstardom. (In French, the idiom is "to turn your jacket over"—to which Serge G. added: "only to discover that its lining is made of mink!")

Miss Gall (in her pre-Michel Berger years) best exhaled a blend of suave sweetness, of childlike kindness, existing in a bittersweet universe that perfectly depicted the hardships of crossing the border between adolescence and adulthood.

A Parisian born and bred, France was the daughter of composer Robert Gall, who notably penned Charles Aznavour's "La Mamma" and Hugues Aufray's "À Bientôt Nous Deux." She was the granddaughter of Paul Berthier, one of the co-founders of Les Petits Chanteurs À La Croix De Bois, the nation's most famous children's choir for years. Between 1963 and 1968, Robert Gall would write songs for his daughter and conduct her career as a family affair, taking advantage of his numerous connections in the music business.

In 1963, *Ne Sois Pas Si Bête* was Gall's first 45, and included the smash hit "Sacré Charlemagne," a fairy-tale song about the emperor of the Franks, who was supposed to have invented school. It sold by the ton: 200,000 copies for just the first pressing! Also featured was a jazz gem, "Pense À Moi" (by Jacques Datin and Maurice Vidalin). The sixteen-year-old Gall was at once established as a serious competitor for Sheila and Sylvie Vartan, in the race toward setting foot on the throne of favorite yé-yé singer.

Enter Gainsbourg, in a rather unexpected move at first view: he was indeed *the* songwriter for older Left Bank chanteuses such as Juliette Gréco, Isabelle Aubret, or Michèle Arnaud.

France Gall remembers the first time she met him: "I was used to seeing people suggesting songs in my producer's office, with my dad attending. In there was a piano for the guy to sing his song and then leave. I'd hardly lend an ear to it all, paying very little attention to the whole process. I remember Gainsbourg was

rather shy, singing with a very softened voice. And I always liked what he did. We'd then only see each other in the studio. Alain Goraguer would do the arrangements for four songs in one morning only, I'd sing my part in the afternoon, the mixing would be done in the evening, and that was it."

France Gall's angelic voice was an ideal match for these sophisticated arrangements and catchy Anglo-Saxon rhythm sections. In 1964, aged seventeen, she sang the wonderful "Laisse Tomber Les Filles," adapted into "Chick Habit" by April March in 1994. Some thirteen years later, Quentin Tarantino would turn the song into a huge hit by featuring it on the soundtrack for *Death Proof*. Gall sang:

> *Laisse tomber les filles*
> *Laisse tomber les filles*
> *Un jour c'est toi qu'on laissera*
> *Laisse tomber les filles*
> *Laisse tomber les filles*
> *Un jour c'est toi qui pleureras*
> *Oui j'ai pleuré mais ce jour-là*
> *Non je ne pleurerai pas*
> *Non je ne pleurerai pas*
> *Je dirai c'est bien fait pour toi*
> *Je dirai ça t'apprendra*
> *Je dirai ça t'apprendra*

As adapted by April March, the lyrics went:

> *Hang up the chick habit*
> *hang it up, daddy,*
> *or you'll be alone quick.*
> *Hang up the chick habit*
> *hang it up, daddy,*
> *or you'll never get another fix.*

I'm telling you it's not a trick
pay attention, don't be thick
or you're liable to get licked.

You're gonna see the reason why
when they're spitting in your eye
they'll be spitting in your eye.

"Laisse Tomber Les Filles" was a feminist song years before Women's Lib existed, a paradox when considering Gainsbourg's misogyny. It was further proof that the man was talented enough to project the personality of the performers—in this case, a melancholy young girl—into his own songs. Gall was a godsend for him: as he confessed years later, it was a way for him to step into the limelight as a commercial artist. Indeed, a few months after "Laisse Tomber," she sold more than 300,000 copies of his "N'Ecoute Pas Les Idoles": Gall-Gainsbourg-Goraguer truly were a successful item.

Of course, it was 1965's Eurovision contest winner, "Poupée De Cire, Poupée De Son," that made her a worldwide star. She went on to record dozens of versions of the song in nearly every foreign language, including Japanese. Backstage, life was not such a bed of roses: the musicians of her backing band would boo the hit during rehearsals because they judged the rhythm too frantic.

Her private life was marked with unhappiness too: she had a secret affair with Claude François, who kept treating her poorly. On the night of her European triumph, as she was calling him to share a bit of enthusiasm, he told her she had been "naff" and sung "completely out of tune." She could later be seen sobbing in Gainsbourg's arms, which everyone mistook for tears of joy. Despite such vicissitudes,

"Poupée" sold like hot cross buns: 20,000 copies a day at one point.

Mes disques sont un miroir
    (My records are a mirror)
Dans lequel chacun peut me voir
    (In which everyone can see me)
Je suis partout à la fois
    (I'm everywhere at the same time)
Brisée en mille éclats de voix
    (Scattered in a thousand shouts)

Autour de moi j'entend rire
    (Around me I can hear the lau
Les poupées de chiffon
    (Rag dolls)
Celles qui dansent sur mes
    (The ones who dance to

Poupée de cire poupée de son
  (I'm a wax doll and a sound doll)
Elles se laissent séduire
  (They let themselves be seduced)
Pour un oui ou pour un non
  (For a serious or no reason)
L'amour n'est pas que dans les chansons
  (Love does not only belong in songs)
Poupée de cire poupée de son
  (I'm a wax doll and a sound doll)
Mes disques sont un miroir
  (My records are a mirror)
Dans lequel ont peut me voir
  (In which everyone can see me)
Je suis partout à la fois
  (I'm everywhere at the same time)
Brisée en mille éclats de voix
  (Scattered in a thousand shouts)

Seule parfois je soupire
  (Sometimes on my own I sigh)
    à quoi bon
      to myself: what's the point)
        ur
          that way)
            ns
              s?)

        ghter of)
        hansons
        my songs)

ament
ppiness
, being a
whose only
ts mindlessly

all are the best-
great songwriters

did do efficient work for her: André Popp ("Deux Oiseaux"), Alain Goraguer ("Mon Bateau De Nuit"), the aforementioned Vidalin and Datin ("Un Prince Charmant," "Faut-Il Que Je T'aime," "La Rose Des Vents," and "La Fille D'Un Garçon," all tremendous efforts). The latter also wrote songs for the likes of Dalida, Nougaro, Barbara, Mireille Darc, Petula Clark, Richard Anthony, J.J. Debout, and Lucky Blondo—and for *filles de la pop* Sophie Darel and Françoise Hardy, of course.

From 1965 onwards, France Gall was a successful export of French pop: she released songs in German (her first hit was "Das war eine schöne party!"), Spanish, and Italian. In 1966, she toured Japan extensively, singing many Japanese adaptations of her songs. Between 1967 and 1972, Germany was like a second home for her: she recorded thirty-six songs

in Goethe's language, among them many originals! The best one was probably "Der Computer Nr. 3," a pre-electro dance number all bathed in Moog synth and Vocoder vocals. Also worth noticing are "Merci, Herr Marquis," a hard-psych killer that was very different from what she was used to doing, as well as gems like "Haifisch Baby" (the German version of "Bébé Requin"), the elegiac "Hippie Hippie," "Love, l'Amour und Liebe," and "Samstag und Sonntag."

Der Computer Nr. 3
   (Computer number three)
Sucht für mich den richtigen Boy
   (Seeks the boy that'll suit me best)
Und die Liebe ist garantiert für beide dabei
   (And love will be guaranteed for us both)

Der Computer weiß genau
   (The computer knows exactly)
Für jeden Mann die richtige Frau
   (Which man corresponds to which woman)
Und das Glück fällt im Augenblick
   (And happiness is drawn instantly)
Aus seiner Kartei
   (From its cards)

Denn einer von vielen Millionen
   (Then amongst millions)
Der wartet auf mich irgendwo
   (Somewhere there'll be the one awaiting me)

Alt: 22 Jahre, schwarze Haare, von Beruf Vertreter, Kennzeichen: Geld wie Heu
   (Age: twenty-two, dark hair, works as a salesman, distinguishing feature: very well-off)

Let's go back to 1966 now, the year when the infamous "Sucettes" song was written. In one interview with Denise Glaser for *Discorama*, the most prestigious talk show of the 1960s, to the interviewer asserting that he had created a factory selling lol lipops to teenagers in the form of yé-yé so Gainsbourg replied that his lollipops were a ginger-flavored. It was a way of insisting on t stant double entendre of his lyrics, particul risqué song.

Years later, France Gall would re bourg with having clearly misund was: "I was really prudish, and innocence, which I'm really p to hear that he was in fact t situation to have a good ships with boys were c

france gall

J'adore assister à des défilés de mode.

J'adore les tee-shirts à lacets.

J'adore la couleur de l'océan Atlantique.

J'adore chanter à tue-tête en voiture avec ma cousine Agnès.

J'adore la place Furstenberg à Paris.

J'adore passer des soirées en famille.

J'adore le patin à glace.

J'adore les tartines de beurre au goûter.

J'adore l'émission de télé « Le mot le plus long ».

J'adore les musiques de Michel Legrand.

J'adore marcher sous la pluie avant d'aller chez le coiffeur.

J'adore circuler à moto dans Paris.

J'adore que les gens qui m'entourent m'aiment.

J'adore danser jusqu'à l'épuisement.

J'adore l'excitation qui précède les départs en vacances.

J'adore râtisser les allées des jardins.

J'adore vivre comme un garçon.

J'adore boire du lait froid en mangeant.

J'adore l'odeur de ma rue au petit matin.

J'adore jouer au tennis quand il fait beau.

J'adore visiter des appartements à louer.

J'adore les filles aux cheveux courts.

J'adore jouer à la belote.

J'adore courir les antiquaires.

ngs,
tually
the con-
arly in that

proach Gains-
erstood who she
sang it with sheer
oud of now. I was sad
aking advantage of the
augh at me. My relation-
omplicated enough: because

Je déteste les gens mous et lents.

Je déteste les photos de moi quand j'avais quinze ans.

Je déteste les situations embarrassantes.

déteste être en retard (et pourtant ça m'arrive souvent).

Je déteste la neige et le froid en général.

Je déteste les répondeurs automatiques.

Je déteste les traits d'eye-liner aux yeux des filles.

Je déteste la musique symphonique moderne.

Je déteste les choux de Bruxelles.

Je déteste ma mère quand elle sort de chez le coiffeur.

Je déteste les travaux ménagers.

déteste qu'on me demande de chanter au cours d'un dîner.

Je déteste Burt Blanca (il comprendra pourquoi).

Je déteste prendre l'avion.

Je déteste mes chiens quand ils hurlent en pleine nuit.

Je déteste faire confiance aux gens.

Je déteste les boîtes à musique.

Je déteste le désordre (chez les autres).

Je déteste les « slips de bains pour garçons ».

Je déteste les blagues grossières.

Je déteste entrer dans un endroit public.

Je déteste faire de la peine.

Je déteste assister aux rites vaudou.

Je déteste les vagues.

I was a famous pop singer, they tended to be a bit scared of me. With 'Sucettes,' I thought I was singing the story of a cute little girl, a Comtesse de Ségur-like kind of a tale. When I eventually figured out what it was all about, I was so ashamed and so frightened of being rejected as a perverse little thing!"

It's true that Gainsbourg didn't particularly spare her as the years went by, each time mainly for the sake of a pun on what she had said in a particular interview. For instance, a journalist asked Gall in 1976 why she wasn't singing "Charlemagne" or "Sucettes" on stage anymore, and she naively answered: "because I'm too old for all this now," before clumsily adding, "well, for 'Charlemagne,' I mean." Of course, Gainsbourg, when he repeated the anecdote on several TV shows, willingly omitted the second part of her answer, which made her seem sillier than she actually was.

The world of artistic creation is full of hits and misses, of successes that should have been but were not. The Beach Boys' *Smile*, Orson Welles' *The Other Side of the Wind*, Alain Resnais' *Mandrake*, a Corto Maltese film version of Hugo Pratt's comic books in which Bowie was supposed to play the lead: none of them saw the light of day when they should have triumphed. France Gall had her share of these lost treasures: Walt Disney seriously envisioned her playing Alice in an adaptation of Lewis Carroll's *Alice in Wonderland*, but his death put an end to the whole project. One can only imagine now how perfect she would have been for the part—much more than Miss What's-her-name in Tim Burton's recent adaptation.

1967 was a turning point for the music industry, with very innovative records: the Beatles' *Sgt. Pepper*, Jimi Hendrix's *Are You Experienced?*, Cream's *Disraeli Gears*, Love's *Forever Changes*, Pink Floyd's *Piper At*

The Gates Of Dawn—to name just a few, all aiming at new directions in terms of arranging and producing.

That's the reason Serge Gainsbourg decided to cease collaborating with Alain Goraguer and cross the Channel to start working with Alan Greenslade and David Whitaker. On January 11, 1967, he'd be headlining on *Dents de Lait, Dents de Loup* (a program inspired by the American shows *Shindig* and *Hullabaloo*), duetting with France Gall on brand-new songs created with his new team. That very same year, Gall would sing "Teenie Weenie Boppie," a semi-prophetic psychedelic song that depicted Mick Jagger drowning in the waters of the Thames (when it'd actually be Brian Jones in his swimming pool two years later, as everyone knows). She remembers the lyrics as very influenced by the era, "people doing

acid and dancing their heads off," Gainsbourg adopting a very sanctimonious tone here, as in American drug scare movies:

Teenie Weenie Boppie
A pris du LSD
  (Has just taken LSD)
Un sucre et la voici
  (One sugar and there she is)
Déjà à l'agonie
  (Almost in agony)

Que sont ces fleurs aux couleurs exquises
  (What kind of exquisite flowers are these?)
Qui dérivent au fil du courant
  (Drifting with the stream)
C'est Mike Jagger qui dans la Tamise
  (It's Mike Jagger inside the Thames)
S'est noyé dans ses beaux vêtements
  (Who's drowned in his beautiful clothes)
Teenie Weenie Boppie
Est morte dans la nuit
  (Died during the night)
De quoi, mais d'avoir pris
  (The cause? Because she took)
Une dose de LSD
  (One dose of LSD)

Gall's "Bébé Requin" (lyrics by Serge Gainsbourg, music by Joe Dassin) was another baroque pop jewel:

Viens suis moi
  (Come follow me)
Je connais une route d'émail
  (I know a road made of enamel)
Qui mène
  (Leading to)
Au pays de perles et de corail
  (A land of pearls and coral)

Je suis un bébé requin
  (I'm a baby shark)
Au ventre blanc aux dents nacrées
  (With a white belly and pearly teeth)
Dans les eaux chaudes
  (In warm waters)
Je t'entraînerai
  (I'll lead you through)
Et sans que tu le sache
  (And without you knowing it)
Avec amour avec douceur
  (With love and tenderness)

Moi vois-tu bébé requin
  (You see, I, being a baby shark)
Je veux te dévorer le cœur
  (I want to eat your heart)

Bébé requin bébé velours
  (Baby shark, velvet baby)
Bébé requin bébé d'amour
  (Baby shark baby love)

Totally unknown in his country of origin, American Joe Dassin was the son of filmmaker Jules Dassin, who left the States to escape Senator Joe McCarthy's witch hunt. Joe Dassin sold millions of records in France, where he's best-known for very light-hearted MOR (middle-of-the-road) hits, which are nonetheless miles away from the more ambitious work he produced at the beginning of his career ("Marie-Jeanne," a cover of Bobbie Gentry's "Ode To Billie Joe" is one example, as is *Blue Country*, a tribute LP to Tony Joe White, recorded one year before his untimely death, which sold very poorly). For France Gall, Dassin wrote "Toi Que Je Veux" in 1967, with "La Vieille Fille," "24/36," and "Souffler Les Bougies," all released the following year. His anthem to Paris as seen in the small hours of the morning, "Aux Champs-Elysées," has been covered by Californian skate-punk band NOFX.

His sister Julie had a less successful career in the music and movie businesses in the mid-'60s (with one hit, "Jock-a-Mo" by Aïko, whose original "Iko Iko" was written by James "Sugar Boy" Crawford in 1953, telling the story of two Indian tribes at war). Strangely enough, following "Teenie Weenie Boppie" and now firmly grounded in Swinging London's sound, France Gall went on to record "Une Chanson Indienne," arranged by Whitaker, with mock Indian sitars and flutes in the foreground.

And then there was May 1968…which she seemed to have been completely unaware of. She sang on *Dim Dam Dom*'s theme tune (written by Michel Colombier, also a collaborator of Gainsbourg's, who later moved to the U.S., met Herb Alpert and Jerry Moss, and found fame with the *Wings* LP starring Paul Williams). A wordless vocals version of *DDD* was then used for a Dim stockings commercial.

No career can go without its slippage in standards, its compromising with pure business. Sometimes even songs recorded with little or no artistic purpose in mind tell us about the historic period in which they were made, and may lead to (good or bad) surprises. "La Petite" was one of those, recorded with Maurice Biraud, a veteran radio DJ and actor who's almost forgotten now.

(Lui)
   (He)
Comment ne pas s'attendrir
   (How not to be taken in)
Devant la petite
   (By this young kid)
Devant ses yeux innocents
   (Her innocent eyes)
Devant son sourire
   (Her smile)
Elle change depuis quelque temps
   (She's been changing for some time now)
Elle pousse la petite
   (That young kid's growing older)
Déjà femme mais pourtant
   (Already a woman, still)
Ce n'est qu'une enfant
   (All but a child)
(Elle)
   (She)
Une enfant on a tout vu
   ("A kid," that's your point of view, not mine)
Qu'est-ce qu'il faut pas entendre
   (I'd rather be deaf than listen to this)
Quand je pense qu'on a failli
   (When thinking that you were about to be)

Hier te surprendre
   (Caught red-handed yesterday)
Essayant de m'embrasser
   (Trying to kiss me)
Moi me laissant faire
   (And me letting you having a go at it)
Il n'est pas si mal
   (He's not that bad-looking indeed)
L'ami, l'ami de mon père
   (The friend, the friend of my father)

Featured on the *Néfertiti* EP, "La Petite" stands on a very thin line between being cryptic or explicitly pedophilic, and would probably be banned today. But as incredible and scandalous as it may seem now, it better "fit" the morals of the time. At the end of the 1960s, though, Gall's career had reached its lowest

point: the hit machine seemed to have seized up, the student revolt having rejected many a yé-yé star, mainly because of their apparent shallowness and refusal to take part in feverish political debates. These downfalls could also be explained by pop music's intrinsic fleeting quality: artists became stars overnight, but the public would soon get bored with them, the record sales diminish, and the labels eventually ditch them.

Gall fell in love with Julien Clerc, an up-and-coming singer-songwriter who played the leading part in the French version of *Hair*. She chose to admire him from behind the scenes, eventually leaving him when she felt guilty about having parenthesized her own career too much. Nevertheless, even though it was not financially rewarding, her 1969–1973 "Clerc period" offered great songs. Her lack of success was easy to explain: people like to pigeonhole artists and performers, and Gall had extreme difficulties in making them accept her new image as a more mature singer, far from the babydoll vignettes for which she once was famous.

In April 1968, she recorded a commercial for Granji wine:

Pour un souper aux chandelles
(For a dinner by candlelight)
Ou un repas entre amis
(Or a meal with friends)
Avec ou sans maître d'hôtel
(With or without a headwaiter)
Je ne veux que du vin Granji.
(I'll only have Granji wine)

It was first featured as a hidden track on a compilation offered to Radio Luxembourg DJs, and was evidence that she was pretty lost, ready to compromise her talent advertising cheap plonk, which her admirers didn't quite get (nowadays, she'd be spared the embarrassment of it all: the Evin Law forbids the promotion of alcoholic drinks on TV or radio channels).

In *Rock & Folk*'s February 1968 issue, Philippe Constantin interviewed Serge Gainsbourg and France Gall. To the journalist asking if he had found in France Gall the ideal interpreter, Gainsbourg replied, "no, *she* has found the ideal composer in me. We form a kind of ideal couple. You know, before I stared writing for her, I'd be very often sneered at—*esoteric*, they'd call me! I can't bear people speaking badly about her—I mean, she's very young, but still, she manages to make a living."

France Gall, meanwhile, assessed her journey on the path to pop stardom so far. Having just turned twenty, she charmingly (and proudly) confessed that she expected to sing "at least until I'm twenty-five." She even related what she deemed to be her "worst memory ever," a TV show with iconoclastic producer Jean-Christophe Averty, on which she was promoting "Sucettes" for the first time:

There were a hundred people on the set. And they were all expecting the same thing from me. It was a nightmare, a real nightmare. Averty had given me that lollipop to suck, and he kept barking at me: "so, little dirty miss Gall, you have never sucked lollipops, have you? I'm going to stick knives and forks into your eyes, you know!" I did not want to do what they all wanted of me, trying to act natural in all that hell. Eventually, Averty asked one of the background dancers to do it, and her take was so perfect that he kept it.

france gall: des cheveux blonds, blonds... blonds..!

was striking was how independent she sounded, especially as far as her relationship to her parents was concerned (perhaps because the latter were all too present at her start?). Merely a month before "the events" (as French politicians called them), Gall showed a disinterest for politics totally at odds with her generation, but very characteristic of the yé-yés (Françoise Hardy, Sylvie Vartan, and Sheila were no more interested—some even left Paris to escape the turmoil).

"I don't give a fig about all things political," she said. "I saw Claude Lelouch's *Vivre Pour Vivre*, and I was amazed by the sequence about the Vietnam war. I didn't know anything about it, it was so overwhelming it spoiled the rest of the movie for me." In the same candid manner, she answered Constantin's question about who she was "living with on that pink cloud of yours above reality" with a discomfiting "my goldfish, two poodles and a cat. You want to meet them?"

In 1970, "Zozoï," by Robert Gall and Angelo, was to be a real move to a funkier direction. But it was a one-shot, unfortunately. Bertrand de Labbey, Julien Clerc's agent and manager, thus agreed to contact Gainsbourg, hoping for a return to form for Gall. Gainsbourg wrote "Frankenstein," a fantasy tale inspired by Mary Shelley's novel, and a rather sexist ditty, "Les Petits Ballons," whose narrator was an inflatable doll obsessed with "petits ballons," that is, "condoms." According to Gall, she turned to Gainsbourg because all of her recent records had flopped, and he quite nicely accepted to help, with Jean-Claude Vannier, his new accomplice (and a true genius himself) arranging. She added that "the lyrics were great, but did not correspond to what I expected. I wasn't particularly happy to sing them. This is when I realized Serge didn't have anything more to say about me—or rather, never had.

The anecdote is not flattering for Averty, who despite his admittedly huge talent, behaved as most men of his generation would have.

In the same article, one learned that Gall's favorite artists were the Beatles and Françoise Hardy, that she envisioned a film career, that her favorite writers were Colette, Daphné du Maurier, Balzac and "stuff like Maurice Druon," that she had read Nabokov's *Lolita* and half of *Trois Filles De Leur Mère* by Pierre Louys, Brigitte Bardot owning the other half. What

He didn't know me, in fact, only projected his own fantasies through me."

In spite of it all, Gall was lucky to work with Vannier, the arranger (and largely uncredited co-writer) of Gainsbourg's *Melody Nelson*. Maritie and Gilbert Carpentier, two major actors of French *variétés* TV shows of the 1970s, loved to suggest unexpected duets for original songs, in the middle of incredibly luxurious sets. On the *Top À Jacques Dutronc* TV show, on March 2, 1974, Gall sang "Frankenstein," in an atmosphere parodying Boris Karloff's Universal movies, with Dutronc pulling faces to try and present himself as a credible monstrous creature. As if displaying some farewell fireworks, she then sang "Cinq Minutes d'Amour," an achingly beautiful folk ballad.

The first part of Gall's career would end with the *Par Plaisir* 45, whose B-side "Plus Haut Que Moi" (originally "Maria Vai Com As Outras") was a cover of a Brazilian song recorded by Toquinho, the famed guitarist who penned marvels with Vinicius de Moraes and accompanied Tom Jobim on stage for so many years.

France Gall et la VW-Porsche. France a été séduite par la Porsche d'avant-garde 914-6. Deux places, 200 km/h et un toit escamotable.

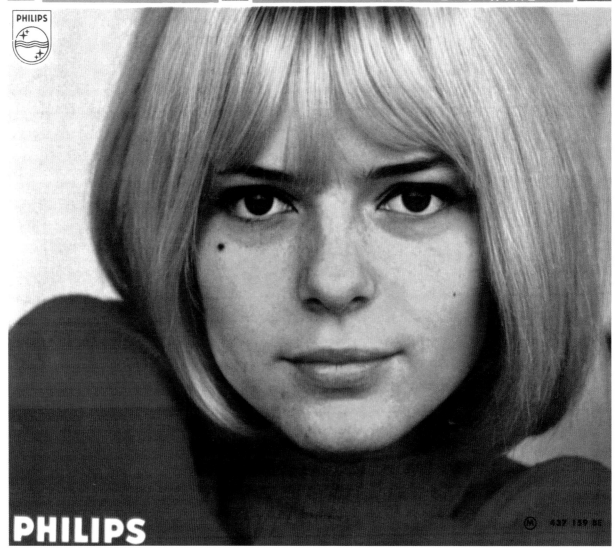

THE FOUR ACES OF HEARTS   55

In 1974, when Gall met Michel Berger, he was clearly on his way up in the charts, and only needed the right singer to hit number one. "La Déclaration" brought him both tremendous commercial success and a partner for life. The couple achieved hit after hit until Berger's death in 1992, the last being "Laissez Passez Les Rêves." If the general public was more than satisfied with Gall's totally different musical direction, fans of adventurous pop couldn't but cry out loud when hearing the results of the alliance: a sub-Elton John grub full of fretless bass and liquid synth—with more groove and efficiency than sensitivity and risk, unfortunately. April March humorously evoked it this way:

C'est Chantal Goya ma chanteuse adorée
    (Chantal Goya is my beloved singer)
J'aime beaucoup Stella
    (I like Stella a lot)
Françoise et Sylvie qui me rendent heureuse
    (Françoise and Sylvie make me happy)
Même France Gall en a fait de si merveilleuses
    (Even France Gall made marvelous ones)
Avant d'être mariée
    (Before she got married)

Some things are seemingly beyond explanation: Michel Berger was the man who produced wonderful singles for Véronique Sanson's group Roche Martin in 1967 (she was Stephen Stills' wife for some time), as well as the gifted musician behind *Puzzle*, an incredible progressive pop LP five years later. How could he then sink in such unpalatable productions for Gall? Just because of the French general public's obvious (bad) taste for those kind of things? Or due to *Puzzle*'s very poor sales? Berger probably couldn't resist the siren call of superstardom (money being a different thing: he was brought up in an upper-class family). If you were to play several France Gall records for a British or American pop music fan, he or she would inevitably prefer Gall's earlier period, and probably make a face while listening to the work produced with Berger.

The gap between what Berger could create and what he actually offered is a real shame: just think of "Message Personnel," which he wrote in 1973 for Françoise Hardy. Maybe it was only a question of bad production choices: his songs, when covered by young artists now, albeit with different arrangements, do not seem as cheesy as they once did, their melodies sounding much fresher.

Françoise Hardy

"Am I difficult to live with? I couldn't say. I'm quite strong-minded, sometimes irritable and moody. I can also be quite chilly with the people around me, but I never do it on purpose. There's one person who knows how to help me find a balance: my mum."
—*Françoise Hardy in 1967, in* Mademoiselle Age Tendre

"With tender, nostalgic air and a voice heard as if through a veil, Françoise manages to attract both kids and their parents, men and women alike. More than a singer, she's becoming an universal myth with whom thousands of young girls dream of identifying."
—Special Pop, *1967*

Françoise Hardy, *the* yé-yé girl from Paris, is one of the few French singers to be internationally famous, including of course in the British Isles and the U.S., two parts of the world normally less than enthusiastic about all things pop from France.

It's not only a matter of good looks—that tall, androgynous beauty, dressed in avant-garde fashion creations by trendy designers such as Courrèges and Paco Rabanne, has had Jagger, Dylan, Bowie, Etienne Daho, and Damon Albarn raving about her melancholy eyes for years now. Obviously, there are the songs, too: magic tracks that have put her in a class of her own, with a finesse and a dreamlike quality that has never quite been emulated since. Although she started in the 1960s, the timelessness of her music is so remarkable that she has managed to continue her career up until now, her image immaculately preserved throughout the years.

Françoise Hardy was brought up by a single mother alongside her sister in a modest family far from any father figure. In her little flat at number 24 rue d'Aumale in Paris, she'd listen to Anglo-Saxon records on Radio Luxembourg: Paul Anka, rock 'n' roll, Brill Building pop, Elvis, Neil Sedaka. As a teenager, she went to Mireille's academy for singers, Le Petit Conservatoire (Mireille Hartuch featured in films starring Buster Keaton and Douglas Fairbanks, and was herself a pianist/singer). Mireille's teaching sessions were broadcast on ORTF at the time, introducing new generations of artists. The timid and sulky type, Françoise Hardy nevertheless made a great impression on her first TV appearance (she wore a V-neck pullover the wrong side out, "just for the fun of it," she said).

Then, at eighteen, she seized the opportunity while still underage (twenty-one was the age of majority) to audition for Vogue Records, Petula Clark's and Johnny Hallyday's label. There she met André Bernot, a sound engineer who introduced her to the mythical Jacques Wolfsohn, the same man who'd launch Jacques Dutronc. Wolfsohn, who had founded Alpha Editions, was one of those fifty-fifty guys: fifty percent for the publisher, fifty percent for the artist. He was used to signing the SACEM (the copyrights) bills for himself, getting credits as an author or composer when he was not.

In 1962, Hardy recorded (in a mere six hours!) a full four-track EP that included "Tous Les Garçons & Les Filles," her first massive hit. Funnily enough, Vogue

had first insisted on promoting "Oh Oh Chéri" on TV and the radio. But in the blink of an eye, "Tous Les Garçons" went up the charts, selling more than a thousand copies a day to finally reach number one, and to be bought by more than a million fans! Françoise Hardy's next single would be a Dutronc composition, "Le Temps De l'Amour" (ironically, this "Time For Love" was recorded way before they were an item), a song covered by (guess who?) April March in 1994. Paradoxically, Françoise now thinks her own version has aged very badly—an opinion one must disagree with: it truly is a poignant ode to youth.

Back to 1962: *Salut Les Copains* provided strong support that Hardy could count on. Both the radio show and the magazine chose to praise her demure behavior instead of the more provocative ways of the rockers. Jean-Marie Périer was summoned for a photo session, which would lead to Françoise falling in love and soon moving in with him. He'd then be both her (almost) exclusive photographer (notably, he created all of her record covers) as well as her agent. Her fame became such that she even made the cover of *Paris Match* with the caption "eighteen-year-old millionaires" (Sylvie Vartan was also featured). Everybody seemed to love her—and as for those who didn't, she seemingly couldn't care less (columnist Philippe Bouvard, who hated the yé-yé girls, nicknamed her "the chicory of twist," referring to her static performances on TV).

That same year, Hardy discovered what was to be a lifetime passion, astrology. Some months later, she made her acting debut in *Château En Suède*, directed by Roger Vadim, of *Barbarella* and *God Created Woman* fame (he was also known for being a womanizer whose conquests included Catherine Deneuve, Bardot, of course, and Jane Fonda). Things

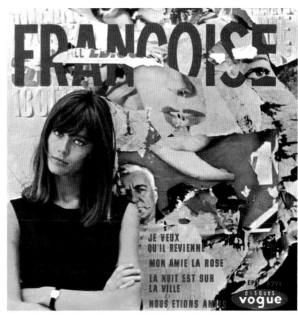

didn't go too well with him: he nicknamed her "my little imperial duckling," mocking her "infinite apathy." It was only the beginning of her dread for filming sessions and the movie business in general.

In 1964, she made the same move as Gainsbourg would make a few years later: she left the poor quality of French studios and sound engineers to go record her songs with the nascent Swinging London musicians; such a demanding attitude was also what made her so different from her French counterparts. Charles Blackwell, once an arranger for Joe Meek, was the man who helped her reach new levels of sophistication.

Mademoiselle Hardy became an overnight sensation among pop stars: Mick Jagger claimed her to be his ideal woman, while Bowie would pretend his radio set was suddenly on fire whenever she was on. Even Malcolm McLaren, the controversial Sex Pistols manager, would add to it, asserting that she represented the "utmost of the pinup girl, pinned to the walls of every trendy pop apprentice's bedroom down in Chelsea. Many bands in their prime, like the Beatles or the Stones, dreamt of dating her." As for Françoise? She went through all this with splendid innocence. She'd laugh about it years later in interviews, remembering for instance being invited over one day by Anita Pallenberg and Brian Jones, and politely refusing the "strange cigarettes" she was offered (cannabis, of course), thus puzzling her hosts, who went on to think she had come for a threesome. (Of course she hadn't, she was just a fan of the Stones, delighted to have a chat with one of them!)

Another striking anecdote is that of Bob Dylan being so taken with Hardy that he quit the stage after just a few mediocre renditions of his songs on May 24, 1966, at the Paris Olympia, demanding that she come to chat with him in his dressing room, or he would refuse to go back and sing for the numerous spectators. Once his whim had been satisfied, a pompous Robert Zimmerman would tell everyone he met "now I'm a star, when asking for the moon, I get the moon! I want Françoise Hardy to appear in the flesh and there she is!" Hardy's memory of the meeting is slightly less enchanting: "I had the impression that his whole life was hanging on a thread, he seemed to be very sick, like the living dead. I was totally unaware of his drug-taking, and was disappointed to see he was in no way the elf that used to appear on his record sleeves."

Even though she was quite taken aback by the habits of the jet set, the lovely mademoiselle was popular enough to remain on the UK charts for fifteen weeks with "All Over The World." Like Gall, she also recorded in German and Italian and developed her sales in different marketplaces. After a cameo in *What's New Pussycat?*, she accepted a role in Jean-Daniel Pollet's *Une Balle Au Cœur*. It was another so-so experience for her: "I'm often clear-sighted enough to see when things are about to fall apart, and it was plain to see that Pollet's film was going nowhere."

In 1966, she nonetheless agreed to another minor role in John Frankenheimer's *Grand Prix*, which became another tainted memory. Her filmography was not to be particularly brilliant—and could have been significantly worse had she agreed to take part in the third-rate *Cherchez l'Idole*, a distressing comedy by Michel Boisrond, starring Johnny Hallyday. However, people with a taste for weird, cosmic B-movies would have loved to see her in Joël Lemoine's psychotronic *Les Poneyttes*, released in 1967, another film she declined, while more serious film

Tous les garçons et les filles de mon âge
se promènent dans les rues deux par deux

Oui, mais moi, je vais seule
dans les rues l'âme en peine

Oh ! quand donc pour
moi brillera le soleil

Je me demande quand viendra le jour où
moi aussi l'ami quelqu'un qui m'aimera

LA CHANSON DANS LE VENT DE...
FRANÇOISE HARDY

Elle l'écrivit il y a trois ans alors qu'elle était l'élève du petit conservatoire de la chanson chez Mireille. Avec ses copains Vic Laurens, Arielle et Zambo, elle l'a mimée pour nous aujourd'hui. Françoise trouve l'accompagnement à la guitare un peu simpliste et préfère maintenant les violons et l'orgue. Son disque, qui doit paraître prochainement, « L'Amour reviendra », vous réserve donc des surprises...

Cinémonde magazine: March 12, 1963

buffs would certainly have enjoyed Jean-Marie Perier's remake of Cocteau's *Enfants Terribles*.

In the second half of the decade, Hardy had become a pop icon, and was consequently made an *égérie* (muse) by top fashion designers. This new status, added to the fact that she was reaching worldwide celebrity (she was even famous in the Middle East!) had her claim more independence—hence the creation of her own publishing company, Asparagus, an allusion to "l'asperge," another one of those derogatory nicknames given to her by critics (in that case, because she was so incredibly thin).

1967 was a period of great change for her: Jacques Dutronc became her new partner (and Jean-Marie Perier's best friend). They formed a couple that was very emblematic of the era: able to find a balance in spite of strong characters and Dutronc's dissolute way of life, full of parties with his mates and temptations of the flesh. Professionally, the two of them were also very successful: as individual singers first, but also when they performed duets.

One example comes to mind: "Les Garçons," a parody of Cléo's (who was also on Vogue) "Et Moi, Et Toi, Et Soie," itself a cover of "Et Moi Et Moi Et Moi" with different lyrics. The song could be seen in *Françoise Hardy Blues*, a program hosted by Michèle Arnaud and directed by French "dada pop" producer Jean-Christophe Averty.

The Pop Revolution Will Be Televised

At the end of the 1960s, there were only two TV channels in France, under French Radio and Television Broadcasting's (RTF) strict regime. The Secretary for Information was reported to have said that RTF's goal was to have the French government in every citizen's

dining room. Colorful programs such as the weekly *Dim Dam Dom* or the special *Dents de Lait, Dents de Loup* were the only ways to escape from such a grasp.

On New Year's Eve 1968, a true live concert, with loads of great French, British, and American bands, was broadcast. It was directed by Guy Job (*Dim Dam Dom*'s cameraman) and looked like a massive psychedelic party. The whole show was produced by André Weinfeld and Michel Taittinger, two rock activists who created the hip "Bouton Rouge" TV show. The emcees were Zouzou and Dani, who introduced songs by Hardy, Dutronc (with fantastic French band Système Crapoutchik backing him), Pink Floyd, the Who, the Small Faces, Les Variations, Marie Laforet, the Equals, and dozens of others. An incredible cast indeed: lucky were those who had the chance to see it!

The same year Pierre Koralnik (who directed the musical *Anna*, starring Anna Karina, Gainsbourg—who wrote the score and the songs—and Jean-Claude Brialy) cast Françoise Hardy and Udo Jürgens in a short film that wasn't released, due to, rumor had it, a scene deemed too erotic.

I Am An Égérie

Françoise Hardy was a muse for numerous creative people. Even though she has always rejected this idea, being too modest, it is a fact that no one can deny. The late 1960s/early 1970s were both an artistic and personal peak for her, a time when she was *the* synonym for "cool." But today she seems to be fed up with constantly answering questions about forty years ago, refusing to be associated with other icons of that age. Does she even remember Guy Peellaert? That's a tricky question indeed.

Guy Peellaert (1934–2008) was a Belgian artist who'd be worthy of the pop Hall of Fame, just like Peter Blake, Jim Steranko, Keiichi Tanaami, or Frank Holmes (creator of the Beach Boys' *Smile* cover art). Drawing his inspiration from American aesthetics, he became very fashionable following the new wave of pop artists, much to his own surprise: "Well, okay then, fine with me—I'm suddenly hip! Just one thing: my main inspiration was Gottlieb pinball machines, you see," he told me during an interview in 2001. "At the end of the 1950s, I used to hang out at the Gymnase all day long. It was a kind of honky-tonk [bar] in which Brussels scoundrels came to play poker. The music was fantastic, the jukebox was full of real American rock records, and the pinball machines were fabulous too, with all these lights! Their fronts had such graphic quality, a real suffocating beauty for me."

Peellaert settled down in Paris and launched his career working for the satirical *Hara-Kiri*, the French equivalent of *Mad*. In 1966, he created the Jodelle character, modeled on Sylvie Vartan, then got inspiration from Françoise Hardy to develop a comic called "Pravda la Survireuse" (Pascal Thomas, now a successful film director, wrote the script). It was a futuristic fable, pop and feminist at the same time. Pravda liked speeding on her motorcycle through an apocalyptic universe, and even if she had a cast of Amazons for followers and sometimes flirted with

pour les filles dans le vent

mademoiselle age tendre

FRANÇOISE HARDY, SHEILA, CATHERINE DENEUVE

UNE JOLIE MODE HIVER

GRAND DEPART DE L'ELECTION M.A.T. 66!

ADAMO REPOND

DEC. 1965, N° 14, 1,50 F. BELGIQUE : 18 FB, SUISSE : 1,80 FS, CANADA : 35 CENTS, ESP. : 23 PESETAS

an imitative Brian Jones, she wasn't used to clinging to other people. Being more and more in demand, Peellaert stopped producing comics for a while to collaborate with director Alain Jessua on *Jeu de Massacre* (screened for the first time in 1967). The following year, he had acquired enough confidence to work on *Les Vénusiennes*, a full-color program made for the second TV channel, and centered on Hardy. The latter was dressed in a bolero and articulated black leather miniskirt designed by Paco Rabanne. She moved, as if by magic, from one set to another, all of them pictures from *Pravda*. The comics heroine and the singer were one now.

From then onward, Peellaert's career would be a stellar one: he made record covers for the Rolling Stones (*It's Only Rock & Roll*), David Bowie (*Diamond Dogs*), Café de Paris (*Les Variations*), Etienne Daho (*Pour Nos Vies Martiennes*), and Lio (*Wandatta*); film

posters for *Taxi Driver* and *Paris, Texas*; and books with essayist and novelist Nik Cohn (*Rock Dreams*, *The Big Room*, and *Rêves Du XXe Siècle*, in which he revisits the figures of pop culture and history with iconoclastic verve and refined aesthetics).

Hardy's image was also a great source of inspiration for Jean-Marie Périer, who loved to play with it, especially when using the fish-eye lens to magnify her, with surreal backgrounds and situations acting as perfect counterparts. Before the CD or the MP3, record covers of course had a huge impact on buyers, and Périer was the right man at the right place at the right time to help promote Françoise's records—not that she needed much help.

Jean-Philippe Goude was a mod hanging out at the Drugstore (headquarters of young Paris trendsetters), as well as Zouzou's boyfriend and Pygmalion. He was another creator of one of those fine record covers Françoise insisted on getting for her singles or LPs, attracting many a talent with her magnetism and androgynous beauty.

Salvador Dali himself admired her, as shown in issue number 75 of *SLC*, dated November 1968, in which she was offered a chance to be editor-in-chief. Her "honor roll" featured Averty ("a madman and a genius"), god of dance Rudolf Nureyev, Nouvelle Vague symbol Jean-Pierre Léaud, stylist Yves Saint Laurent ("the Polnareff of haute couture"), Warren Beatty, Rosco (the poppiest French DJ), and Veruschka, the lanky fashion icon who once had a film made about her (with a ravishing soundtrack by Ennio Morricone). This is what Hardy wrote about Dali:

"I like Salvador Dali. Because he's my favorite painter, because his strong accent is charming when he speaks French, because what he writes is generally very seductive, and because he's the most intriguing public persona I ever met, there's a great place in my heart for him. This is why I agreed to spend a whole week with him in Cadaquès, in his wonderful, bizarre universe."

This special issue was a good pretext for Périer to suggest taking a batch of totally unusual pictures. Dali can be seen rising out of an egg alongside Françoise, getting dressed as a hippie, and so on. Hardy declared, "It was very simple to get a good picture of Dali. All you had to do was give him free rein to let his imagination flow, and he'd always come up with the weirdest of ideas."

Weird gags also characterized the series "Quand Françoise fait des plans pour les couvrantes" ("When Françoise has plans for magazine covers"). Photographed by Périer, Hardy "remade" *SLC*'s most famous front-page pictures, impersonating the likes of Michel Polnareff, Eddy Mitchell, Salvatore Adamo, France Gall, Johnny Hallyday, Claude François, Sylvie Vartan, Sheila, Antoine, Jacques Dutronc, and Mireille Mathieu. Beyond the funny idea, such love for the pastiche showed that French teenage pop culture had become self-referential in just a few years. Its symbolic domain had largely penetrated the unconscious. Another clear fact was that genres now judged as different as rock, *variété*, and pop music then still belonged to the same field.

We Loved The Pop Revolution So Much!

For a majority of Hardyology scholars, her 1966–74 period, as already noted, was the best. Her 1966 LP, simply called *Françoise*, was overflowing with pearls such as "Je Changerais d 'Avis," "Comme," "Rendez-vous d'Automne," "Peut-Être Que Je T'Aime,"

"Si C'est Ça," "Surtout Ne Vous Retournez Pas," "Je Serai Là Pour Toi," and "Qu'ils Sont Heureux"…well, the whole record was tremendous, in fact! In 1967, Hardy interpreted the *SLC* radio show's new theme song, with new psychedelic pop jerk overtones. The next LP, *Ma Jeunesse Fout Le Camp*, was a beautiful journey through bittersweet lands, as was *Comment Te Dire Adieu*, with its titular hit song, one of her most moving ones (it was a Gainsbourg adaptation of a tune by Jack Gold). From that moment on, she tended to leave the Kinks' Pye Records studios in London in favor of Bernard Estardy's CBE in Paris. Estardy had been Nino Ferrer's organist before he began producing countless artists, as well as recording under his own name (*La Formule Du Baron* is his lone LP).

In 1970, Françoise set sail from Vogue and launched her own label, Hypopotam, linked to Kundalini publishing company. The same year, she recorded the album *Soleil*—with the help of novelist Patrick Modiano, Jean-Pierre Sabar, Jean-Claude Vannier (both Gainsbourg regulars), Bernard Ilous (of Ilous and Decuyper), Étienne Roda-Gil, and Micky Jones and Tommy Brown, who'd form the substandard band Foreigner later on. *Soleil* was a strange thing, being an adaptation of an LP sung in English that she had recorded some months before. It corresponded to the rising of a new dawn, when teenagers had grown up and were more attracted by longer pieces and neglected 45s. Trapped in the meanderings of a legal case with Vogue, Hardy chose to stop playing live. Freed from any commercial constraint, she would now record what she still thinks was her best work. She'd sell less, but that was the price to pay for newly-gained independence and more complex songs.

Sylvie Vartan

Born on August 15, 1944, in Iskretz, Bulgaria, Sylvie Vartan (née Sylvie Vartanian) is a child of exile, her parents having fled the Communist regime. They were also Francophile, her father being an attaché at the French embassy in Sofia. Sylvie nonetheless spent her first years as a refugee in a very modest dwelling on rue Montmartre. But providence came to knock on her door one day, as her older brother Eddie, a fan of jazz, became a DJ on *SLC* and a producer at RCA. He once asked his sibling to replace Gillian Hills on "Panne d'Essence," a duet with Frankie Jordan, a fleeting yé-yé idol who soon was to become a dentist. Against all odds, the track was a hit, Vartan's very thin voice attracting the ears of both the professionals and the general public. She was so young and cutesy that the press called her "the junior high school girl of twist." Of course, she benefited from the strength of *SLC*'s mini-empire, which was all that was needed: remember there were only three big radio and TV channels in the country at the time! Vartan was an overnight sensation, just like Hardy and Sheila, singing at the Olympia as early as 1962.

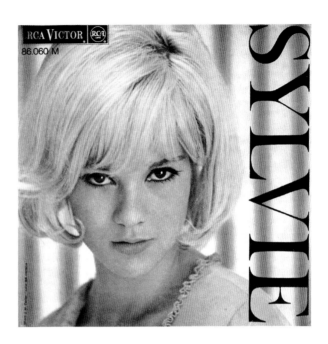

She topped the bill there in 1964, alongside none other than the Beatles. A funny memory: France in the mid-'60s was so unhip that the audience preferred her, some spectators booing the Fab Four and trying to get them off the stage. Before the yé-yés, in accordance with General de Gaulle's policy, French citizens were wary of an English-speaking world, and a new music with crazed rhythms played by long-haired musicians was in many ways very frightening—the first step, adults thought, toward estranging their children from their own homes.

With Vartan-mania in full bloom in France, Sylvie went to Nashville to record *A Gift Wrapped From Paris*. Like fellow yé-yé girls, she was asked to perform in exploitation movies (just like American teenage stars, actually), most of them atrocious, the others mediocre: let's just cite *Patate* or *Cherchez l'Idole*, with Johnny Hallyday. Their romance was a media bonanza, attracting numerous reports and the papers' front pages. In 1965, their marriage was treated as some sort of national event, as were their disputes and reconciliations, and the birth of their son David in 1966.

Hallyday, often mocked as a poor man's Elvis, liked to wallow in rock clichés (never-ending touring, partying, getting drunk…the usual). Vartan eventually got bored and left. A tragicomic episode in the saga occurred when Johnny tried to kill himself on September 10, 1966, just hours before climbing on stage for the (then immensely) popular Fête de l'Humanité organized by the Communist Party. This is how he described it in his autobiography:

> In the morning of the 10th, I was in the Caravelle plane getting me back to Paris Orly airport and not particularly flourishing. I'd lost touch with Sylvie and had just had a dreadful night in London: drugs, alcohol, red pills being passed over in the studio. I took one, and being kind of depressed, I had a nightmarish trip, with visions, distortions, the room shrinking back and forth, snakes on the walls, or seeing myself leaving the place while totally unable to move. That was the first and last time I did acid. My manager welcomed me at the airport: news was bad—in fact it was the worst I could imagine: Sylvie was asking for a divorce, and the Inland Revenue were harassing me with four million in unpaid taxes.

Eventually, Johnny's suicide attempt bonded the couple further for another fifteen years.

In November 1968, when *Rock & Folk* journalist Pierre Chatenier tried to interview her, Vartan was so caught in the hustle and bustle of rehearsing, recording, and touring that he could only ask his questions in Orly airport's arrivals lounge. The essential part of the article was thus centered on the singer's hectic life (at the time she had much credibility as a pop and rock singer—this was before she turned into a MOR chanteuse in the 1970s).

As Chatenier rightfully noticed, Sylvie, who had just come back from Milan, looked a lot like Peellaert's Jodelle, with "loose gray trousers and black,

Johnny Hallyday and Sylvie Vartan

life of a star—we know now how the pressure and, consequently, the military organization of things are much worse for stars like Madonna or Lady Gaga.

However, the late 1960s were still a period when artists were quite accessible. Here's an extract from the interview, dealing with what Vartan's new *à l'américaine* (American-style) show looked like (cabaret would be a suitable term):

Rehearsal starts straight away. Carlos has brought all the props. Walking sticks, straw hats. Someone puts on a record: Comme Un Garçon. *Jean-Pierre carefully measures up the light, adjusts the overture of his camera irises, the speed, chooses the lenses. Wide angle, telephoto. Holding a walking stick, facing a mirror, Sylvie is rehearsing, Arthur watching. In a corner, Carlos practices his tap dance. There's a Fred Astaire mood in the air. Jean-Pierre, his cameras on his belly, hides behind pillars to avoid taking a picture of his own reflection. The others are observing the whole scene. Sylvie dances, again and again, looking elegant, with her long legs, her high-heel shoes. She repeats her entrance move over and over. The stage is a fiction, as well as the wings. The audience is in front of her, facing the mirror. Cocteau would surely have liked such ballet, such* pas-de-deux *of the singer and her double. The photographer takes advantage of the depth of field, given by the duality of the place. The journalist just watches the scene, leaning against the window offering an incredible view on Paris.*
—Rock & Folk, *December 1968*

well-polished shoes, a Marine-blue scarf with yellow stripes, a black velvet jacket and her hair parted in pig-tails." Accompanied by her "odd job man" and best friend Carlos, the son of famous child psychiatrist Françoise Dolto and who himself had a successful career as a comedy singer, Sylvie Vartan was in no mood to confide, torn as she was between preparing for her guest appearance on a TV show and having a break on her own to regain strength. The talent of the journalist was to make his readers subtly understand what the other side of the picture could be in the

Was Sylvie Vartan A Reactionary Singer?

Yé-yé and pop singers brought freshness to the music business and their youth to the duller world of the adults. But they were no revolutionaries at all, Miss Vartan included—even though she started as a rock singer and covered the Byrds. This becomes quite clear when one takes a closer look at how her career changed in 1968, which was *the* year to adopt anti-establishment views if there ever was one.

In April, she was involved in a terrible road accident and had to undergo plastic surgery to avoid being permanently disfigured. This automobile crash was also a psychological trauma, since her beloved assistant Mercedes met her death there:

Fifteen minutes later, as we were going up Bois-d'Arcy hill, me sitting behind the wheel of my Ford Osi, Mercedes to my right, a car suddenly appeared in front of us, from behind a truck, driving real fast, in the middle lane (the road there was a three-lane one). But it instantly changed paths, and in the few seconds it took me to understand the driver had lost control, I didn't have time to drive in the berm and it crashed into us, at full speed.
—*From Vartan's autobiography* Entre L'Ombre Et La Lumière

A convalescent Sylvie Vartan would look at May 1968 with global indifference, as she would confess on many occasions. She was more focused on getting back to business and developing as a *variétés* artist. Feminists must have been horrified to discover what her songs were about:

Comme un garçon j'ai les cheveux long
(Like a boy my hair is long)
Comme un garçon je porte un blouson
(Like a boy I wear a jacket)
Un médaillon, un gros ceinturon, comme un garçon
(A medal, big buckles, like a boy)
Comme un garçon moi je suis têtue
(Like a boy I am stubborn)
Et bien souvent moi je distribue
(And often I distribute)
Des corrections faut faire attention
(Punishments, you gotta be careful)
Comme un garçon
(Like a boy)

Pourtant je ne suis qu'une fille
(Still I'm only a girl)
Et quand je suis dans tes bras
(And when I'm in your arms)
Je n'suis qu'une petite fille
(I'm only a little girl)
Perdue, quand tu n'es plus là
(So lost when you're not there anymore)
from "Comme Un Garçon"

Moi aussi je voudrais
(I'd like it too)
Pouvoir te dire ce soir je sors sans toi
(To say "I'm going out without you")
Moi aussi je voudrais
(I'd like it too)
Pouvoir te dire ce soir ne m'attends pas
(To say "don't wait for me tonight")
Te faire pleurer
(To make you cry)   →

Te torturer
   (To torture you)
Oui parfois je voudrais
   (Yes sometimes I'd like to)
Être un garçon comme toi
   (Be a boy just like you)
from "Je Voudrais Être Un Garçon"

On a toutes besoin d'un garçon
   (We girls all need a boy)
On a toutes besoin d'un homme
   (We girls all need a man)
Faudra bien nous supporter
   (You'll have to stand us)
Laver, repasser, cuisiner, travailler
   (Washing up, ironing, cooking, working)
Nous les filles on saura vous aimer
   (Us girls will know how to love you)
Laver, repasser, cuisiner, travailler
   (Washing up, ironing, cooking, working)
Nous les filles on saura vous garder!
   (Us girls will know how to keep you)
from "On A Toutes Besoin d'Un Homme"

Vartan was clearly no leftist, Left Bank singer. For that matter, in 1974 her then-husband Johnny would officially support Valery Giscard d'Estaing, the right-wing (Republican) candidate. In 1981, when socialist François Mitterrand got elected, she had to reassure her mother, who was scared that Russian tanks might invade Paris, as she had witnessed when still in Bulgaria under the Communist regime.

From The Best to the Worst!

As Sylvie once sang, *"il y a deux filles en moi"* (there are two girls in me). So it went for her career: *before* and *after* 1968. Her repertoire was initially full of charming little ditties, up until 1964 and the Nashville recordings. Then there'd be *A Gift Wrapped From Paris*, an EP with a cover of Roy Orbison's "Pretty Woman" called "L'Homme En Noir," and two great rock numbers, "Oui, Prends-Moi Dans Tes Bras" and "N'oublie Pas Qu'il Est A Moi." Some critics went as far as comparing the guitar playing on those tracks with Jimmy Page's own technique. In 1966, while still hip, she would go R&B with "De Ma Vie," soul with "Sauve-Toi," and even baroque pop when covering Left Banke's "Walk Away Renée (Quand Un Amour Renaît)." In '68, she was even offered a chance to sing "L'Oiseau," on an instrumental track full of mellow bass guitar and beat rhythms:

Sur un rayon de lune
   (On a moonlight ray)
Qui traverse les rideaux
   (Going through the curtains)
Chante un oiseau
   (There is a bird singing)
Effleurant d'une plume
   (One of its feathers lightly touching)
Quelques touches de piano
   (Some piano keys)
Chante un oiseau
   (There is a bird)
Qui fait comme ça
   (Going:)
Tip tip tip tip tip tip tip
   (Chirp chirp chirp chirp chirp chirp chirp)

Comment vivent vos vedettes préférées ?

Sylvie Vartan

Elle a une vie trépidante. Entre un passage à la Télé et l'enregistrement d'une chanson, on ne sait pas comment elle trouve le temps d'aller marcher une heure à la campagne ou de passer à sa boutique de mode pour choisir des modèles de Prêt à Porter.

"J'aime les choses simples et de bon goût", nous dit-elle, "ce ne sont pas toujours les plus chères. Dans tous les domaines. Comme savon de toilette, par exemple, je sais que je préfère Lux, une fois pour toutes.

Il fait tant de bien à la peau et son parfum est tellement raffiné. Avez vous remarqué comme sa mousse est douce et pure?"

LUX
le savon de beauté des vedettes

part of the *Harry Dickson* series—Dickson being an American detective grappling with obscure forces), revealed Vartan as a very good actress indeed. Playing a singer in a brothel, she proved herself worthy of co-stars Orson Welles and Susan Hampshire (an English actress who had played alongside Patrick McGoohan in TV series *Danger Man*). It wasn't until 1994 and Jean-Claude Brisseau's *L'Ange Noir* that Vartan was allowed to display her abilities as a truly gifted comedian again.

That same year, she covered "Turn, Turn, Turn," which was among her last singles to be really interesting, a few months before 1969's swan song, "Ballade Pour Une Fugue" and the heavy rock "C'est Un Jour À Rester Couché."

The rest of her public appearances, as far as this writer is concerned, are worth noting primarily for her part in *Malpertuis* by Belgian director Harry Kümel (who also made *Les Lèvres Rouges*, starring Delphine Seyrig). *Malpertuis*, adapted from the novel of the same name by Jean Ray (who wrote the best

Chantal Goya

Chantal was educated at the Couvent des Oiseaux. There, she dreamt of becoming an actress, but prudently chose to pursue a degree in translation at Cambridge University. Languages, when one stops studying them, decidedly lead to pop music. In Chantal's case, it was meeting Jean-Jacques Debout that changed her destiny. By marrying him, she married music. Along with Mickey Baker, he opened the doors for her. Her first record, *C'est Bien Bernard*, didn't sell. Jean-Luc Godard then gave her an opportunity at the movies, playing in *Masculin Féminin*. Girl magazines are more interested now in "Chantal as a mum," and have taken nice pictures of Mrs. Debout (born on June 10, 1946) and her son Pimpin. (*Spécial Pop*, 1967)

Chantal Goya (née Deguerre) was born in Saigon, where her father owned a plantation. Following the war of independence in Indochina, the family left for Paris. While still a teenager, on a trip spent as an au pair at the Duke and Duchess of Bedford's Woburn Abbey, she had dinner with the Beatles:

I'll never forget the arriving of a limo in the yard, and these four young artists who had just finished a record considered an international event. They were called the Beatles, and the song was 'She Loves You.' Throughout the meal, which was very intimate—we were only eight at the table—Paul, John, George, and Ringo would chat with me as if we were old friends, and we parted ways promising to see each other very soon. But that would never happen, of course. Not only because their career prevented them from doing so, but also because my parents wanted me to come back to France and I had to obey them.

—Des Poussières Pleins Les Yeux,
Chantal's autobiography

This sweet memory is typical of her career: meeting people unexpectedly and relying on pure chance helped her take important steps. With her naiveté and genuine innocence about show business, she was very representative of all these *filles de la pop*. They would absorb everything they learned with a great deal of desire to improve, and that pleased the producers very much. The latter could mold them, and put them on the covers of magazines at a very young age, exploiting their image. Chantal was one of the most charming of these little girls immersed in an adult world. She was only sixteen when she met Jean-Jacques Debout, a successful singer-songwriter whose moment of glory came when he was Marlene Dietrich's secretary. He was also good friends with the Hallyday-Vartan duo. Chantal remembers the circumstances of their first meeting in her autobiography, and the dialogue that followed:

I had never even heard his name. I was just back from England, where I never listened to the radio, and of course I totally ignored the fact that there was a weekly hit parade on a show called Salut Les Copains. *Someone told me that this twenty-something boy was an up-and-coming artist with a noticeable song, "En Casquette À Galons Dorés," the one he was performing at the piano right now, with the audience raving and wanting an encore. Falsely hesitating, he was about to accept, when our eyes met. Without even introducing himself or asking for my name, he told me: "I've got the impression I've known you forever. You and I are going to get married soon. We'll have two kids, you'll be famous by thirty, and you'll sing at the Opera." Which made me laugh, obviously, and I replied: "Getting married and having kids is a possibility. Being famous at thirty I cannot see how. And as for the Opera, I'm no Maria Callas!"*

—*From* Des Poussières Pleins Les Yeux

In 1962, Jean-Jacques Debout had a crush on Sylvie Vartan and had been writing songs for her. But the *belle* preferred Hallyday, and Debout then met Chantal, whose *nom de scène*, Goya, came from a famous painting of a child by the renowned Spanish painter, whom Debout was fascinated with. Chantal, still dreaming of being a comedian, had a cameo in 1963's *Charade* by Stanley Donen, starring Gary Grant and Audrey Hepburn, which was partly shot in Paris. But once she had met her Pygmalion in the form of Debout, she signed a recording contract with RCA, although she had to get authorization from her parents because she was still underage.

C'est Bien Bernard, her debut, was not very different from the hundreds of records being released in 1964, but because of Debout's connections (Filipacchi, as ever!), she got a spot in a TV show singing the song. *Une Echarpe Une Rose*, which was out the following year, was far more convincing. She was now benefiting from African-American guitarist Mickey Baker's help. The latter was a blues musician who had left his country to escape segregation laws, although he had a promising career waiting for him, having scored a hit in 1956 as part of the duo Mickey & Sylvia with "Love Is Strange" (he even had the immense honor of working for Elvis Presley). With the addition of "La Pluie Du Ciel," "Comment Le Revoir," and "Sois Gentil," Goya's repertoire suddenly made a giant leap toward quality. (In fact, Baker was so influential that his method for beginning guitarists was published by *SLC*.) In 1965 she also released a Spectorian Wall

of Sound-inspired EP, with "Si Tu Gagnes Au Flipper" as the most remarkable title. It smelled of milkshake bars and teenage passions, just like a British or American single. Jean Bouchety, who worked for Michel Polnareff for years, did the uplifting arrangements—as the great man in the shadow he was at the time, not only for Polnareff, but also for the likes of Jacqueline Taïeb, Eric St-Laurent (a one-man French Beatles), Eddy Mitchell, and Eric Charden.

Of course, Chantal Goya was a regular feature in the teenage press, especially in *MAT*. As early as January 1965, she was on the cover of the magazine, participating in fashion columns that were actually aimed at promoting her records. No *Vogue* mag sophistication there, obviously, even though reports with stronger purposes and characters did appear—in January 1966, she posed under flashy neon lights alongside Ronnie Bird, a French R&B icon worth rediscovering.

Godard & Me

There couldn't be two personalities more opposed than Jean-Luc Godard's and Goya's. The Nouvelle Vague director of *Le Mépris*, *À Bout de Souffle*, *La Chinoise*, and *Sympathy for the Devil* was taciturn, cerebral, and complex, whereas the singer was solar, instinctive, and naive. Even if opposites do attract, Chantal was more than surprised in 1965 to get a call from Daniel Filipacchi informing her that Godard had seen her on television and wanted her to feature in his new film *Masculin Féminin*.

Godard being famed for not giving any developed script to his actors, she was a bit puzzled on the set at first, but soon realized the man was a genius. The black-and-white movie told the story of the unrequited

Jean-Pierre Léaud, Chantal Goya and Catherine-Isabelle Duport in *Masculin Féminin*

love affair between a young iconoclast, played by Jean-Pierre Léaud, and one disdainful Madeleine (Chantal Goya). Léaud's character would eventually commit suicide. The cast also featured Marlène Jobert and cameos by Brigitte Bardot and Françoise Hardy. The film was a pretext to draw a bittersweet portrait of urban youth in the mid-'60s.

Godard's opinion of yé-yé girls and boys was rather abrasive, as shown in his attempts to trap young Elsa Leroy with puzzling questions. He tried to film Chantal Goya in moments of intimacy, predating reality TV by forty years. Throughout the shooting, he provoked minor incidents to obtain "moments of truth" from the actors. Goya got infuriated when he asked her to appear in the nude, hidden by the glass of a window, which she couldn't accept because of her very strict upbringing. She had Marlène Jobert replace her, which deeply annoyed Godard, who became mad with rage and declared she'd never be a true actress. Despite this, the film carried on, with Godard sometimes including his actresses' remarks or anecdotes in the script.

A few months before, Chantal had met a Japanese man on the Champs-Elysées who told her he was looking for the RCA offices. She gracefully agreed to show him the way and before she left, gave him her brand new record. In just a few weeks, *Une Echarpe Une Rose* was number three on the Japanese charts, just behind Presley's *It's Now or Never* and *Satisfaction* by the Rolling Stones; the man was the owner of fifteen radio stations there and had promoted her heavily as a reward for her kindness!

She told this episode to an unimpressed Godard, who recycled the anecdote to paint the picture of a dumb singer, with no particular gift for her art, who became big in Japan out of sheer good luck. His talent

set the film in a category of its own, though, far from any yé-yéxploitation movie, despite its cruel tones. It was also the opportunity to discover five new songs by Chantal and to see her in the studio, rehearsing with Mickey Baker. In 1966, as the walls of Paris were covered with posters advertising the film, an EP would be released, with the songs "D'abord Dis-Moi Ton Nom" (re-arranged by Baker), "Comment Le Revoir," "Sois Gentil," "Laisse-moi," and "Si Tu Gagnes Au Flipper."

A few months later, Goya would publish her last two pop EPs: the first included "Laisse-Moi," "Dans La Nuit," "Ce Soir On Danse" and "Mon Ange Gardien." (Written by Baker, the latter was a melancholic gem that went unnoticed. It took April March's cover on the *Chrominance Decoder* LP for Tricatel Records to do it justice and help it earn new fame.) The second LP featured the unremarkable "Pense Pas Trop" and "La Flamme Et Le Feu." She had decided to raise a family and retired for a while.

I'm On Television Now!

The young singer topped the bill in two episodes of *Dim Dam Dom*. In December of 1966, she played Mary in a fable about nativity alongside Gainsbourg, who didn't seem overly enthusiastic about the whole thing. Years later, he'd confess to not remembering anything about *Noël à Vaugirard*: "Did I play Joseph or the donkey?" A harsh judgment on what was but a thumbnail sketch with an interesting cast: Sylvie Vartan, Jacques Dutronc, Régine (high priestess of Paris nights, also a singer of many of Gainsbourg's songs), Georges Ulmer, Dirk Sanders' dancers, Dominique Grange (a folk protest singer), a gospel choir dressed up as nuns, and Guy Marchand. The short film, which was directed by Jacques Espagne at the rue de Vaugirard's abattoir, was not to be taken too seriously: it was a period piece from a time when cynicism hadn't yet begun to reign. Its surreal scenes were numerous: to see, for instance, the jet-set of Biblical times surrounded with carcasses of meat had its charm. Near the end of it all, Espagne even had a go at mixing Dutronc's "Et Moi Et Moi Et Moi" with Gainsbourg's "Qui Est In, Qui Est Out?," which led to a Fellinian sort of oddity. In an interview with a Gainsbourg fan website, Espagne remembers the experience this way:

Robe
en pure laine,
95 F

> *Yes, I was delighted to work with Chantal Goya, who is far more interesting as an artist than what people usually say of her. Godard hired her, for God's sake! I remember Gainsbourg chatting her up as we were preparing to shoot the scene with Mary and Joseph: he was there, dressed up as Joseph, smoking his usual Gitane fag, and that was extraordinary, because he was trying everything and anything to seduce her, being totally unaware that the sound engineer had installed a very powerful mike which had everyone hear all of their conversation! But nothing happened between them. Chantal also had fond memories of* Noël à Vaugirard: *each time we meet, she will tell me about it and ask why we all don't see each other more often.*

Daisy de Galard (DDD's producer) had one rule: the more stars there are, the better it is for the show! It was a kind of passage obligé for famous people of the moment. The atmosphere of the shootings was crazy, a real party time it was, with a young crew [who] decided to innovate and try everything that was possible. Those were the days, as they say...

Chantal Goya was also the host of a *Dim Dam Dom* show in 1968 (when she had already stopped singing), then played in an episode of the TV series *Les Dossiers de l'Agence O*, with Marlène Jobert as well as Serge Gainsbourg. In 1969, it was back to the cinema with *Tout Peut Arriver* (with a young Fabrice Luchini), then one had to wait until 1971 to see her again, in *L'amour C'est Gai, L'Amour C'est Triste*, alongside Bernadette Lafont. Three more years passed before 1974's comedy *Les Gaspards* (in which a young Gérard Depardieu appeared too). And that was it for her acting career.

The second half of the 1970s would see Chantal Goya turn into a singer for children, often mocked for her cheesiness. Strangely enough, she went from über-square to über-hip twenty years later, owing to the post-modernist irony of her seventies fans' own kids, who

created techno or house music versions of her songs. This tended (and still tends) to overshadow her 1960s work. Fifteen years ago, it took courage for April March to sing her ode to Mickey & Chantal in front of a puzzled French audience, who were convinced it was all just sarcastic humor.

"Do's and Don'ts"
Mademoiselle Age Tendre, No. 14, December 1965

5
SERGE GAINSBOURG'S
FILLES DE LA POP

From Literary *Chanteur* to Pop Entrepreneur

SERGE GAINSBOURG OFFICIALLY LAUNCHED HIS career as a singer, writer, and composer in 1954, when he registered at the SACEM (the French equivalent of the American Society of Composers, Authors, and Publishers). In 1958, *Du chant à la une!*…was his first LP. After those early beginnings, Gainsbourg offered songs to female performers, for example Michèle Arnaud, a cabaret singer who had noticed him when he was a shy piano player working in bars. Once she had become a successful television producer, Arnaud would keep helping him out, for instance by agreeing to produce *Anna*. The musical featured great songs now considered classics, such as "Sous Le Soleil Exactement," sung by Anna Karina.

Marianne Faithfull's "Hier Ou Demain," also penned by Gainsbourg, was another highlight. The story is of a man working in the advertising business (Jean-Claude Brialy) who has fallen in love with the girl on an advertising poster (Karina) and tries desperately to find out her name and whereabouts (she is actually his bespectacled secretary, to whom he pays no attention). The film was clearly alluding to the cover girls of the era, to this whole business centered on the image of young stars who seemed to have come out of the blue. Gainsbourg's music was at its best, and Michel Colombier's arrangements were simply superb.

In the late 1950s and early 1960s, Gainsbourg was still under the influence of traditional French chanson, though veering toward Boris Vian-influenced jazz, and miles away from the world of pop. His crossover only happened some years later, for example, when his "Javanaise" was covered by Avengers actress Honor

Blackman as "Men Will Deceive You." (Gainsbourg's original was sung by Juliette Gréco, the "muse of Saint-Germain," a district of artists, poets, and existentialists dear to Jean-Paul Sartre.) The early songs were great, that's a fact, but had more to do with yesteryear sensitivity and surroundings (think of "L'Accordéon" or "Le Poinçonneur Des Lilas"), and their singers were all mature ladies (Catherine Sauvage was another particularly good one). 1963 marked a hint of change, with Brigitte Bardot singing "L'Appareil À Sous," which sounded very poppy indeed:

Tu n'es qu'un appareil à sou-pir
    (You're all but a sighing machine)
Un appareil à sou-rire
    (A smiling machine)
À ce jeu je ne joue pas, je n'aime pas.
    (This game I won't play, 'cos I don't like it)
Cet opéra de quatre sou-pirs
    (This threepenny sighing opera)
Cet air que tu as de sou-rire
    (The look in your eyes when you're smiling)
Je ne pourrais qu'en sou-ffrir
    (I couldn't do anything but suffer from it)
On ne gagne que des gros sou-pirs
    (One only gains big sighs)
À vouloir tant assouvir
    (Wanting to fulfill that much)
Tout ce je ne sais quoi d'animal en soi
    (All this je ne sais quoi of an inside animal)

A note for those unfamiliar with French: the *appareil à sous* is a slot machine that could be a jukebox or a "what-the-butler-saw" machine. Here, Gainsbourg is playing with words starting with the syllable "sou," a word itself meaning "dime."

In 1964 the yé-yé sound invaded the nation and swept away a whole generation of singers. Gainsbourg sang "Chez Les Yéyés" and immediately tried to ride the new wave, adding a touch of Anglo-Saxon pop to his tunes. In one finger-click, he managed to reach a new market: all these youngsters willing to start fresh and buy music resembling them. Gainsbourg scored big with "Poupée De Cire" and France Gall's numerous hits, then it was "Les P'tits Papiers," "La Guérilla" for Valérie Lagrange, "Les Incorruptibles" for Petula Clark, and on and on it went!

In the 1965 interview with Denise Glaser mentioned earlier, he said he regretted having told the yé-yés to "go buy yourselves entire wagons of lollipops and leave us alone!", asserting that this new trend of singers was "finally a good thing, because it has put an end to very painful songs with literary presumptions such as those of old-fashioned Left Bank protesters," claiming that rock was "more sincere and acceptable." This complete change of opinions

Anna Karina

showed that Gainsbourg was a) an opportunist, and b) totally clear-sighted about the current situation in the music business.

To put these new ideas into practice, Gainsbourg wrote "Bubble Gum" for Brigitte Bardot, a charming little song that was the basis for a fruitful personal and artistic relationship between the two of them.

1966 saw him working in Swinging London, doing "exercises in style, trying to adapt to everything and everyone: I can write for Greco or Gall, I have no pretension to be myself, as writing songs is pure entertainment for me. The Anglo-Saxon influence has stayed, establishing new artists—all these little girls with a pink carnation, so fresh and studious…you know, they are often decried, France Gall and all, and it really makes me sick because they're not stealing their money at all, they're doing a difficult job and are

charming people—Françoise Hardy is charming, and Sylvie Vartan too!"

Hits kept coming: "Baby Pop" and "Les Sucettes" (Gall), "La Gadoue" (Petula Clark), "Pourquoi Un Pyjama?" (Régine), "Les Papillons Noirs" (Michèle Arnaud): all in 1966!

La nuit, tous les chagrins se grisent
    (At night sorrows turn gray)
De tout son cœur, on aimerait
    (With all your heart, you'd like to have)
Que disparaissent à jamais
    (Forever disappearing)

Les papillons noirs
    (Black butterflies)
Les papillons noirs
    (Black butterflies)
Les papillons noirs
    (Black butterflies)

Les autres filles te séduisent
    (Other girls are attracting you)
De mille feux leurs pierreries
    (Their jewels with a thousand lights)
Attirent au cœur de la nuit
    (Attract in the middle of the night)
Les papillons noirs
    (Black butterflies) x 3

The year 1967 saw no pause: Anna Karina became a pop idol thanks to Gainsbourg, and "Boum-Badaboum" by Minouche Barelli also went to Eurovision—another forgotten gem in Serge's catalogue.

Initials B.B.

The affair between Serge and Brigitte started after an ordinary lunch in October 1967, during which they were supposed to discuss plans for the *Brigitte Bardot Show*, soon to be broadcast on television. As they were rehearsing vocals for "Harley Davidson" and "Contact," Bardot had some champagne to break the ice, and then decided to invite Serge along with a couple of friends, notably her Chilean assistant Gloria and her husband, actor Gérard Klein. When seeing Gloria's obvious happiness, Bardot…well, the rest is history. As she writes in her autobiography:

> *I had an urge to be loved, to be desired, to belong body and soul to a man I admired, cherished and respected. My hand into his provoked a shock for the both of us, a kind of never-ending welding, an uncontrollable electrocution, a wish to mash up something, to melt, a rare, magic alchemy. Our eyes met, and couldn't look at anywhere or anyone else. We were alone in the whole universe, on our own, alone…) This minute seemed to have lasted for centuries, and it still seems to be lasting. I've never left Serge since, and he's never left me.*

Gainsbourg and Bardot would then be immersed in passion. The funny thing is that all of the musicians in the studio were also in love with Bardot, and would carefully choose their best clothes for the sessions, to look as good as they could in front of her! For the *Brigitte Bardot Show*, the star wore thigh-high boots and a black leather miniskirt, posing beside a Harley-Davidson in a set looking like a real garage. The

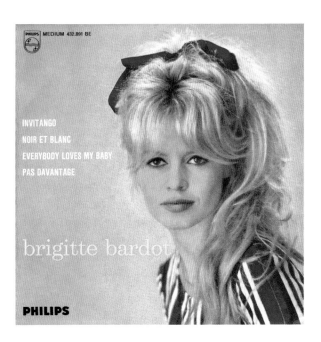

images would be so internationally famous (noticeably reproduced in magazines such as *Playboy*) that thousands of posters were printed for young men to pin up in their rooms. On "Contact," she was wearing a space outfit designed by Paco Rabanne. The song, which depicted the feelings of an extraterrestrial woman, is now a classic, covered in recent years by Japanese band Pizzicato Five. Gainsbourg really had a knack for writing songs that corresponded to the moods of the day (another example: for an episode of the *Sacha Show*, Bardot and Sacha Distel sang his mockingly psychedelic "La Bise Aux Hippies," when flower power was already starting to decline).

But there was a snag: Bardot had been married to German billionaire Gunther Sachs since the summer of 1966. And the golden-boy businessman couldn't put up with seeing his wife on the front page of tabloids with a man he thought looked like Quasimodo.

Overloaded with work, overwhelmed by passion, Gainsbourg couldn't face the pressure. He even complained to Michel Colombier "each time I put my shirt back on, she has me take it off again!"

He had been very much involved in the *Brigitte Bardot Show*, choosing costumes or conducting the recording sessions for the songs. Even the idea of having Bardot doing her best Barbarella in "Comic Strip" was his, as was the set full of balloons decorated with onomatopoeic phrases in psychedelic lettering. Impressed by Arthur Penn's *Bonnie & Clyde*, he also wrote the eponymous song especially for the program, largely drawing inspiration from the famous poem Bonnie Parker had sent to the newspapers to advocate the couple she formed with Clyde Barrow:

Vous avez lu l'histoire de Jesse James
 (You read the story of Jesse James)
Comment il vécu, comment il est mort
 (Of how he lived and died)
Ça vous a plus, hein?
Vous en demandez encore
 (Well you liked it, eh? You want some
 more?)
Eh bien écoutez l'histoire de Bonnie and Clyde
 (Well, here's the story of Bonnie and Clyde)

Alors voilà, Clyde a une petite amie
 (Clyde's got a girlfriend)
Elle est belle, et son nom c'est Bonnie
 (She's beautiful, and her name's Bonnie)
À eux deux ils forment le gang Barrow
 (The two of them form the Barrow gang)
Bonnie Parker et Clyde Barrow
 (Bonnie Parker and Clyde Barrow)

In a kind of teaser for the show, Bardot and Gainsbourg were seen dressed as Beatty and Dunaway in the movie—with Brigitte no less sex-kitten than Faye!

As the days went by, Bardot was less and less torn with guilt about neglecting her husband, no matter how severe the comments from the media could be. Paparazzi harassed her and couldn't stand that she felt so independent and free—so free to love whoever she wanted to love that she asked Gainsbourg to write her "the most sublime love song ever."

"He spent hours composing on my little Pleyel piano. One morning, he played what sounded like a love present to me: 'Je T'aime Moi Non Plus.'" Of course it was an international success, partly due to its being banned by the Vatican—but not Bardot's

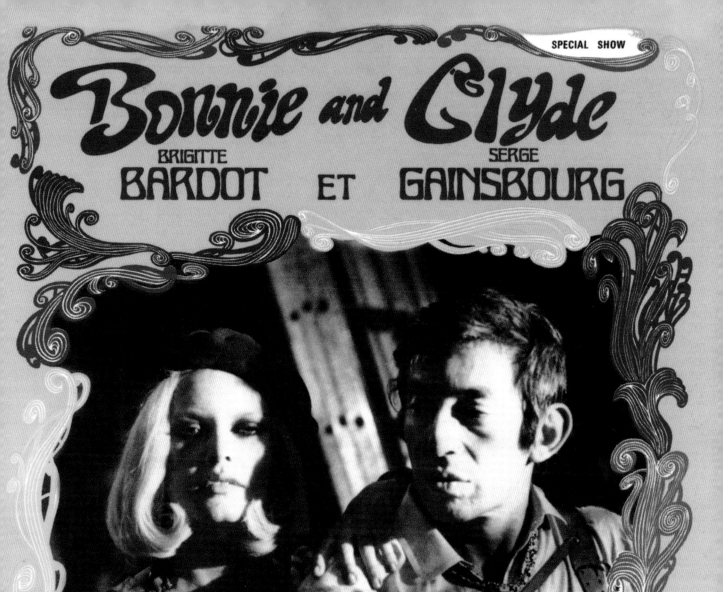

version, Jane Birkin's! The two were quite different, with Bardot's sounding even more erotic, if possible.

Brigitte was mistaken, though, in thinking Serge had composed it especially for her: as a cunning entertainer, he was used to recycling material or "borrowing" from others, when he was not getting all the credit for music actually written by his arrangers. "Je T'Aime" had seen the light of day in 1966, to general indifference, as an instrumental track played by obscure band the Jets in a film that is now a cult classic, *Les Cœurs Verts*, directed by Édouard Luntz. Fortunately for Gainsbourg, the film flopped, and he could re-use his tune.

On the day when the single was going to be pressed, the studio got an injunction from Bardot to stop publishing it. There had been leaks in the papers about the content of the song: *France Dimanche* was talking of "4:35 minutes of groaning and love sighs." Olga, Brigitte's housekeeper, had been pestering her about "good Christian morals," convincing her that Sachs would ask for a divorce were the song to be released.

The lovers could not resist the gossip, goody-goody columns in the media, and pressure from both family and friends. But Gainsbourg didn't understand why he couldn't publish the song. He felt the situation was appalling, telling a French journalist: "There's been some gossip in a gossip paper, but getting a scandal with such a beautiful song is out of the question, because it's too beautiful for that. Of course it is erotic, but it'd have been X-rated. Its music is so pure! For the first time in my life I've written a love song, and this is what's going on, people can't accept it. Bardot interpreted it so well. I'm delighted to have been working with her, I had her sing in a more dramatic way, and that was very fine."

To a journalist who later asked him, "Are you having a good Christmas?" he would answer "yes, sure—on my own!"

When the *Brigitte Bardot Show* was broadcast on January 1, 1968, Brigitte was back home, and she watched it on TV with Gunther Sachs and his friends. She'd later remember the whole situation: "I was there in Foch avenue, with everybody shouting how beautiful I was and [how I] sang well—even Gunther was proud. Serge was the only one to get bad remarks. Gunther's friends would yell at him, saying how ugly he was. It was horrible, I had tears in my eyes. Where was he at that moment? Surely he was really down, all alone in the messy student room he was renting, with his large piano for sole companion."

On January 2, 1968, the record shops would get the *Bonnie and Clyde* LP, rush-released after the TV show. The sleeve notes sounded like Gainsbourg's farewell to his now-former lover: "These twelve tracks by Brigitte and myself are only but love songs. Fighting love, passionate love, physical love, fictitious love. Moral or amoral ones, it doesn't matter: they're all marked with absolute sincerity."

Bardot then left to shoot *Shalako* in Alméria, Andalucia, with Sean Connery as her male co-star. She'd often have long conversations on the phone with Serge, but they didn't see each other in the flesh, to avoid the paparazzi and Sachs' spies.

Michel Colombier witnessed Serge's unhappy moments at the time: "I felt Bardot was a woman who needed to love someone very much. And Serge was totally different from the men she had previously met. I saw him in total confusion: he wanted to go see her in Spain while we had so much work to do here in Paris. He even had this crazy idea of bringing us all, him, me and my whole family, to live there, so that he might be nearer to Brigitte. We had to dissuade him from doing so."

Even Serge's own father was not mistaken by his son's jokes, when he pretended he was perfectly fine: "He suffered a lot, that's the truth, it was a real agony, the martyrdom of a bashful lover who was waiting in vain, all alone. Alone, alone, alone! And no sympathetic soul to confide in! He spent days locked up in the apartment, until he saw her one day at her dressmaker's."

To exorcise his grief, Gainsbourg would write "Initials B.B.," whose melody is a rip-off of Anton Dvořák's Symphony No. 9 (this was common practice for Gainsbourg; Chopin was also a treasure trove of inspiration):

Jusques en haut des cuisses
  (Up to top of her thighs)
Elle est bottée
  (She's in boots)
Et c'est comme un calice
  (And it's like a chalice)
À sa beauté
  (To her beauty)
Elle ne porte rien
  (She wears nothing)
D'autre qu'un peu
  (But some)
D'essence de Guerlain
  (Fragrance by Guerlain)
Dans les cheveux
  (In her hair)

B.B. Initials B.B. (x3)

À chaque mouvement
  (With each movement)
On entendait
  (One could hear)

Les clochettes d'argent
  (The little silver bells)
De ses poignets
  (At her wrists)
Agitant ses grelots
  (Shaking them all)
Elle avança
  (She took a step further)
Et prononça ce mot:
  (And uttered this word:)
Alméria!
  (Alméria!)

Broken-hearted, Gainsbourg's womanizing was as prevalent as ever as he tried to find comfort in numerous love affairs. To a friend, he said he wanted to drown in the river Seine. He had always considered himself a very ugly man, and suddenly he had been singled out as the lover of a beautiful woman who sincerely loved him. The narcissistic wound had left a gaping hole.

Jane B.: Nationality: British Sex: Female

Ironically enough (or was it fate?), Bardot would meet Gainsbourg's partner-to-be Jane Birkin in Alméria, during a party given after the shooting of *The Magic*, starring Michael Caine. Birkin, who had just broken up with John Barry, had been invited there by her brother, who was an assistant on the set. She herself had already been seen in small roles in *Blow-Up* (Gillian Hills, another *fille de la pop*, had a small role in it too) and *Wonderwall*. She was then of course far from knowing that she would in some way replace Bardot the star: she was just a twenty-something with an estranged spouse and a nine-month-old baby to care for.

Birkin had led a very domestic life in the second half of the 1960s, married to a man she seldom saw, mainly due to his hectic way of life, and she was very unhappy with it. She thought she was made to be "the perfect housewife, easily satisfied with preparing her husband's turtle soup and steak in the evening, some sort of an ideal woman." *Newsweek* unwillingly added insult to injury when describing John Barry as "arriving home in his Type-E Jaguar beside his Type-E wife." Even though she was an up-and-coming young actress in the Swinging London scene, her life was a very traditional one, and her dreams were slowly fading away. This was strengthened by Sharon Tate's murder; suddenly Charles Manson had put an end to the Flower Power era:

That was the end of what seemed so nice and beneficial with Flower Power...When Sharon Tate got killed, there was an immediate disgust with long dresses, bells and smoking pot. Nothing of this seemed to be fresh and joyful anymore. Maybe it was because I knew her a bit. It was irrational, she was a symbol for innocence, and then...Enthusiasm had completely disappeared overnight, everybody had a very bad taste in their mouths.

Birkin's very short British career would be attached to these two films, *Blow-Up* and *Wonderwall*. The former was directed by Michelangelo Antonioni, and featured the Yardbirds imitating the Who smashing up their gear, as well as David Hemmings, whose character was modeled on the most famous photographer of the period, Catherine Deneuve's husband David Bailey. The most controversial scene was the one some called "pornographic": for the first time in a film rated "general public," pubic hair could be seen! A blonde Jane Birkin and a brunette Gillian Hills played two Dolly girls harassing photographer Thomas (David Hemmings), who had them come to his studio, where he tore their clothes off and forced them to climb into his bed.

Wonderwall was shot by relatively unknown Joe Massot, who made this surreal pop pastiche full of slapstick moments and then vanished into thin air. The film was very psychedelic in mood, with drawings by the Fool (the painters/musicians who designed the Apple boutique in London and put out an LP in 1968), wide-angle lenses, and an Indian-sounding soundtrack by George Harrison. Jane played Penny Lane (see the hint?), a young maid spending her nights out at trendy hippie parties, among

David Hemmings and Jane Birkin in *Blow-Up*

people smoking joints, playing the sitar or banging on bongos, with semi-naked girls and loose morals. Her neighbor was an old professor who spied on her so much it drove him mad. Anita Pallenberg made a cameo, and Penny's boyfriend had a strong accent from Liverpool; the film was also a tribute to rock stars of the moment, even if it wasn't well-received by the general public. Birkin thought it was "a period piece, with all its charms and faults—the original idea was great, but the result just followed the trend too much."

She might have been too harsh when remembering this part of her life. After all, Mick Jagger and Keith Richard react the same way when they claim to hate *Their Satanic Majesties Request*: they were surely too busy living their youth at full speed to really appreciate what they were doing. It took a generation to do so.

In February 1968, filmmaker Pierre Grimblat, who used to work in the advertising business, wrote a script for a film to be called *Slogan,* and offered Gainsbourg the lead as one Serge Faberger, a man disillusioned with everything who nevertheless finds love in the character of Evelyne, a much younger woman from across the Channel. On Grimblat's initiative, Birkin was invited for an audition with Gainsbourg, who was living at the time with his parents, while his new house on rue de Verneuil (now a pilgrimage destination for fans) was being refurbished. On that first meeting, Gainsbourg was surrounded by journalists in his childhood bedroom covered with posters and photographs of Bardot, whose version of "Je T'aime" was being played on the hi-fi speakers.

Years later, Jane would confide: "I was so embarrassed, but also very excited, because it was so puzzling. Bardot was so great in that song, the arrangements fantastic, the whole buzzing inside my head!"

As he usually was under those circumstances, Serge got very unpleasant with her. As she politely asked him how he was, he dryly answered "Who cares how we both are?" Grimblat even said that Gainsbourg was "a perfect bastard" during screen tests.

In spite of these initial difficulties with her partner (who wanted Marisa Berenson to play opposite him), Birkin got the job. Although she didn't speak good French at all, she spent the events of May 1968 in an ecstatic state, eagerly waiting for the shooting to begin the next summer. But reality was very different from what she had expected: Grimblat had to comfort her every evening when filming stopped, as Gainsbourg became more and more aggressive toward her during the day. But true life and fiction intermingled when—as unexpected as it was by everyone who witnessed their daily quarrels on set—Serge and Jane started a relationship after a drunken night out at the New Jimmy's, a place owned by Régine, the pagan goddess to the stars' lonely hearts club band.

Birkin started to realize that Gainsbourg's personality was one of extreme sensitivity and charm: "we had a dance together, and he was so clumsy he kept stepping on my feet, which I found irresistible. I thought it was marvelous to see, that cynical, seemingly blasé man who couldn't dance! We had such a very good laugh!" They ended up in a hotel bedroom in which Serge immediately fell asleep. Jane left him, not too disappointed—as a joke, she put *Yummy Yummy Yummy* by Ohio Express between his toes (she happened to have the record in her handbag). The most famous couple of France's pop was born, with great "love in their tummies," as the fifteen years to follow would show.

One funny anecdote: Birkin very soon afterwards was chosen by Jacques Deray to play with Alain Delon in *La Piscine*. Each morning, the actors and crew would be amazed to see a jealous Gainsbourg arriving on the set with a Rolls or a Bentley, just to show off a bit and impress his potential rival.

Slogan was very successful with the general public and the critics alike, with the exception of some intellectual leftists, who were wary of a film made by a former advertising executive. In *Télérama*, a weekly aimed at both Catholic and left-wing obedience, Jean Collet wrote that this "so-called anti-advertising movie actually looked like an advertising slot, something wanting to fight the stupefying effects of the mass media but being stupefying itself." As for film monthly *Positive*, it saw Jean-Paul Török judge Grimblat's whole confession to have "the thinness of an anecdote, the feelings described here no stronger than sharp-figured miss Birkin, the directing of the actors gone with the wind."

However, *Slogan* acquired something of a cult status as the decades passed by. It was visually very imaginative, bordering on psych. Grimblat managed to grasp the mood of the day, the "good vibes" of innovation and adventure that still prevailed. A single was released in 1969, featuring two extracts from the soundtrack, written by Serge and Jean-Claude Vannier.

The beautiful *Chanson De Slogan/Evelyne* 45 was the first time Birkin and Gainsbourg recorded a duet. The main track was free from any cynicism,

and adopted the same path from sadness toward a better future as the script did:

> *Tu es faible tu es fourbe tu es fou*
>   (You're weak, you're deceitful, you're mad)
> *Tu es froid tu es faux tu t'en fous*
>   (You're cold, you're false, you don't care)
> *Évelyne je t'en pris Évelyne dis pas ça*
>   (Evelyne, please, Evelyne don't say that)
> *Évelyne tu m'as aimé crois-moi*
>   (Evelyne you once loved me, believe me)
>
> *Tu es vil tu es veule tu es vain*
>   (You're vile, you're spineless, you're vain)
> *Tu es vieux tu es vide tu n'es rien*
>   (You're old, you're shallow, you're nothing)
> *Évelyne tu es injuste Évelyne tu as tort*
>   (Evelyne, you're unfair, you're wrong)
> *Évelyne tu vois tu m'aimes encore*
>   (Evelyne, you see, you love me still)

Birkin soon moved in at 5 bis, rue de Verneuil, in a house Serge had decorated with obsessive care, as if it were a curiosity store. A place in which every object had an aesthetic function, in which black and white were predominant. The atypical young woman (she always carried a wicker basket, even in clubs) agreed to record her own version of "Je T'Aime, Moi Non Plus," whose initial version was heard only by a few privileged people. As it was of course no less shocking than Bardot's take, Georges Meyerstein, the manager of Serge's label Philips told him: "You may go to prison. The publishing company's MD may go to prison. I may go to prison. Releasing just one single is not worth the risk. Go to London and come back with a full album." An LP was thus recorded which saw the light of day in 1969, simply called *Jane Birkin-Serge Gainsbourg*, one half of the album being dedicated to each singer, with duets "Je T'Aime" and "69, Année Erotique."

The most brilliant tracks were "Orang-Outang," a wonderful stab at Serge's complex about ugliness, "Jane B" (with a prelude by Chopin), and the heartbreaking "Le Canari Est Sur Le Balcon" (about a young lass who, before her suicide by gas, writes a note to help save the canary she had left on the balcony). Rather expectedly, "Je T'Aime" was the one that raised passions. It was banned by the BBC, as well as by other radio stations across the world (as far away as Brazil!).

The Vatican excommunicated the A&R man responsible for having imported the song into Italy. Its official newspaper, *L'Osservatore Romano*, claimed the song was "obscene and unlistenable by underage kids." The publisher was even condemned to a two-month sentence. In England, despite the ban, the song reached number two, just behind "Bad Moon Rising" by Creedence Clearwater Revival. However, Fontana agreed to stop pressing it, in accordance with Queen of the Netherlands Juliana's demand (she was a shareholder in the company). Irish label Major Minor took advantage of the situation and bought the licensing back. In France, Philips sold the rights to Gainsbourg, who then negotiated with label AZ.

Such controversy was all the more beneficial for the song: in Italy alone, the single was exchanged for 50,000 liras (a huge sum then) on the black market, hidden under Maria Callas record covers. The ban had the opposite effect of its intention: the song sold by the ton throughout the world, with the considerable exception of the U.S., where it only reached number sixty-nine! Numerous covers or parodies were made, some of them huge hits as well. It became a part of the

collective unconscious in France. People were proud to say they had conceived their children to that song. As for him, Gainsbourg would later confess that he had no intention of writing an erotic song, but aimed on the contrary at underlining the despair of sexual practices. He added that "Je T'Aime" was "the shortest aphorism about incommunicability. Everything was wrapped in sighs, but, you know…"

Whatever. The song made him a rich(er) man: the year it was released alone, it earned him 69.2 million francs in songwriting royalties (Birkin earned one million as its singer). The spiciest anecdote is of the day young Jane had her parents listen to the record: she'd stop the record player each time the groans of pleasure were to happen, and her mum, actress Judy Campbell, in typically stolid British manner, declared the melody to be "very pretty indeed!"

The Gainsbourg/Birkin duo would be, for the ten years to follow at least, the subject of countless reports in newspapers or on TV, magazine covers, and radio interviews. Beyond the gossip columns, they were embodying a new freedom of morals after years of the stricter Gaullist way of life. TV director André Flédérick saw them as very symbolic of the desires and wishes of the era:

Everyone remembers those pictures of Jane with a see-through mini-dress showing her breasts and mini-knickers. For the people of my generation, Jane and Serge brought along very good things. They were daring what we were not used to daring, they were contributing to make the boundaries of what was acceptable stretch: lovers at the time almost felt they couldn't freely kiss in the street, let's all remember that! One could sense there was extraordinary love and complete liberty in their relationship. And Jane, of course, with her openness and frank character, was the exact opposite of a sex object without autonomy. She had come a long way from the pretty English doll she used to be. She was blossoming with Serge.

Birkin instantly became a star, posing with her companion for *Rock & Folk* in September, then on her own for *Lui*, the "modern man magazine" (as the slogan claimed) in December. *Lui* was directed by Jacques

Lanzmann (Dutronc's lyricist) and was a serious rival for *Playboy*, its laid-back yet sophisticated tone a favorite among young, educated bachelors who wanted to be attractive. It once featured articles by people such as François Truffaut or Michel Mardore, illustrations by Jean-Paul Goude, and interviews with Belmondo or Sacha Distel, NRF head Jean Paulhan, film directors Jean-Pierre Melville or writer Maurice Clavel, even protean artist Boris Vian, without forgetting the pinup girls painted by Aslan and an impressive cast of French stars: Brigitte Bardot, Mireille Darc, Dani, Valérie Lagrange, or Marlène Jobert.

The cinema got interested in Serge and Jane as a couple: in 1969, they starred in *Les Chemins de Katmandou* by André Cayatte, a turkey of a film riding the dying wave of fear the hippies had inspired in the bourgeois. Jane remembers being "probably a bit ridiculous with my posh English accent. All these hippies in Katmandou, they were really naff and sad to see, with their slippers, their dysentery, their poverty. Flower power was real gone and pitiful. When compared to Barbet Schroeder's *More*, *Katmandou* was a very conventional film." During the shooting, Gainsbourg had a really bad trip after he had smoked very strong hash, and Birkin could not enjoy the sheer beauty of India, traumatized as she was by the extreme destitution surrounding them.

That same year, Jane and Serge shot the tedious *Cannabis*, directed by Pierre Koralnik, a gangster movie that was some kind of exploitation film and turned out to be a flop, despite the fact that Birkin appeared naked! Its soundtrack, a true classic, was co-written with Vannier. In 1970, Birkin played in famous French critic Henry Chapier's post-psych *Sex Power*, with former Aphrodite's Child's keyboard player Vangelis writing a magnificent score.

The pace of productions then went down, with Birkin less and less interested in shooting new films just for the sake of it. Her reputation was still that of the sex kitten singing in "that song 'Je T'aime'" and of Serge's ready-for-another-scandal partner.

That leads us to 1971 and "Décadanse," which saw Birkin and Gainsbourg at their provocative peak, with a not-so-discreet hymn to sodomy (they were seen performing this new dance on TV—in full clothes, mind you!). Here's the translation of the lyrics:

Turn
No
Against me
No, not like that
And dance
The decadance
Move your hips
Slowly
In front of mine
Stay there
Behind me
And sway
The decadance
Let your hands
Brush against my breast
And my heart
Which is yours
My love
Forever
Patience
The decadance
Under my fingers
Will lead you
Toward faraway
Afterlives

This was covered in 2007 by Alain Chamfort, duetting with young actress Mylène Jampanoï. Chamfort's artistic destiny was linked to some *filles de la pop*: he worked with Lio and her younger sister Helena Noguerra, who can be seen as having inherited the spirit and charm of 1960s icons.

Also in 1971, there was of course *Histoire de Melody Nelson*, Gainsbourg's most famous LP, done with Jean-Claude Vannier and the crème de la crème of British studio musicians. Always the opportunistic type, Serge had decided to follow the trend and have a go at his own concept album. Although her vocal involvement was less than minimal, Jane was at the center of the whole thing, as a personal projection of Nabokov's young heroine Lolita. Gainsbourg staged himself starting with the very first song, in which he drives a Rolls-Royce that bumps into a teenager riding her bike ("aged fourteen springs and fifteen summers," the lyrics go):

Un petit animal
    (A small animal)
Que cette Melody Nelson
    (That Melody Nelson)
Une adorable garçonne
    (Such an adorable tomboy)
Et si délicieuse enfant
    (And such a delightful child)
Que je n'ai con-
    (That I on-)
-Nue qu'un instant.
    (-Ly knew for a while)
Oh! Ma Melody
    (Oh! My Melody)
Ma Melody Nelson
    (My Melody Nelson)

→

Aimable petite conne
   (Amiable little bastard)
Tu étais la condition
   (You were the sine qua non condition)
Sine qua non
De ma raison
   (To my reason)

Would such a record be possible today after Polanski's case? It's doubtful. But at the time, record companies had decided to invest in more mature projects, such as pop operas like *Melody Nelson*. EMI thus funded Gérard Manset's *La Mort d'Orion*, Igor Wakhevitch's *Hathor*, Guy Skornik's *Pour Pauwels*, and Michel Berger's *Puzzle*, while CBS released William Sheller's *Lux Aeterna* and LPs by songwriters such as François Wertheimer. (These albums, now much sought after by collectors, all flopped. This would explain why the major labels then chose to limit themselves to MOR music, which in turn led to the creation of smaller independent labels.)

Melody Nelson has recently been reissued as a luxurious box set with unreleased material, which looks like a very late kind of celebration. Jean-Claude Vannier was the arranger of the original recording sessions. Jane Birkin said one day that "he was decisive on *Melody*—there was a very peculiar *color* attached to Serge's Vannier years. He was a modest, very touching young man who suffered a lot because Serge was in the limelight and he wasn't—which of course was quite easy to understand."

I met Jean-Claude Vannier in the early 2000s, as I was planning to reissue his *L'Enfant Assassin Des Mouches*, and was surprised to see how bitter he still was and how harshly he criticized Gainsbourg, "who did zilch music-wise on *Melody Nelson,*" while Vannier

"had to put into shape the four or five notes Serge had hastily written." The man was visibly very much in pain when reminded of his (great but obscure) 1960s arrangements with some *filles de la pop*, and preferred to evoke his (arguably mediocre) hits of the following decades. Some years later, as a new generation of pop lovers had reached the mainstream (people like Beck or Jarvis Cocker), Vannier got some kind of revenge when was invited to conduct his music at the Hollywood Bowl in Los Angeles and the Barbican Centre in London. At the Cité de la musique in Paris in 2008, where he was supposed to honor the memory of his "best enemy," he didn't even utter Gainsbourg's name once in between songs. Perhaps this goes to show that some periods of time have more talent, so to speak, than the people who defined them—or that 1960s yé-yé and pop music still suffer from the same prejudice today as it did then.

On the sleeve of *Melody Nelson* was a topless Jane Birkin, her breasts carefully hidden by a chimp cuddly toy, wearing casual jeans but with the makeup of a baby doll. The photograph was taken by Tony Frank, who worked for Polnareff and Hallyday, but also Dylan, Hendrix, and The Who, and it played a major role in the LP's reception. People who thought it'd be a very domestic record were bewildered by its content. Conversely, others simply didn't buy it because they wanted something more extreme, more scandalous, and were given a mistaken impression by such an "innocent" photograph. Now, Gainsbourg scholars cite the sleeve as one of the best they have ever seen. Perhaps the music was disconcerting too: its hypnotic violin layers, roaring bass, Serge's Gitanes-damaged voice doing more talking than singing, the unusual pattern of the songs akin to a Baudelaire-meets-Pink-Floyd project; all of this was too avant-garde for French audiences (it sold only five thousand copies).

The narration was simple: a chance meeting between a jaded, well-off forty-something man and a four-teen-year-old Lolita, their love at first sight, their carnal passion in a luxury hotel used by prostitutes, eventually grinding to a halt in a pagan cere-mony, some sort of a voodoo cult in the jungle of New Guinea. Melody Nelson dies in a plane crash, which Gainsbourg would justify this way: "I wrecked her so that our love would be an everlasting one."

His misogyny would reach further heights in an interview with *Super-hebdo*: "Women's lib? Don't give…! Male and female equality? Don't give… either! It'll never exist anyway. There must be one domineering and one being dominated, that's a natu-ral law. In the U.S., women are boss. Here, men are—which I find better, of course." Despite such provoca-tive remarks, a woman is the central figure of *Melody Nelson*: Birkin, of course. In July 1971, she gave birth to their daughter Charlotte, just months before the album was set to pictures by Jean-Christophe Averty. Working, as film critic Jacques Siclier wrote, "quite stubbornly on a creation fed with his own dreams, his own tastes and his passion for the televisual medium, which he wanted to make

SERGE GAINSBOURG
JANE BIRKIN
PAUL NICHOLAS
ET
CURD JURGENS
DANS

Cannabis

INTERDIT
AUX MOINS 18 ANS

UN FILM DE
PIERRE KORALNIK

ROGER DUCHET
ET NAT WACHSBERGER

D'APRÈS LE ROMAN DE
F.S. GILBERT
"ET PUIS S'EN VONT!…"
(ÉDIT GALLIMARD SÉRIE NOIRE)

AVEC LA PARTICIPATION DE
GABRIELE FERZETTI

ADATATION DE
PIERRE KORALNIK ET FRANTZ-ANDRÉ BURGET
DIALOGUES DE
FRANTZ-ANDRÉ BURGET

MUSIQUE DE
SERGE GAINSBOURG
IMAGES DE
WILLY KURRANT

TECHNISCOPE
EASTMANCOLOR
DIRECTION DE LA PRODUCTION
ANDRÉE DÉBAR
UNE SÉLECTION
OCEANIC FILMS
(RAYMOND GAUTREAU)

the ideal means of expression for the general public, Averty didn't want to deliver a message and was this way totally unique."

As a true connoisseur of surrealism, Averty used paintings by Belgian Paul Delvaux, with dehumanized naked women seemingly posing in very stagey settings. As a result, journalists and the public alike would write infuriated letters to the editor about the film—which didn't impress Averty, who had created a scandal years before by pretending to be crunching babies on a vegetable mill live on TV.

As time passed, Gainsbourg got frustrated, because he was becoming "Mr. Birkin" more and more: his career had come to a halt, whereas Jane kept being offered film roles. In 1972, though, the

Brigitte Bardot and Jane Birkin in *Don Juan '73*

pair were reunited for the appalling comedy *Trop Jolies Pour Être Honnêtess* by veteran Richard Balducci (the immortal director behind the mega-kitsch *La face Cachée d'Hitler* with porn star Brigitte Lahaie). In spite of Elisabeth Wiener and Bernadette Lafont completing the cast, the film flopped, but was an opportunity to have Serge write a song for the soundtrack, called "Moogy-Woogy," and obviously very influenced by hearing Gershon Kingsley's "Popcorn" on the radio.

In 1973, Birkin was featured in Brigitte Bardot's last movie ever before she decided to retire: Roger Vadim's *Don Juan '73*. The result was disappointing, although the script (written by Jean-Paul Sartre's former secretary turned extreme right-wing novelist Jean Cau) was a promising one—imagining Don Juan as a woman. The most interesting part was the score, written by Michel Magne, and one sequence in which Bardot and Birkin were seen rolling naked together on a fur carpet.

The music of those years had changed, many a yé-yé girl having completely sunk without a trace. Vartan and Sheila were trapped in MOR treacle, Gall and Hardy doing totally different things, and a new generation of female singer-songwriters was arriving: Véronique Sanson was a French Carole King, Catherine Ribeiro and Brigitte Fontaine were more radical, while former *filles de la pop* like Valérie Lagrange or Dominique Grange completely changed styles (the former from poppy songs to *hippie* folk and the latter becoming a protest singer).

Jane Birkin became a regular guest on the Carpentiers' TV shows, doing numerous funny duets or trios. On *Top À Sylvie Vartan*, Sylvie, Jane, and Serge sang "Les Filles N'ont Aucun Dégoût," a very ironic (and slightly male-chauvinist) ditty:

Jane Birkin:
Oh c'qu'il est moche
    (Oh, how ugly he is)
Avec son pif et ses poches
    (With that conk and those bags)
Sous ses yeux blasés
    (Under his blasé eyes)

Sylvie Vartan:
Oh quel physique
    (Oh, what a physique!)
Toujours son p'tit air cynique
    (Always that little cynical air with him)
Et jamais rasé
    (And never clean-shaven)

To which Serge replied:

Oui mais les filles n'ont aucun dégoût
    (Yes but girls have no disgust)
Pour l'amour celui des sous
    (When it comes to love—love of money)
Elles se vautrent dans la boue
    (They'd wallow in the mud)
Les filles n'ont aucun dégoût
    (They have no disgust)
J'ai qu'une sale gueule j'suis qu'un voyou
    (I've got an ugly face, I'm just a rogue)
Mais elles se pendent toutes à mon cou
    (But they all hang on to my neck)

That year, 1973, was the last occasion when Vannier did arrangements for Gainsbourg: for Jane's wonderful *Di Doo Dah* album. The atmosphere was tense between the two men, and one clash too many led to a separation. Gainsbourg admitted that "he

was a great musician, but one day, after we had drunk very, very much, he told me that I was overshadowing him, to which I replied: *well, get off and leave me then!* He could have been one of the greatest orchestrators ever, but sensing he'd then take the risk of doing the same things over and over again, and being a very intelligent and hyper-sensitive guy, he decided to move on and stage himself with his own material."

Paradoxically, the LP would be full of very laid-back moments and hints of self-mockery, as evidenced by the similarly-named hit single:

Di doo di doo di daho di doo di doo dah
Je suis l'portrait d'mon père tout craché
    (I'm a spitting image of my dad)

Il chantait
    (He'd sing)
Di doo di doo di daho di doo di doo dah   →

Quand il m'accompagnait au lycée
    (When he was dropping me off at
    high school)
Les autres filles ont de beaux nichons
    (Other girls have nice tits)
Et moi moi je reste aussi aussi plate
qu'un garçon
    (But I'm as flat as a boy)
Que c'est con
    (How dumb that is!)
Di doo di doo di daho di doo di doo dah
Difficile de m'imaginer
    (It's hard to imagine)
En chantant
    (When singing)
Di doo di doo di daho di doo di doo dah
Qu'un de ces quatre ça va m'arriver
    (That it's gonna happen to me one day)

The *Di Dooh Dah* LP sounded like a bittersweet existential ballad, a kind of end-of-term assessment: "Help Camionneur" described a woman grown tired of love, "Puisque Je Te Le Dis" talked about the dissatisfaction of sex, "Leur Plaisir Sans Moi" adopted the point of view of a woman disillusioned with all men, "Kawasaki" was a *Bonnie and Clyde*-meets-*The Wild Bunch* motorcycle odyssey, and "C'est La Vie Qui Veut Ça" concluded with a "take it or leave it" ultimatum. Although the tunes and the lyrics were top-notch, the record didn't sell well.

Birkin was then much more respected as a powerful comedy actress. In 1974, *Comment Réussir Quand On Est Con Et Pleurnichard* by Michel Audiard saw her play a dancer making a living in shady cabaret clubs. It was a very incisive criticism of the average French male's conduct. Jean-Pierre Marielle, Jean

Carmet, and Jean Rochefort were perfect playing middle-aged boors leading the dismaying lives of losers. Jane's character being only attracted to pathetic men, this led to such dialogues as:

JANE: *J'étais sûre que t'étais formidable. Je suis pas déçue. Tu m'as loupée comme un chef. T'as pas arrêté de dire des conneries. T'as failli mettre le feu au paddock avec ta cigarette. Tu portes un maillot de corps. Tu gardes tes chaussettes.*
    (I was sure you were gonna be great! I'm not disappointed at all. You missed me big time. You kept talking nonsense. You almost set the paddock on fire with your cigarette. You're wearing an undershirt only. And you kept your shoes...)

MADAME ROBINEAU: *Antoine!*
    (Antoine!)
ANTOINE: *Oui maman?*
    (Yes mum?)

MADAME ROBINEAU: *Quand t'auras fini de tringler, tu viendras ranger ta voiture qu'est dans le passage!*
    (When you're finished getting laid, come down and park your car, it's in my way!)

ANTOINE: *J'arrive, maman!*
    (Coming, mum!)

JANE: *Et y a même ta maman...tout! T'es une synthèse.*
    (And there's your mum! You've got it all! You're the total package!)

The rest of the female cast included Stéphane Audran (Claude Chabrol's muse and wife) as an upper-class twat, and Evelyne Buyle as a receptionist obsessed with power. A very funny film and a great role for Jane!

According to her fans, the latter had found her way as the cute, amusing English girl with a strong accent: Claude Zidi's 1974 *La Moutarde Me Monte Au Nez* (with big 1970s star Pierre Richard) was thus a hit. Jean-Paul Belmondo and Brigitte Bardot had first been cast for the leading roles of this slapstick comedy, but their replacements were so successful that the Birkin-Richard duo had another go and shot *La Course A L'Echalote* the following year.

In the mid-1970s, trendy people such as the "gang" of La Coupole café and restaurant (Zouzou, Jean-Pierre Kalfon, Pierre Clémenti, Tina Aumont, Philippe Garrel and Nico, Valérie Lagrange, and Maria Schneider) cut their hair shorter, and started to be crazy about all things "decadent," being both society men and women and underground artists. Gay club Le Sept, owned by Fabrice Emaer (who'd open Le Palace, the temple of cool, in 1977) and driven by Guy Cuevas (a DJ who later played in *Jewel of the Nile* and in Prince's *Under The Cherry Moon*), became *the* place to be in between the Flower Power and punk movements. Marie-France, the glamorous androgynous creature who was their muse, and her friends from the Gazolines, pop and queer activists with the FHAR (Homosexual Front For Revolutionary Liberation), were also regulars who instilled some glitter in a post-1968 gray (and dull) everyday life.

Jane Birkin, though a night owl herself, was not necessarily fond of counterculture excesses, even when Swinging London was happening (this was mainly due to her very upper-class upbringing). Serge Gainsbourg himself was more preoccupied with shooting his first movie as a director, *Je T'Aime, Moi Non Plus*. For Jane's new LP, which was all but ready to go to print, he had so little time that he handed over production matters to Jean-Pierre Sabar (who had replaced Vannier), and even invited journalist, writer, and filmmaker Philippe Labro to offer lyrics. In fact, Serge had only firmly decided its title: *Lolita Go Home*, and laid down just a few chords and scattered words. During various meetings with Gainsbourg at rue de Verneuil, Labro thus tried to find his own way through Serge's morbid universe, the latter writing the melodies as his guest created the lyrics, in a tennis-like exchange of ideas. The LP was rushed through its release, with a sleeve taken from Jane's *Lui* magazine photo sessions.

Pressure was very strong when Gainsbourg and Birkin started *Je T'Aime* the movie, initiated by producer Jacques-Éric Strauss. Instead of the expected witty musical, Gainsbourg wrote a very gloomy fable about a diner waitress infatuated with a gay truck driver named Krassky (Joe Dalessandro, of Warhol movies fame), himself in love with his colleague Padovan (Hugues Quester). Jane's character was named Johnny, and was an androgynous girl with short hair who'd end up being sodomized near a garbage dumpster. A young Gérard Depardieu had a part, but Gainsbourg mostly paid attention to d'Alessandro, who seemed to have a crush on his British partner: Hugues Quester remembers "some fuss as Jane was very much involved in her role and quite troubled herself with Joe's good looks, which led to Serge being very jealous. To stage somebody that you love in situations like these can be a very dangerous game indeed."

Gainsbourg and Birkin had a symbolic S&M relationship on the set and in between the scenes: he would drink so much that he'd become both verbally and physically very violent, and she would be in tears almost every day. Things would always be the same: he'd hit her, and she'd go to her friend publisher Eric Losfeld and complain, before trying to find every kind of excuse to explain his attitude—and then go back to the set and have another quarrel.

Je T'aime, though, had pictures as magnificent as its purpose was crude. It was an uncompromising essay on luxury underground. When released, it was assassinated by the critics, who judged it "unbearable" (*Le Figaro*), "not worth commenting at all" (*La Croix*), or "disgusting" (*Libération*). Amidst such disgrace, *France Soir* found "tragic grandeur" and *Le Quotidien de Paris* "pitiless lucidity." The general public wasn't really interested—in 1976, the audience for such films was limited. Following the scandal, chief cameraman Willy Kurant left for the States, where he'd find a job as Willy Kurtis, working for Roger Corman. Jane Birkin, meanwhile, had managed to escape from her nutty Brit-girl image, which probably enabled her to be part of the cast of *Death on the Nile* (shot by John Guillermin), among Peter Ustinov, Bette Davis, Mia Farrow, and Maggie Smith. By then, the youngster who had played in *Blow-Up* had been completely forgotten.

In 1978, Jane recorded the "Ex-Fan Des Sixties" single that gave its name to the album. It's a beautiful song, enumerating names belonging to the golden age of rock and pop, which had disappeared for years:

> *Ex-fan des sixties*
> *(Ex-fan of the sixties)*
> *Petite Baby Doll*
> *(Little Baby Doll)*
> *Comme tu dansais bien le Rock 'n' Roll*
> *(Oh, how you danced to rock 'n' roll so well!)*

> *Ex-fan des sixties*
> *(Ex-fan of the sixties)*
> *Où sont tes années folles*
> *(Where have your crazy years gone?)*
> *Que sont devenues toutes tes idoles?*
> *(Where have all your idols been?)*
> *Disparus Brian Jones*
> *(Gone Brian Jones)*
> *Jim Morrison*
> *Eddie Cochran*
> *Buddy Holly*
> *Idem Jimi Hendrix*
> *(Ditto Jimi Hendrix)*
> *Otis Redding*
> *Janis Joplin*
> *T. Rex*
> *Elvis*

Also worth noticing on the same abum is "L'Aquoi-boniste," which Françoise Hardy had turned down, and which draws a portrait of a man who couldn't care less (modeled on Dutronc). The word "aquoiboniste" instantly became an all-purpose term for rock journalists to describe any depressed, cynical musician. "Dépressive" showed a side of Birkin that people were not aware of, while "Classée X" and "Exercice En Forme De Z" were wonderful exercises in style with alliterations in Y and Z. "Le Velours Des Vierges" sounded like a romantic poem set to Apollinaire's "11,000 Verges," and "Rocking Chair" recycled the track sung by Isabelle Adjani four years before.

In 1979, Alain Legovic's artistic life was heading in a completely different direction. He had started as a keyboard player in Les Mods (1966-67), and appeared in Dutronc's backing band (1967-68) as well as in Système Crapoutchik (1968-69). He then

embraced a career as a singer under the stage name of Chamfort (1968-70) and became a favorite of girly popsters signed to Claude François' Flarenasch record company (1972-76). Eventually, he would opt for more ambitious songs, and began a successful songwriting partnership with Jacques Duvall (who wrote "Banana Split" for Lio). Gainsbourg wrote the words for Chamfort's "Manureva," a synth pop lament that went to number one (Jane did the same for the B-side, "Let Me Try It Again," which was very charming).

The end of the 1970s would witness Serge's slow downfall: he had "created" his doppelgänger, Gainsbarre, a grotesque wino wallowing in childish provocation ("*Gainsbourg se barre quand Gainsbarre*

Released in 1984, this single, performed by Gainsbourg with his and Jane's daughter, Charlotte, was accused of glamorizing pedophilia and incest.

se bourre," he used to say—Gainsbourg clears off when Gainsbarre gets drunk). Sadly, this was at the same time as he had at long last achieved success with the teenagers: surprisingly enough, the latter were not repelled by singles and albums that were more and more botchy. He had come full circle from selling lollipops to (and thanks to) yé-yé girls and being considered a sell-out by the elite, to being successful (commercially speaking) with the children of the same yé-yés and being admired as an "agent provocateur" by the masses! He was like a permanent guest on the most popular talk shows, where he was invited by the hosts to "do something outrageous." And because he was too drunk to react and think correctly, he would oblige—and tell Whitney Houston he wanted to…her on prime time, set fire to three-quarters of a 500-franc banknote to show how the Tax & Income Administration Office was unfair to him, call Les Rita Mitsouko's Catherine Ringer "a whore," and on and on.

Watching this, Jane Birkin left him for intellectual filmmaker Jacques Doillon. In 1980, Gainsbourg would confess that "she was right to leave me: I was permanently drunk, beating her up over and over again. But the feeling of sheer love we have for each other will last forever." The same year, he met his new muse, Bambou, and immediately set sail for a sublime mansion in Beverly Hills to record a new album with Chamfort and his then-partner Lio. But nothing came of it, because of Serge's usual unpredictability. In spite of having split up, he carried on writing for Jane: LPs *Baby Alone In Babylone* (1983), *Lost Song* (1987), and *Amours Des Feintes* (1990) all contained great songs but also more pedestrian material.

His Majesty Serge's Court of (Other) Favorites

Let's go back to 1967, which was a pinnacle year for Gainsbourg. In addition to composing for Minouche Barelli, he wrote many hits: "Nefertiti" for France Gall, "Loulou" for Régine, and "Buffalo Bill" for Stone. In 1968, Mireille Darc was another lucky one: the now-cult star of Georges Lautner's films *La Grande Sauterelle* and *Les Barbouzes* (both with scripts by Michel Audiard) was given the tremendous songs "Hélicoptère" and "Drapeau Noir":

Mon lit est un radeau qui dérive sur l'eau
    (My bed is like a raft drifting on water)
Et là-haut, là-haut, tout là-haut
    (And over there, over there at the very top)
Là-haut flotte ma culotte
    (Over there float my knickers)
Un petit drapeau noir dans le vent du soir
    (A small black flag in the evening wind)

Sometimes, bad jokes were the basis for great songs: Régine's "Capone Et Sa P'tite Phyllis" was evidence of Serge's taste for spoonerisms. 1969's "Comment Te Dire Adieu" was a more serious matter, and Françoise Hardy a perhaps much better performer. Zizi Jeanmaire's "L'oiseau De Paradis" was perfect for the famous dancer and music hall captain, and "La Fille Qui Fait Tchic-ti-tchic" was unexpectedly fitting for Michèle Mercier.

The latter had achieved huge commercial success with the *Angélique* movies from 1964 to 1968, and was considered a new Bardot because her character embodied the ideal of a sexy woman with a strong personality, leading a life full of adventures. Even though the role eventually put an end to a greater career with more diverse jobs, Mercier had nonetheless played for Truffaut alongside Jean Gabin, and had real success in Italy with Mario Bava's film *Trois Visages De La Peur*, as well as in France with Robert Hossein's western *Une Corde, Un Colt* (its title song sung by none other than Scott Walker!). In Michel Audiard's *Une Femme En Or*, she had real presence onscreen, dressed in pop art clothes and posing in front of late '60s sets. Its most prominent musical moment was definitely "La Fille Qui Fait":

Je suis la fille qui fait
    (I'm the girl who goes)
(tchic ti tchic)
Ma robe de métal fait
    (My metal dress goes)
(tchic ti tchic)
Oui c'est elle qui fait
    (Yes it really goes)
(tchic ti tchic)
À chaque mouvement qu'je fais
    (With each movement I make)
(tchic ti tchic)
Quand tu n'l'entendras plus
    (When you don't hear it any longer)
(tchic ti tchic)
Quand elle se sera tue
    (When it stops)

→

(tchic ti tchic)
C'est que je n'aurai plus
  (It means that I won't wear any longer)
(tchic ti tchic)

Ma p'tite robe en alu
  (My small aluminum dress)
(tchic ti tchic)

The B-side of the 45, "Six Huit," written by Guy Skornik, was also very Gainsbourgian in its inspiration and result. After Bertrand de Labey's 1972 attempt to relaunch France Gall's career by way of Serge's songs (see earlier in the book), someone got the latter to try and do the same (if possible with more success this time) for Dani—funnily enough, with the Eurovision Song Contest in mind. Serge chose to develop one of the themes he had already been using, the image of the boomerang. Here's what he came up with:

Je sens des boum et des bang
  (I feel booms and bangs)
Agiter mon cœur blessé
  (Shaking my wounded heart)
L'amour comme un boomerang
  (Love, like a boomerang)
Me revient des jours passés
  (Me coming back from long-gone days)
À pleurer les larmes dingues
  (Spent crying the crazy tears)
D'un corps que je t'avais donné
  (Off a body I once gave to you)

The song, though harrowing, was turned down by the jury because it was deemed too provocative, and Gainsbourg refused to soften his lyrics. "Comme Un

Boomerang" went unreleased, until it became a surprise hit in the 2000s thanks to Etienne Daho, who
recorded it in a duet with Dani (the latter gaining a
new, younger audience on that occasion). The track
was even released in 2011.

In 1982, Lio covered Alain Chamfort's "Baby Lou"
(which initially appeared on his Gainsbourg-pro-
duced and largely co-written *Rock & Rose*). She
insisted on having it on the album *Mona Lisa*. This
gem was written by Chamfort and old accomplice
Michel Pelay (from Système Crapoutchik), with Gainsbourg adding lyrics to what seemed to have been
everybody's favorite back then (Jane Birkin would
also cover it the following year):

Sur les abords du périphérique
   (*Just near the ring road*)
Tu m'as aperçue par la vitre
   (*You saw me through your car window*)

On aurait dit comme le générique
   (*It looked like the credits*)
D'un film ricain sans sous-titres
   (*Of a Yank film without subtitles*)
Tu n'm'as même pas d'mandé où j'allais
   (*You didn't even ask where I was going*)
On aurait dit que tu t'en foutais
   (*You seemed like you didn't care*)
Toi, tu filais droit sur l'Atlantique
   (*You were heading for the Atlantic coast*)
Voir les bateaux qui chavirent
   (*To see a shipwreck*)
Moi, j'voulais m'noyer dans l'romantique
   (*I wanted to drown in romanticism*)
L'idée semblait te séduire
   (*The idea seemed to be to your liking*)

J't'ai dit "J'ai jamais vu l'océan
   (*I told you "I've never been to the ocean"*)
Qui sait, là-bas c'est p't-êt' plus marrant!"
   (*Who knows, things might be more
   fun there!*)
T'as compris ma philosophie, Baby Lou
   (*You got my philosophy, Baby Lou*)
Et ma façon de voir la vie, Baby Lou
   (*And the way I'm seeing life*)
Et pourquoi pas si c'est c'qui m'va?
   (*Why not then, if it does suit me?*)
Je n'suis pas concerné
   (*I'm not involved*)
Putôt du genre consternée
   (*Rather the appalled type*)
Et pourquoi pas si c'est c'qui m'va?
   (*Why not then, if it does suit me?*)

This wonderful track, sung gracefully by Lio, was
Gainsbourg's swan song with the *filles de la pop*. What
he offered Catherine Deneuve, Isabelle Adjani (with
the exception of "Rocking Chair"), or Vanessa Paradis
(without even mentioning Joelle Ursull) was no match
for his earlier career. Arrangements sounded instantly
outmoded, with overuse of Fairlight or DX7 synths.
But whatever the end of the story, Gainsbourg left a
very profound mark on French female pop history—a
funny thing for someone who did his best to appear
like such a misogynist, and once stated that "writing
pop songs definitely belongs to the minor arts."

6
MORE POP MADEMOISELLES

Gillian Hills

FIFI CHACHNIL IS A FAMOUS STYLIST WHO HAS worked for Lio, Mikado, Marc Almond, Pierre & Gilles, and Arielle Dombasle. In 2011, in a performance that made her seem like a post-punk Tinkerbell, she covered a bunch of Gillian Hills' songs onstage (the songs will also feature on her forthcoming album). Charmed by the naughty tongue-in-cheek freshness of the set, the audience wondered: *who the heck is Gillian Hills*? Marie-France herself had once covered the young British-French singer with the early Bardot hairdo, doe-eyed makeup, and a childlike smile.

Let's go back in time then. Cairo, 1944: Gillian was born. Her grandmother was a painter who counted Modigliani among her friends, while her grandfather was a famous Polish poet who had revolutionized the language of his country. Her father Dennis was both a writer and a secret agent for the UK. After years spent in a convent in Switzerland, the young Gillian settled with her divorced mother in Nice. While only fourteen, she met Roger Vadim, who was looking for an actress to play in his adaptation of Choderlos de Laclos' *Liaisons Dangereuses*. Gillian's mom later sent him a photograph of her daughter in a bikini, via Christian Marquand, a mutual friend. The irony of the situation was that Gillian wanted to carry on with her studies, while her mum wanted to push her forward in the film business. Five hundred girls auditioned, but Gillian got the part of Cécile de Volange.

She soon became a favorite of the media, and even appeared on the cover of *Paris Match*. Such unexpected fame finally alarmed her mother, who got scared that her daughter might follow the same path as Bardot, whom Vadim had met when she was fifteen. After Jeanne Moreau, the leading actress of *Liaisons*, began having problems accepting that she could be overshadowed by a debutante, everything led to Gillian being given a smaller role, that of a friend of Cécile's. But other actors nevertheless gave her the cold shoulder on set, with the exception of a caring Gérard Philipe.

To change people's ideas about her, Gillian left for London to star in *Beat Girl* by Edmond T. Gréville. The film perfectly depicted the pivotal years between the end of the rock pioneers and the arrival of the Beatles, when beatnik teenagers used to go to bars and listen to Elvis or his British counterpart, Adam Faith. The John Barry Seven appeared in a bewitching rock performance that saw Hills' character dancing with a haughtiness that was a real dramatic creation for such a shy girl. Noëlle Adam, singer Serge Reggiani's partner, played her mother, though with a strong French accent. Christopher Lee was a blackmailer threatening to reveal everything about the young alley cat's nightlife. Hills' character, Jennifer Liden, was a spoiled child who would do anything not to go study at St. Martin's College of Arts, where she had registered. "If mum could be a stripper, so can I now," she declared.

When the film was released, the British press nicknamed her "the sex kitten." Hills would comment about this years later, in *Jukebox Magazine*: "It was so restrictive! As if I just had cotton inside my brains! What was worse is that one may tend to conform to that sort of image: at the beginning, I refused to wear makeup

because I thought it didn't fit me. Then I saw Pascale Petit and wanted to be the same."

Once back in France in the spring of 1960, she had an audition for Eddie Barclay, a famed producer who ruled the roost at the time. Between 1960 and 1961, he'd have Hills put out five EPs in which her childlike voice excelled. With Jean Yanne and Henri Salvador, Gillian sang "Cha Cha Stop," pretending to be a British hitchhiker with a foreign accent. She had singing lessons, improved a lot, and was daring enough to interpret "Ma Première Cigarette," which advocated

the discovery of tobacco smoking for teens. This was one of the songs covered by Fifi Chachnil on that famous night—a song she didn't pick with a tribute to Gillian Hills in mind, but because it had remained very modern indeed:

Puff, puff...
Si moi j'avais 16 ans lui en avait autant
   (If I was sixteen, he was no older)
En cette pension ou tous deux étudions
   (In this boarding school where we
   were studying)
Mon ami Jimmy
   (My friend Jimmy)
Jimmy, Jimmy
C'était un champion
   (He was a champion)
Puff, puff...
Je me souviens d'un soir
   (I remember one evening)
Où tout près du parloir
   (When, very near the parlor)
Pour la première fois
   (For the first time in my life)
J'ai tenu dans mes doigts
   (Between my fingers I held)
Une cigarette
   (A cigarette)

Gillian Hills reached new levels of fame when duetting with American actor-singer Eddie Constantine on "Spécialisation" and "Aimons-Nous" (though unknown in the U.S., he was very popular in France—and really convincing in Godard's *Alphaville*). She of course soon became a regular guest on *SLC* and *MAT*, as a singer as well as a model.

But "the 1960s Lolita" suffered from an artistic dictatorship under her manager Jean Fernandez. She has more recently confessed to Jean-William Thoury that she "didn't choose which song she would sing or not, and rehearsed them only the day before they were recorded. 'Ma Première Cigarette' was OK to me—as for the rest…I wanted to do other things but couldn't, for being a singer required a certain amount of discipline."

"Si Tu Veux Que Je Te Dise," written by Aimé Barelli, was one of the highlights of those days. In 1961, Hills met Charles Aznavour, who was looking for singers from the new generation to place songs with. As he had shares in *Music Hall* magazine, he took advantage of the situation to promote his new protégé in an article that said it all: "Charles Aznavour is now writing songs for Gillian Hills, who's been rejected by Vadim." Gillian remembers him well: "Barclay told me Charles Aznavour was composing for me and my heart melted. He was such a warm personality, such a charming, handsome man that it was all but too easy to fall in love with him. As I hadn't lived with my dad very much, I liked the fact Charles was a sort of father figure. One detail which had its importance was that we were both of the same height: it created a kind of intimacy in the eye-meeting." With "Jean-Lou" and "Ne Crois Surtout Pas," Aznavour managed to both adapt to Hills' own personality and stay true to his own way of writing.

The same article informed its readers that Hills had recorded three singles in six months, was leading a very domestic life at the Hôtel du Bois away from parties and cocktails, and that she was fond of "Marlon Brando, Sinatra, Jeanne Moreau, and Brialy." She confessed to "holding a grudge against people who mystified me," which was no doubt aimed at Vadim, and to being "superstitious and frightened of roller coasters."

As months went by, she abandoned her cha-cha style to record twist songs, as witnessed by her EP "Tu Mens," on which the title track was the gem, with Mickey Baker writing the arrangements. In 1961, she played alongside Catherine Deneuve and Johnny Hallyday in "Sophie," one of the sketches in Marc Allegret's episodic film *Les Parisiennes*. Vetoed by Barclay, she had also missed a great opportunity to sing "Panne d'Essence" with Frankie Jordan, being replaced by Sylvie Vartan, who launched her career that way. But in 1963, Gillian's duet with Serge Gainsbourg on TV for the song "Une Petite Tasse d'Anxiété" was her fifteen minutes of fame:

Elle: (Her:)
Monsieur, s'il vous plaît,
    (Please, Sir)
J'vais être en retard au lycée!
    (I'm going to be late for school!)

Lui: (Him:)
Faites comme les copains
    (Do as your friends do)
Prenez le métropolitain!
    (Just take the Underground!)

Elle: (Her:)
Monsieur, je vous en prie!
    (Please, Sir, please!)

Je n'arrive pas à avoir un taxi
    (I can't manage to get a cab!)

→

Lui: (Him:)
Bon, montez
    (OK, hop on)
Prenons le chemin des écoliers
    (Let's take the long way round)
Vous prendrez bien
    (What about you having)
Une petite tasse d'anxiété
    (A little cup of anxiety)
Avant de vous rendre au lycée
    (Before getting to school?)

Elle: (Her:)
Où m'emmenez-vous?
    (Where are you driving me to?)
Etes-vous donc devenu fou?
    (Have you lost your mind?)

Lui: (Him:)
Un p'tit tour au bois
    (Let's go for a stroll in the woods)
Si vous n'avez pas peur de moi
    (That is, if you're not afraid of me)

Elle: (Her:)
Mais vous vous trompez
    (But you're being mistaken)
Je n' suis pas celle que vous croyez
    (I'm not the kind you're thinking of)

Lui: (Him:)
C'est ce qu'on verra
    (We'll see about that)
Si cela n' vous dérange pas!
    (If you don't mind!)

Vous prendrez bien
    (What about you having)
Une petite tasse d'anxiété
    (A little cup of anxiety)
Avant de vous rendre au lycée
    (Before getting to school?)

Surprisingly enough, she got sacked from Barclay's record company: other yé-yé figures, having started in more recent years, were better sellers—Hardy, Vartan, Gall. Hills then went to Brazil to shoot *Lana: Queen of the Amazons*, co-starring with Catherine Schell (who played a James Bond girl in *On Her Majesty's Secret Service*); Gillian was Maya, an alien who could turn into any creature at will. A year later, in 1965, she changed looks, with shorter hair and lighter make-up, just before she signed a recording contract with Lucien Morisse's AZ label. The man was heading Europe n°1 and had discovered talents such as Dalida (with whom he was living), Michel Polnareff, Christophe, and Petula Clark. Gillian's first EP on AZ saw her move toward poppier, more up-to-date sounds, although "Tut, Tut, Tut" made use of the same onomatopeia gimmick that she was so good at:

Tut tut tut tut tut tut tut
    (Beep, beep, beep...)
Voilà c'est comme ça depuis dix heures
ce matin
    (It's been the same since ten in
    the morning)
Ce n'est pas libre, ce n'est pas libre
    (Line is busy, line is busy)

Je sens la colère qui me fait trembler les mains
    (My hands are shaking with anger)

Ce n'est pas libre, ce n'est pas libre
     (Line is busy, line is busy)
Je perd mon sang froid en écoutant cet air-là
     (I'm losing my nerves on that tune)
Tut tut tut tut tut tut tut
     (Beep, beep, beep...)

J'ai tout essayé, mais c'est pareil chaque fois
     (I tried everything, but it's always the same)
Ce n'est pas libre, ce n'est pas libre
     (Line is busy, line is busy)
J'ai téléphoné du petit café en bas
     (I phoned from the café on the ground floor)
Ce n'est pas libre, ce n'est pas libre
     (Line is busy, line is busy)
Se moquant de moi chaque fois j'entends
cet air-là
     (Laughing at me, over and over the
     same tune)
Tut tut tut tut tut tut tut
     (Beep, beep, beep...)

The other tracks, "Oublie Oublie-La," "Rien N'est Changé," and "Rentre Sans Moi" were very influenced by the Beatles, and not quite far from Vashti Bunyan or early Marianne Faithfull. Logically enough, Hills went to England to record two songs for Vogue UK called "Look At Them" and "Tomorrow," carrying on with this new folky style of hers. But poorer and poorer sales made her quit the music business and become a full-time actress. After *Blow-Up*, she came back to France to play in the popular TV series *Les Globes-Trotters* in 1967. Her next interesting role was that of Albine in Georges Franju's 1970 adaptation of Zola's *La Faute De l'Abbé Mouret*. Francis Huster co-starred in the title role, as the abbot yielding to

the sins of the flesh. In 1971, a semi-naked Gillian Hills performed an infamous love scene with Malcolm McDowell in *A Clockwork Orange*.

More obscure but no less fascinating was *Demons of the Mind* in 1972, a curio of late-period Hammer, which was trying to revive *Dracula*'s years of fame by adding a touch of sex and violence to its movies—in this case incest and possession by evil forces. Two noteworthy facts: Patrick Macnee (John Steed in *The Avengers*) featured in the leading role, and it was directed by Peter Sykes, responsible for the incredible *The Committee*. (That film, with a script by Max Steuer, featured songs by Arthur Brown and Pink Floyd in its soundtrack and was a paranoid crossover between Orson Welles' *The Trial* and Patrick McGoohan's *The Prisoner*.) In 1974, Gillian Hills was already nearing the end of her acting career: a Spanish *giallo* shot in London, *La Muerte Llamas A Las 10*, and a minor spaghetti western called *Dallas* (shot by Juan Bosch) were her last contacts with the industry. Exhausted

Jessica Paré singing "Zou Bisou Bisou" on *Mad Men*

by showbiz, she became an illustrator, moved to New York in the late 1970s, and married Stewart Young, the manager of numerous rock bands. She has since moved back to London, and has enjoyed getting more and more young admirers.

Katty Line

Coming from Switzerland, where he used to manage Les Aiglons, René Porchet (a.k.a. Ken Lean) became an overnight sensation and a French showbiz wunderkind when his instrumental *Stalactite* (1963) sold 100,000 copies. A handsome kid in a leather jacket, he could have been a Gallic Phil Spector. Driven by his lust for life, he was unfortunately so unpredictable

that he made many enemies—he had, for instance, to leave Barclay for Pathé (EMI). In the studio, Lean would distance himself from his French counterparts by insisting on bass and drums in the mix. Musicians loved him, in spite of his Homeric fits of anger and control-freak attitudes, because he knew what sound he wanted and knew how to obtain it.

As a little girl, Catherine Boloban wasn't dreaming of becoming a singer, but an artist in the circus. She was born in 1947 to a working-class family living in the suburbs of Paris. Then she heard Vince Taylor and Ray Charles on *SLC*, and met Lean through a mutual friend. The beautiful blonde and the producer immediately clicked and became partners. Their romance would beget a bunch of very good songs indeed. After a turn as a backing singer for Les Dauphins on a cover of Bobby Goldsboro, Catherine, rechristened Katty Line by her boyfriend-mentor, released her first EP. The year was 1965, and the best track was a very convincing adaptation of the Supremes' "Back In My Arms Again" ("N'hésite Pas Quand L'amour T'appelle"). The rest was well above par, with a groovy composition by Lean, "Avec Toi Je Veux Danser," and a catchy number by Mort Shuman (once Doc Pomus' writing partner) who had just come to live in France: "Si Je Sors Avec Toi Le Samedi Soir."

Katty Line's image was carefully designed to position her as a sexy pop icon in op-art miniskirts. Sounding fresh and optimistic, she had even more success with her second single in 1966, "Je Cherche Un Petit Homme," and her third, Graham Bonney's hit "Super Girl," sung in French as "Les Garçons." On this, with a canvas of superb vocal harmonies, the lyrics (here translated from the French) went: "Hey, boys, despite our miniskirts, we'll never be taken in, you just have to wake up!" Katty would then travel across Europe and sing on Spanish or Polish television shows, and would of course be hugely promoted by *SLC* and *MAT* and get vast amounts of fan mail.

She also successfully covered Ann-Margret's "I Just Don't Understand" ("Je N'y Comprends Rien," written by Pierre Delanoë, who penned hundreds of songs). After a triumphant tour of Spain, she released "Un Mini Cœur," a song predating girl power, in which the narrator was settling a score with an ex-boyfriend. The funny "Les Mots Croisés," written by André Salvet and Sheila's producer Claude Carrère, was also very good:

Horizontalement
   (Across)
Un mot de sept lettres
   (A word in seven letters)
Et verticalement
   (Down)
Un mot de huit lettres
   (A word in eight letters)
Horizontalement
   (Across)
Un mot de trois lettres
   (A word in three letters)
Et verticalement
   (Down)
Un mot de
   (A word in...)

Ah! C'est trop compliqué!
   (Oh, that's too complex!)

Et je n'y arriverai jamais, jamais
   (I'll never ever manage)
Non, je n'ai pas besoin
   (No, I don't need to)

Pas besoin des mots croisés
   (Don't need to do crosswords)
Pour dire que tu me plais
   (To tell that I like you)

"How Does That Grab You, Darlin'" (written by Lee Hazlewood, sung by Nancy Sinatra) enabled an interesting comparison: on January 22, 1967, the DJ Rosco-hosted TV program *A Tous Vents* showed that Line's "Ne Fais Pas La Tête" was a good match for Ol' Blue Eyes' daughter's original version. And of course it didn't hurt that Katty was gorgeous, which people at her Olympia concert or watching her on television could easily see.

Her fifth EP marked a change: the tracks were folkier and there wasn't a single cover to be seen, a clear sign that she wanted to find her own way through. "Mon Cœur N'a Pas Dormi" was a dreamlike little jewel, to which Gilles Thibaut and Jean Renard (the team behind most of Vartan's songs) had added "C'est En Quoi?" and "L'amour Ne Tombe Pas Du Ciel." Thanks to them, Line started work as Johnny Hallyday's secretary, just before her last records were made.

It was 1968 and back to covers for a while, with the Easybeats' "Bring A Little Lovin'" brilliantly turned into "Un Petit Peu d'Amour." The following year, "Sans Un Adieu (Il Ne Faut Pas Pleurer)" and "Quand S'en Vont Les Framboises" were her tremendous baroque pop farewells to the French music business (the former wonderfully arranged by Jean-Claude Vannier). Katty and Ken settled in Italy, where four MOR singles saw the light of day between 1969 and 1971. After a visit to the Midem music festival in Cannes, they signed a contract with Adriano Celentano's label Clan, which led to a mellow version of the Doors' "Touch Me" ("Tu Vinci Sempre").

Line and Lane would then be caught in a terrible road accident. Lane lost his life, while Line was in the hospital for eighteen months being looked after by nuns. She came back to France and, hoping she'd resume her career, started a working relationship with the transplanted Italian singer Miro. But as she still suffered from her accident, she had to give it up. She told *Jukebox Magazine*: "I'm not the conservative/curator kind of woman: I haven't kept any of my own records, I gave them all to a friend. Being onstage was much more important to me, I don't even have a record or a CD player at home. When [I was] in the hospital, I started to read a Bible that had been given to me by Ken's parents. It was full of annotations, which was really touching. I've read many books about religion since then, especially about

Buddhism. I really feel home in a monastery. Today, I want to understand things a bit more." Katty Line's wrecked career paralleled surf rockers Jan & Dean and their famous song "Dead Man's Curve," as if to remind one of how chaotic the lush world of pop could actually be.

Chantal Kelly

Gimmick is a 1967 gem to be found in INA's archives. It was a narration-free report from the series *Le Monde De La Musique*, directed by Jacques Rozier (who shot *Maine-Océan* and *Du Côté d'Orouët*). It started with Dani and host Hubert Wayaffe having a

chat in the Europe No. 1 studios, but was especially worth watching because of its long sequence about Chantal Kelly. Born in Corsica, Kelly was the wonderful singer of "Caribou," written by Cris Carol, one of the rare female songwriters then:

Il est perdu le temps déjà
    (That time is already gone)
Où nous jouions toi et moi
    (When you and I were playing)
Aux Indiens dans la forêt
    (Indians in the forest)

Nous avions construit dans les bois
    (We had built a cabin)
Une cabane de bois
    (In the woods)
Où nous allions nous cacher
    (Where we used to hide)

Tu allumais du feu pour nous
    (You would set a firecamp for us both)
Tu t'appelais Caribou
    (Your name was Cariboo)
Tu étais le roi des Sioux
    (You were the chief of the Sioux)

On faisait la chasse aux oiseaux
    (We would hunt birds)
On descendait le ruisseau
    (Go down the river)
Dans notre petit canot
    (In our little canoe)

Ensemble nous étions heureux
    (We were happy together)

J'accrochais après nos jeux
    (After our games I would put)
Une plume à mes cheveux
    (A flower in my hair)

What was remarkable was Kelly's little nephew, nicknamed "Mini Michel," having a go at singing "Pas d'Excès," a swinging song produced by Richard Bennett. The whole process had been filmed, from Cris Carol's early hesitating chords on the

piano to rehearsals, through to unruly sessions in the studio, and ending with a broadcast on Hubert Wayaffe's program. Chantal Kelly, the girl with the pink knot in her hair, only lasted five 45s and a full LP. In 1980, she tried for a comeback with a New Wave record under her real name, Chantal Bassi. She wasn't very fond of her 1960s songs, which is a shame: "Le Château de Sable" was reminiscent of the Shangri-Las' "Remember (Walking In The Sand)," and "Les Poupées d'Aujourd'hui" was very popular as the theme tune for the Bella dolls commercials. Besides Cris Carol, her songwriters included Charles Level, Claude Bolling, and Joe Dassin ("Je N'ai Jamais Vraiment Pleuré"). Even Gérard Manset obliged for the magnificent "Toi Mon Magicien." Chantal became very popular in Japan, more than she ever was in her own country, unfortunately.

Cléo

In 1969, *Les Blousons Noirs*, a made-for-TV movie directed by one Paul Paviot, was made about Cléo. Born Chantal Rousselot, she was, along with Clothilde and Stella, a perfect illustration of caustic humor applied to pop music, in many ways closer to Dutronc than Vartan. She was part of the Vogue stable and had the privilege of having Hardy's beau compose for her, as well as Gérard Rinaldi and Luis Rego from Antoine's backing band Les Problèmes, plus her husband-to-be Herbert Léonard and the duo Bourgeois and Rivière, names closely linked to Brigitte Bardot's music career. The film was a fiction (at some point, Cléo was abducted by rockers) and clearly no classic, but it was efficient enough to let the viewers imagine the hardships faced by the young woman when on tour, singing in small towns in the middle of nowhere, facing an audience of bumpkins.

Clothilde

Elisabeth Beauvais, a.k.a. Clothilde, was born near Paris to a family of artists; her parents, actress Gisèle Parry and producer and playwright Robert Beauvais, were used to inviting famous people home, noticeably the movie star Michel Simon. At the tender age of eight, Elizabeth recorded her first song, for her mother's radio show. Ten years later, she met producer-musician Germinal Tenas from Toulouse, once one of the youngest rockers in France with his band Les Caïds. As early as 1963, he had been working with Antoine's producer-to-be Christian Fechner, and had soon established himself as a French Joe Meek. He'd become a reference for twisted psychedelic yé-yé sound in the years to come, working with Antoine, Jean-Bernard de Libreville, and Christine Delaroche, among others (Delaroche was at the time starring opposite Juliette Greco in the fantastic series *Belphegor*, broadcast on French TV). Germinal Tenas also took part in pure beat-pop artifacts such as Chorus Reverendus' single in 1967. As for Clothilde, she left a mark in history with only two 45s, made after she had met Tenas (then just nineteen) on the set of *Vient De Paraître* in 1965. The show featured Ronnie Bird, Michel Polnareff, Stone, and Eric Charden. Clothilde was to sing very ironic lyrics on a background of baroque pop arranged with a plethora of French horns and harpsichords. Following the "dumb and nasty" trend, the song was "Fallait Pas Ecraser La Queue Du Chat":

L'était pas superstitieux
  (Wasn't superstitious)
L'aurait dû l'être un p'tit peu
  (Shoulda been a bit)
L'aurait mieux fait d'éviter
  (Had better avoid)
L'innocent petit minet
  (The innocent little kitten)

Fallait surtout pas
  (Shouldn't have)
Ecraser la queue du chat
  (Crushed the kitten's tail)
Non,non, fallait pas
  (No, really shouldn't have)
Hep!
  (Hey!)

Il travaillait dans le bois
  (He was working in the woods)
C'était un garçon adroit
  (He was a skillful boy)
Qu'arriva-t-il ce jour-là?
  (What happened to him that day?)
La scie lui coupa le bras!
  (The saw cut his arm off!)
Fallait surtout pas
  (Really shouldn't have)
Ecraser la queue du chat
  (Crushed the kitten's tail)
Non, non, fallait pas
  (No, really shouldn't have)
Hep!
  (Hey!)

Comme il sortait d' l'hôpital
    (As he was leaving the hospital)
Une voiture l'accrocha
    (He got bumped into by a car)
Sa jambe droite lui faisait mal
    (His right leg hurt)
C'est la gauche qu'on amputa!
    (But it's the left one they amputated!)

The combination of Tenas' humor and Clothilde's pouting attitudes proved irresistible. Behind the scenes, though, the young girl felt ill at ease: she hated what she was singing, the hip clothes she had to wear, and the sometimes-high-school wit that lay beneath the words she had to perform. Her adolescent crisis and the mockery of her schoolmates developed her anguish further. In recent interviews, she confessed that she and Tenas went well outside the studio, but that their strong personalities regularly clashed inside of it. He would very often force her to

sing, to which she'd reply by demanding to be alone during sessions.

The public of course didn't know anything of it, and she was launched as a new face in a snap, starring alongside Les Charlots, Pierre Dac, or her rival in sarcastic songs, Cléo, sharing the same musicians and arrangers. The working-class Cléo would reproach Clothilde about her middle-class origins and insist on her family connections, which made her feel more depressed than she should have been. "Fallait Pas Ecraser," "La Chanson Bête Et Méchante," "La Ballade Du Bossu" and "102, 103" were indeed jewels she should have been very proud of. Éric Demarsan, who was to write scores for Jean-Pierre Melville (and, as Jason Havelock, published a great LP on Pierre Cardin's label), added his talent to give the songs mini pop-symphony leanings.

But in 1967, Elizabeth Beauvais had become so fed up with being Clothilde that she started to act very cold to people in the business and fans alike. Nobody at the time was clear-sighted enough to realize how frightened she was of fame. Her self-destruction as an artist went as far as not answering the phone when her own label, Vogue, was trying to reach her. It took her years after the end of her career before she was able to talk about those days as Clothilde again. Her two EPs were like a beautiful Hollywood set hiding a desolate landscape, or a nice little semi-detached house in a very cozy suburb, in which a desperate housewife has just turned on the gas and is hesitating before striking a full box of matches.

Clothilde

7
GIRL BANDS

FRANCE HAD ITS SHARE OF GIRL BANDS IN THE 1960s. To list them all would be impossible. I'll thus focus on the most important ones, starting with Les Parisiennes, who lasted from 1964 to 1971. Its four members—Raymonde Bronstein, Hélène Longuet, Anne Lefébure, and Anne-Marie Royer—were originally dancers who started their career with famous choreographer Roland Petit. They starred at the Olympia for three years with him (and on numerous TV shows), before they began singing, after meeting jazz band leader and composer Claude Bolling. The latter had primarily worked for Boris Vian and Sacha Distel, but also with Juliette Gréco and Brigitte Bardot. A very popular musician at the time, he advocated a ragtime jazz far from more adventurous hard bop and free jazz. Eager to develop a pop project, he pushed Raymonde to the forefront, knowing she could sing, then hired lyricist Franck Gérald (a songwriter for Polnareff, Bardot, Clark, Hardy, Gall, Greco, etc.) who tried to put himself in the young ladies' shoes and imagine what their day-to-day preoccupations could be:

On fait peur aux garçons
  (Boys are afraid of us)
Ça nous étonne mais c'est comme ça.
  (It surprises us, but that's the way it is)
On fait peur aux garçons
  (Boys are afraid of us)
C'est à croire qu'ils ne nous voient pas
  (It's as if they weren't seeing us)
On fait peur aux garçons
  (Boys are afraid of us)
Devant nous ils sont hébétés
  (Before us they look stupid)

→

Bien sûr nous recevons
  (Of course we get)
Des bouquets de fleurs, des billets doux
  (Bunches of flowers and love letters)

Tout pleins de mots enchanteurs
  (Full of enchanting words)
Mais comme on est quatre il faut se les partager
  (But being four of us we have to share them)

Even if, musically speaking, Les Parisiennes were quite inspired by the 1930s, their texts (and even the titles of the songs) were very modern, witty, and iconoclastic. Just listen to "Les Zozos," "Repassez Plutôt À La Saint Glin-Glin"and "C'est Tout de Même Malheureux (De Ne Pas Pouvoir Se Promener Tranquille)" and you'll see!

C'est bien normal d'avoir envie d'aller seul au cinéma
  (It's pretty normal to fancy going to the cinema on your own)
Oui mais le soir nous les filles on n' peut pas
  (Yes but us girls can't do that)
A peine a-t-on mis dehors le bout du nez
  (Just minutes after we've gone out)
Qu'on n'arrête pas de se faire accoster
  (We keep being accosted)
Alors on reste à la maison devant la télévision
  (So we stay home in front of the TV)
En pantoufles et en peignoir
  (In our slippers and dressing gowns)
C'est tout de même malheureux qu'on n' puisse pas
  (It's a shame not to be able to)
S' promener tranquillement dans les rues
Après 9 h du soir
  (Have a quiet walk in the streets after 9 p.m.)

In 1967, Les Parisiennes had a huge success with their cover of Sandie Shaw's "Puppet On A String," called "Un Tout Petit Pantin."

State radio France Inter was a great support for the band—even offering them a chance to write the theme tune to José Artur's *Pop Club* (which they did, their introduction to the program alternating with Serge Gainsbourg's). Their best songs were nonetheless ahead of them: "Il Flotte" in 1970, and "Un Rayon De Soleil" the following year. Claude Bolling had been replaced by trendier Georges Costa, who wrote psych pop numbers with loads of Hammond organ. Oddly enough, this marked the end of the band. Anne Lefébure became a host on TV for the next two decades, while Raymonde married singer Daniel Beretta (who had written fabulous psychedelic ditties with Richard de Bordeaux).

In spite of their all-too-brief career, which spanned 1962 to 1964, Les Gam's were the second most important girls group of the decade. They used to be Gilbert Becaud's and Sylvie Vartan's backup singers, under the Jinns moniker. The "Les Gam's" name was inspired by their initials: Graziella Portail, Annie Markan, Michèle Léger, and Suzi Gorini. Johnny Hallyday's cousin Lee decided to produce them, and they were part of the infamous concert at the Place de la Nation. Their repertoire was mainly covers of English-speaking singers, in French: "Il A Le Truc" (the Exciters' "He's Got The Power"), "C'est Bien Fait Pour Toi" (Lesley Gore's "Judy's Turn To Cry"), "Toi L'Ami" or "Attention, Accident!" (the Beatles' "All My Loving" and the Beach Boys' "Shut Down!"). "My Boy Lollipop," by Anglo-Jamaican Millie Small was also a hit, as "C'est Toi Mon Idole."

After touring with Claude François from 1964–1965, Les Gam's released an EP under the band name "Les Gam's with Annie Markan" (reminiscent of when the Supremes billed themselves as "Diana Ross and the Supremes"). "Une Petite Larme M'a Trahie" (Hank Cochran's "A Little Bitty Tear") was the most prominent song on the record, which featured country-pop items such as "Toujours Un Coin Qui Me Rappelle" ("Always Something There To Remind Me," written by Burt Bacharach). But in 1965, Annie Markan went solo, releasing four EPs before 1966. The record company wanted her to start fresh, to the point that her past with Les Gam's was never mentioned in interviews. The sound evolved from bossa nova (Tom Jobim's "Agua De Beber") to R&B ("Mon Obsession Me Poursuit," the Vandellas' "Nowhere

To Run"). Though Lee Hallyday tried to advertise Markan as "the first true French R&B singer," she went nowhere. Her last EP, featuring a catchy version of Charlie Rich's "Mohair Sam" ("Fière Allure Et Cheveux Longs") didn't sell as much as expected, and Annie chose to become a press attaché for Polygram. She'd end up promoting Sheila's disco comeback in the 1970s. Suzie Gorini eventually married Lee Hallyday, and Graziella Portail tried to carry on in the business but sank without a trace.

Another group, Les Petites Souris, released only one 45 on RCA. What's remarkable is that the five members of the group all played on this record, which was very rare at the time! They were led by Evelyne Courtois, who decided to take a chance in music after going to a gig by Dany Logan and the Pirates. A gifted

multi-instrumentalist, Evelyne met Gérard Hugé, a young producer totally in awe of Phil Spector, who used to play the drums and sing with Les Pingouins, and would pen songs for Stella, Alain Bashung, Ronnie Bird, and Noël Deschamps. Although Evelyne wrote two tracks on the EP, its best song was Gérard's "Ce N'est Pas Triste," a gem of a romantic teenage pop dream. Evelyne's vocals contributed a lot to the Petites Souris' charm, which would explain why, aided by Hugé, she quit the band to start a solo career as Pussy Cat (the name was a homage to the Tom Jones song).

Les Fizz had a very brief existence too. They had found a competent producer, arranger, and conductor in Jacques Denjean, a man who originally sang with the Double Six jazz vocal sextet, founded in 1959 by Mimi Perrin. At one time produced by

Quincy Jones, the Double Six also featured Michel Legrand's sister, Christiane. All through the 1960s, Denjean recorded his own compositions, which are now highly sought after by collectors ("Névrose," for instance, which was written in 1968—all sitars, smooth basses, and fuzzy guitars). Jacques Denjean's name is also found on numerous records by Charles Aznavour, Hallyday, Bashung, Christophe, and *filles de la pop* like Liz Brady or Elsa.

Danielle Licari, Jackie Castan, and Nadine Doukhan had started as background singers, just like the Gam's (in this case, for Sacha Distel). Their first EP, in 1965, had a tune written by Sacha, "Trois Filles Pour Un Garçon," which was an attempt at the Brill Building sound, though the best was "Tut Tut Tut Tut" (the Lollipops' "Busy Signal"), also in Gillian Hills' repertoire. "Stop, Tu N'as Plus Fait Ça" was their take at the Supremes' "Stop!" later in the year. It was quite good, as was their cover of "You Can't Do That" by Lennon-McCartney ("Si Tu Fais Ça").

In March 1966, Claude François invited them on a prime-time TV show, after which they released (in October of the same year) "Toute Ma Vie," an original slow dance number to make all teenage hearts cry… and that was it, basically! Danielle Licari went solo but completely changed styles, adopting a baroque-pop and jazz sound akin to the Swingle Singers.

It'd be unfair not to mention Les OP'4, whose lineup was made up of four cousins: Francine Chabot, sixteen, Martine Lejeune, nineteen, Dominique Poulain, seventeen, and Catherine Bonnevay, fourteen. They had trained by performing at marriages and first communion gigs, where Gérard Hugé discovered them. He and Eric Charden (before he had met Stone) teamed up to adapt standards for them, such as "You're Ready Now" by Frankie Valli & The Four

Seasons (which sold really well as "T'es Pas Malin").

Claude François signed the band on his Flèche label in 1968, and decided to change their name to Les Fléchettes. The girls were hired as part of his backing singers, and their records were then left in the shadow, becoming more and more…well, MOR! When asked years later about that period, the cousins admitted having learned a lot professionally with François, but wished they hadn't had to face his tyrannical behavior and innumerable fits of anger.

At the end of the sixties, composer, singer, and producer Billy Nencioli was slowly moving away from the Left Bank style on which he had built his reputation in the previous decade (in 1955, he and Serge Gainsbourg co-wrote an anti-army protest song, "On Lui A Donné," which was banned due to its reference to the war for independence in Algeria). In 1965, he recorded a pretty good bossa nova LP with Baden Powell, using arrangements by Michel Colombier. He also became a children's TV favorite as Samsong, a troubadour dressed in Napoleonic-era clothing (a French Willy Wonka?). This was just before he created Les Chimeriennes, four girls he recruited to sing marvelously surreal pop songs such as "Monsieur Cyber" and "Chimeria," distributed by obscure label Princess. Jean Morlier handled the arrangements: he had written an EP for Christine Pilzer's sister, Violaine, who was one of the most surprising of the swinging beatnik mademoiselles.

Les Chimeriennes' whole concept was developed into a satirical film, *Poussez Pas Grand-Père Dans Les Cactus*, in which they could be seen dancing to cosmic sounds—the best part of the film, actually. In June 1969 their robotic performance, under the baton of Morlier, was the best of the *Musicolor* TV program. A Proustian madeleine for those who watched it

then, their song "Monsieur Cyber" has recently been reissued on the *Groove Club Vol. 1: La Confiserie Magique* compilation:

> *Monsieur Cyber, je voudrais*
>   *(Mr. Cyber, I'd like)*
> *Monsieur Cyber, je voudrais savoir*
>   *(Mr. Cyber I'd like to know)*
> *Qui je suis, qui je suis*
>   *(Who I am, who I am)*
> *D'ou je viens, où je vais*
>   *(Where I come from, where I'm going to)*
> *Monsieur cyber, comment ça*
>   *(Mr. Cyber, how is it)*
> *Monsieur cyber, comment ça se fait*
>   *(Mr. Cyber, how is it that)*
> *Que mes yeux restent ouvert*
>   *(My eyes stay open)*
> *Quand je dors, quand je dors*
>   *(When I sleep, when I sleep?)*
> *Vous êtes des machines*
>   *(You're machines)*
> *Fabriquées en usine*
>   *(Made in a factory)*
> *Ca dure ce que ça dure*
>   *(It won't last forever)*
> *Mais la vie, elle vous est garantie sur facture*
>   *(But life is paid upon receipt)*

8
FRANCOPHILE *FILLES*

IN THE 1960S, ANGLO-SAXON HITS HAD TO BE adapted into French to reach a wide audience. Publishing companies established a hierarchy of songs to be sung and singers to promote them, in accordance with their status: Johnny Hallyday, Claude François, Richard Anthony, and Eddy Mitchell on one side, and Sylvie Vartan and Françoise Hardy on the other, got the lion's share of the more prestigious titles. Girls from abroad had to sing their hits in French versions too—that is, if they wanted their records to sell well.

Petula Clark

She became more famous in France than many of her British counterparts (she was nicknamed "the most French of the British girls"), because she was one of the first to adapt to the situation described above after she met press attaché Claude Wolff, whom she soon married. Her first French hits were "Chariot," "Ya Ya Twist," "Marin" and "Roméo," written by Tony Hatch of Pye Records. She attracted older women to her songs as well as teenage girls—perhaps due to her unaggressive exoticism and her gentle manners (she looked a bit like a nice, middle-class *au pair*), or her 1950s music-hall style. Her repertoire had mellow Swinging London leanings, far from the violence of the beatniks that frightened the French audiences so much. She was a kind of "older sister" to the younger British Beat bands (she was almost thirty when they all started to find success); she paved the way for them, actually.

In 1964, she released the more modern "Downtown," which became a number one hit as "Dans Le Temps" in France. Serge Gainsbourg gave her "O

Sheriff" and "La Gadoue," a huge hit in 1966. To carry on with adaptations, she even dared to turn the Kinks' "A Well Respected Man" into "Un Jeune Homme Bien"—which sold much more than the original, of course! Petula's 1964-1967 period included a streak of good songs: "Un Doigt De Champagne," "Puisque Tu Pars," "Il Faut Revenir." Then it all faded out, mainly because she decided to focus on her private life more than her career (she settled in Switzerland).

Nonetheless, she released almost eighty EPs in France from 1958 to 1970, with each one selling an average 500,000 copies! Her good friend Sacha Distel played a part in all this, regularly inviting her on his immensely popular *Sacha Show* on TV, in which artists were often asked to play in sketches, sing duets, or simply cover songs—which the audience loved, and which greatly increased sales.

Sandie Shaw

Née Sandra Goodrich, the barefoot brunette started with Pye Records and had a hit with her second single for them, Hal David/Burt Bacharach's "(There's) Always Something There to Remind Me" (Eddy Mitchell was even more successful in France with its adaptation, "Toujours Un Coin"). Sandie had an impressive career in France, where she released eight EPs and one LP from 1965 to 1967, all sung in French! Chris Andrews' "Girl Don't Come" and "Long Live Love" became "Mais Tu L'Aimes" and "Pourvu Que Ça Dure," among many others. Her style, her freshness, her kindness too, were decisive in establishing her as a favorite of the French market. This was how *SLC* depicted her in a 1967 article:

*Sandie Shaw is a curious, paradoxical charac-
ter: her blasé attitude offers deep contrast with
the freshness of her songs. She's not taken in
with her wealth, fame, or love, even though she
drives a Rolls (or rather, her chauffeur drives
it!) or has recently been brought to court for
some private affair. She hasn't got a particular
home, leaves her belongings with friends, only
taking her hair-dryer, her record player and
her records everywhere with her. As indeci-
pherable as she may seem, though, she always
shows total frankness and honesty.*

Shaw was often invited to guest star on TV shows
(such as *Age Tendre Et Tête De Bois* and the *Sacha
Show*), she opened tours for Richard Anthony or Hallyday, and was even the subject of a lengthy television
news report from the Bourget airport, in which she
was seen arriving bare-footed (her signature) and
greeted by a huge number of fans. As a true pop icon,
she was also a guest host once on *Dim, Dam, Dom*,
singing "Mais Tu L'Aimes" and introducing herself in
French with a charming "*je suis Sandie Shaw, j'ai 18
ans et maintenant regardons*" (I'm Sandie Shaw, I'm
eighteen, let's just watch the show) then taking a bite
from a baguette.

In a later episode of *Discorama*, one would learn
that her single had sold 250,000 copies in only two
weeks, the presenter insisting on the fact that her
foreign accent was actually an asset (something Jane
Birkin used to her advantage too). After her career
had reached a (relative) low in 1967, Shaw took part
in the Eurovision Song Contest with the infamous
"Puppet On a String" (which scored twice in France:
with its original version, and its adaptation, "Un Tout
Petit Pantin"). The same year, she'd sing "Une Anglaise

Aime Un Français," which also proved irresistible in
its use of clichés:

Quand je bois mon thé à 17 H
    (When I have my 5 o'clock tea)
Tu manges du pain, saucisson et beurre
    (You have bread, sausage, and butter)
Pour me faire plaisir tu apprends l'anglais
    (To please me you're learning English)
Mais avec l'accent de Saint Germain des Prés
    (But with a Saint Germain accent)
C'est comme ça qu'une anglaise
    (That's the way an English girl)
Aime un français
    (Loves a French boy)
C'est comme ça que je vais t'aimer
    (That's the way I'm going to love you)
Toi où que tu sois, tu es décontracté
    (Wherever you are, you're laid-back)
C'est tous les jours, le 14 juillet
    (It's the 14th of July everyday)
Les gens dans la rue sont tous tes amis
    (People in the street are all your friends)
C'est écrit dans tes yeux que tu aimes la vie
    (It's written in your eyes that you love life)

In 1968, Sandie Shaw was invited on Claude
François' *Music Hall De France*, in which she performed a heart-wrenching duet with Michel Polnareff
on his "Love Me Please Love Me." Then she adapted
Mary Hopkin's "Those Were The Days" ("Le Temps Des
Fleurs"), before scoring big with "Monsieur Dupont"
(whose original performer was the German Manuela).
She sang the song in both French and English; here
are the two versions:

La pluie dégoulinait lorsque mon petit pied
A touché le sol de Paris
Je me sentais perdue quand soudain, j'aperçus
Deux gentlemen très chics et identiques
Monsieur Dupont, la la la la
Monsieur Dupont, la la la la
Une demoiselle si jolie aurait besoin de
compagnie
Monsieur Dupont, la la la la
Monsieur Dupont, la la la la
Je vous en prie, prenez mon bras et suivez-moi

Ils étaient si mignons sous leur chapeau melon
Oh, c'étaient de charmants garçons
Je n'ai pu faire de choix et j'ai gardé pour moi
Deux gentlemen très chics et identiques

* * *

The rain was falling down, as I flew out of town
I went to Paris for the day.
And there I got to know a certain Romeo
With oh so gentle continental ways

Monsieur Dupont, la la ta ta, Monsieur
Dupont, la la la la
You made me see so tenderly that I was never
loved before
Monsieur Dupont, la la ta ta, I know it's wrong,
la la la la
That I don't ever want to go home anymore

You said "Hello" to me, and I began to see
That I could fall in love with you
I seemed to realize the kind of paradise
Your continental kiss could lead me to

In 1969, *Dieu Seul Sait* (*Heaven Knows I'm Missing Him Now*) was her last 45 but one, featuring Bernard Ilous (listen to his records or his duet with Patrice Decuyper), weeks before she covered Michel Delpech's "Wight Is Wight." She then turned to a job in psychiatry, before the Smiths' Morrissey convinced her out to come back and record one single with them.

Marianne Faithfull

Even though she didn't mention it in her autobiography, Marianne Faithfull always had a very strong link to France. Born in 1946, she was the daughter of an Austrian aristocrat and a British officer, as well as the grand-niece of Leopold Ritter von Sacher-Masoch, writer of *Venus In Furs*, who gave his name to masochism. French being the official language at the British court until 1480, it has left deep marks in Britain, and like any other upper-class girl her age, Faithfull was immersed in French culture.

At the beginning of the 1960s, when she was still singing folk music in tiny coffee bars in Reading, she met the Stones' manager, Andrew Loog Oldham. The rest is history: Jagger-Richard, "As Tears Go By," the charts, fame, scandals, the lot. Her adventures in France (from 1965-67) are less well-documented. She often crossed the Channel to take part in TV shows, recording French versions of her hits in the process—or doing the exact opposite, which was more original. In April 1965, Decca released two of her albums. On one, France Gall's "A Bientôt Nous Deux" and Chantal Goya's "Emporte Avec Toi" had become "He'll Come Back to Me," and "They Will Never Leave You." She then released an EP with "Nuit D'été," "Là Devant Toi," "Comme Une Aube Nouvelle," and "Si Demain." In 1966, Michel Legrand offered her a song, and she starred at the Olympia.

Still, the highest point in her French career was *Anna*. Koralnik, the director, was at the origin of her starring role in the movie: "Marianne Faithfull was an idea of mine," Koralnik told Gainsbourg biographer Gilles Verlant. "In the script, there was this strange, beautiful but wild girl, whose beauty was to contrast with Anna Karina's sophistication."

Marianne sang the strongly emotional "Hier Ou Demain," released on its own as a 45:

> *Écoute mon cœur qui bat*
>   *(Listen to my heart beating)*
> *Il ne bat pas pour toi*
>   *(It doesn't beat for you)*
> *Mais pour un autre que toi*
>   *(But for another man)*
> *Que je ne connais pas*
>   *(That I don't know)*

Hier ou demain
   (Yesterday or tomorrow)
Je t'aurais dit oui
   (I'd have said "yes" to you)
Hier ou demain
   (Yesterday or tomorrow)
Mais pas aujourd'hui
(But not today)

Oui, j'aurais pu être à toi
   (Yes, I could have been yours)
Mais tu n'étais pas là
   (But you were not there)

J'étais libre comme toi
   (I was free just like you)
Mais ne le savais pas
   (But I didn't know of it)

Newly divorced from Jean-Luc Godard, Karina nevertheless played in his *Made in USA*, with Faithfull playing her own role, in French! Freely adapted from Richard Stark's novel *The Jugger*, it was a political movie dealing with the Black Panthers movement, the Ben Barka affair, the Vietnam war and "American imperialism." Faithfull was seen singing "As Tears Go By" in front of indifferent Jean-Pierre Léaud and Karina, sitting on a couch.

But it was Marianne who had actually got fed up with it all. Just after the film was released, she answered interview questions about her recent teenage years as if they had happened in ancient times. Pretending to be all smiles and enthusiasm, but appearing sad and exhausted, she confessed to "hating playing live and getting bored by the music business." With a blank stare, she finished the interview with "I'm twenty, and am very tired" (two years later, she'd try to take her own life, just after Brian Jones' death).

Nico

Born Christa Päffgen in Nazi Germany, she was rechristened "Nico" by photographer Herbert Tobias as a tribute to filmmaker Nikos Papatakis. On a trip to Paris, she was noticed by Catherine Harlé's modeling agency (a prestigious one indeed, which had Dani, Marianne Faithfull, Anna Karina, Zouzou, Verushka, Amanda Lear, and Anita Pallenberg working for them). In 1959, she had a small part in Fellini's *La Dolce Vita*, then moved to New York to study at Lee Strasberg's Actors Studio. In 1962, her immaculate beauty was featured on Bill Evans' *Moon Beams* record cover, just before she gave birth to Ari, her son with Alain Delon. The actor refused to admit he was the father of the child, and Nico turned to his parents, who adopted the infant—which led Delon to break away from his family. Little by little, Nico would lose her brightness after years of intense drug addiction.

Nico and Darry Cowl in *Strip-Tease*

In 1962, though, she starred in Jacques Poitrenaud's *Strip-Tease*, with Dany Saval and a fixture of Parisian nights, Jean-Marie Rivière.

On June 16, 1963, in *Discorama*, Gainsbourg was interviewed about the film, whose score he had written, and images of Nico (as the *femme du monde* Ariane starting a striptease) appeared onscreen. She'd then record the song for a forecast release on a 45:

> *Ici s'achève le strip-tease*
>   (Here's where my striptease ends)
> *Qui te grise et m'idéalise*
>   (Which intoxicates you and idealizes me)
> *Voici la chair de la poupée*
>   (Here's the flesh of the doll)
> *Ses vêtements éparpillés*
>   (Her scattered clothes)
> *Pourtant si je suis toute nue*
>   (However, though I'm stark naked)
> *Je garde mon âme ingénue*
>   (I keep the soul of an ingénue)
> *Et je reste en tous points pareille*
>   (And I remain the same)
> *Là, dans le plus simple appareil*
>   (There, totally in the nude)

Eventually finding her voice to be too low-pitched for that song, Gainsbourg would ask Juliette Gréco to record it. Nico's version remained unreleased until 2001, when an anthology of Gainsbourg's film work was published. The rest is much better-known: Bob Dylan writing "I'll Keep It With Mine" for her, Warhol and the Factory, the Velvet Underground, *The Marble Index* and *Desertshore*, the throes of self-destruction with heroin, that fatal bicycle ride in Ibiza. Nico would

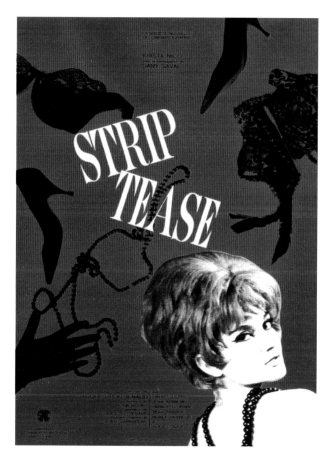

as Zouzou, Tina Aumont, or Valérie Lagrange. In the 1980s, he'd work with their heiresses: Elli Medeiros and Mathématiques Modernes' Edwige.

A cult French TV program about rock and pop, *POP 2*, presented an interview with Nico by Patrice Blanc-Francard, in which she said that meeting the Velvets' Lou Reed and John Cale at the Café Bizarre in Greenwich Village in 1967 was the best thing that ever happened to her; that and "dancing those perverse little dances with Andy Warhol on the tables at Castel's in Paris." When asked about the records she would like to record now, she smiled: "I've done three which are not too bad—I think I could be entitled to retire, couldn't I?" She then mentioned her latest film, *La Cicatrice Intérieure*, shot mainly in deserted landscapes, in which she was seen playing "Janitor Of Lunacy" at the harmonium. The general impression was that of an overwhelming sadness: just like Marianne Faithfull, Nico came too close to the sun and burnt out.

be closely linked to France along the years, because of Ari of course, and also when she was living and working with movie director Philippe Garrel, shooting experimental films such as *La Cicatrice Intérieure* (1972), *Athanor* (1973), *Les Hautes Solitudes* (1974), and *Le Berceau De Cristal* (1976), to name a few. Garrel was part of the Zanzibar group, produced by wealthy Sylvina Boissonnas, which included misfits, intellectual actors, and former *filles de la pop* such

9
THEY SANG IN FRENCH FOR A SEASON

Louise Cordet

BORN LOUISE BOISOT TO FRENCH PARENTS WHO had immigrated to England, she was brought up in Kensington, London. Mom Hélène was an actress and TV host (her *Café Continental* was one of the most popular programs on the BBC) and ran the prestigious Saddle Room club in London, while dad Marcel had been a pilot in the French Air Force for General de Gaulle. Cordet herself was Prince Philip's goddaughter, which allowed her to meet a lot of celebrities while still a child.

Her brief career (spanning 1962 to 1964) contained some gold nuggets. In July 1962, she climbed up the British charts with "I'm Just A Baby," written by Jerry Lordan. In France, it became "Je N'Suis Qu'un Baby." The lyrics and atmosphere seemed to perfectly fit who she was then: "I just got out of convent in Lausanne, Switzerland. I thought the song was cute, I was so naive at the time," she says in the liner notes of her reissue CD.

Louise toured with the Beatles in England and Johnny Hallyday in France. She hadn't heard of the former before seeing them onstage, which was rather funny in 1964!

Apart from "Je N'Suis Qu'Un Baby," she had other hits with "Faire Le Grand Voyage," "Que M'a-t-il Fait?," "L'Amour Tourne En Rond," "Pour Toi," "J'aime Trop Johnny," "Laisse Le Soleil Secher Tes Larmes," and "Dix Mille Fois"—all catchy pop songs bathed in romanticism. Special mention went to "J'aime Trop Johnny (Have You Ever Been Lonely?)," which could have been written with Johnny Hallyday in mind—or not:

J'aime trop Johnny
      (I like Johnny too much)
Il en profite un peu
      (He takes advantage of it a bit)
J'aime trop Johnny
      (I like Johnny too much)
Et ses yeux sont bleus
      (And his eyes are blue)
Et j'y vois mon ciel
      (And I see my own sky in them)
A moi
      (My own)
C'est déjà beaucoup je crois
      (That's too much I think)
J'aime trop Johnny
      (I like Johnny too much)
Mais Johnny c'est ma vie
      (But Johnny is my life)

Carol Friday

A shooting star of English pop, Carol Friday started when she was only seventeen. Between 1965 and 1967, she released three EPs on Parlophone, containing the charming songs "Gone Tomorrow," "Show Me The Way," "Everybody I Know," "Wasted Days," "I Look Around Me," and "Big Sister." All were immediately seductive with their candid vocals and silky arrangements. But her inclusion in this book is due to her brilliant rendition of "Everybody I Know," rechristened "Toutes Mes Amies," in 1965, when she was just seventeen years old. The song passed unnoticed though, despite gigs with Liverpudlian band Remo Four and being invited on the Belgian

TV program *Parapluie Des Vedettes*. She turned to an acting career, appearing in the famous series *The Saint*, starring Roger Moore.

Astrud Gilberto

A favorite of bossa nova and late 1960s pop connoisseurs, Astrud Gilberto released titles in French such as "Vivre Seul" (Tim Hardin's "Misty Roses") and "Le Sourire De Mon Amour" (Johnny Mandel's "The Shadow Of Your Smile"). Eddy Marnay, who had written lyrics for France Gall, did a great job adapting these two songs without trying to translate them literally, but by keeping their true feeling.

Mary Hopkin

Coming from Wales, Mary Hopkin was a folk singer with an angelic voice who was noticed by supermodel Twiggy while singing for a local contest, and then introduced to Paul McCartney, who was looking for artists to sign to newly-founded Apple. Eddy Marnay adapted "Those Were The Days" (itself based on Russian folklore) into "Les Temps Des Fleurs," while Jean-Michel Rivat, Jean-Pierre Bourtayre, and Frank Thomas wrote "Prince en Avignon," which launched her career in France:

photo bob lampard

> *Il était un prince en Avignon*
>   *(There was a prince in Avignon)*
> *Sans royaume, sans château, ni donjon*
>   *(Without a realm, a castle or a dungeon)*
> *Là-bas tout au fond de la province*
>   *(There lost in the remote province)*
> *Il était un prince*
>   *(There was a prince)*
>
> *Et l'enfant que j'étais*
>   *(And the child I was)*
> *Cueillait pour lui bien des roses*
>   *(Would pick up many a rose for him)*
> *En ce temps le bonheur était bien peu*
> *de choses*
>   *(In those days happiness didn't*
>   *mean much)*

In 1968 Mary Hopkin sang "Plaisir d'Amour," (a song belonging to the more traditional French repertoire) for a concert in London, then released "Quand Je Te Regarde Vivre," written by Nino Ferrer's

right-hand man Bernard Estardy for Françoise Hardy. Its melancholy fit Hopkin particularly well, so well she even sang its English version, "Let My Name Be Sorrow" (which Hardy would in turn record).

"Goodbye"—an offering by Paul McCartney—was Mary's next big hit, and it was also adapted into French, for Régine's repertoire this time, though a mock-suburban feel in both the singing and arrangements did it no further credit.

Lulu

Lulu was a Scottish girl who reigned on the British charts for years. She sang "To Sir With Love" and was number one in the U.S. In 1969, she won the Eurovision Song Contest with "Boom Bang-A-Bang." As there were four Eurovision winners in total that year, Lulu released multiple versions of the song in different languages—Claude Rivat adapted the French one for her to sing.

Sonny & Cher

Sonny & Cher, though huge stars in the U.S. and many other countries, nonetheless had to start almost from scratch when their "French career" was launched. It was (still) a case of "sing in French so we understand the lyrics, or your records won't sell." A whole bunch of French singers thus adapted their songs: Sylvie Vartan's "C'était Trop Beau" ("Baby Don't Go") in 1965, Sheila's "Bang Bang" in 1966, and Dalida's "Petit Homme" ("Little Man") in 1967, to name but a few. Sonny & Cher would eventually record their own French version of "Petit Homme," but in the decidedly strange world of French pop, it flopped! Not holding any grudge, they recorded Gilbert Becaud's standard "Et Maintenant," and had a hit with "What Now My Love," proving that sometimes, venturing into territories far away from the pop universe could be a good idea.

Dusty Springfield

Dusty Springfield sang a French version of Goffin & King's "Will You Love Me Tomorrow" ("Demain Tu Peux Changer") and "Reste Encore Un Instant" ("Stay Awhile"), both issued in 1964. The latter was

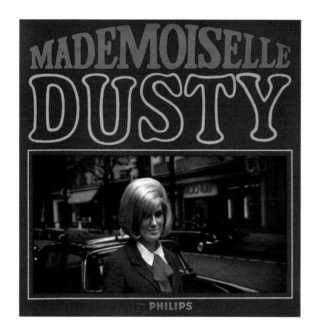

the clever work of Jacques Revaux, the man behind international standard "Comme D'Habitude" ("My Way"—which I'm sure pretty everyone in the world has heard at least once in their lives, haven't they?).

Dana Gillespie

The woman born Richenda Antoinette de Winterstein Gillespie had multiple careers. For the latter half of the 1960s, she sang psych folk-pop such as "Thank You Boy," produced by Jimmy Page. In the early 1970s, she was a regular at David and Angie Bowie's, reinventing herself as a glam rock singer (covering the song "Andy Warhol"). She took part in the *Jesus Christ Superstar* musical, and played numerous parts in B movies, sometimes surprisingly good ones (such as Alberto Sordi's *Fumo Di Londra* in 1966). Decca France released her version of Donovan's highly energetic "You Just Gotta Know My Mind" ("Tu N'as Vraiment Pas Changé") with incredible fuzz guitar by Jimmy Page, the B-side being Dana's own "Il M'aime, Il M'aime Pas."

Mary Roos

Mary Roos was a German *variétés* artist who's still very popular in her native country today. Her repertoire was full of *joie de vivre*, which charmed all audiences alike and assured her numerous spots on TV. In 1972, she attempted to penetrate the French market, playing the lead in *Un Enfant Dans La Ville*, a musical written by Michel Fugain, who believed in her potential so much that he helped her get a contract with CBS for an LP. The most remarkable song on it was "L'Autoroute," written by Georges Costa (who had a band with his brother and film-composer-to-be Gabriel Yared, and went on writing for Vartan and Laforêt). Lyrics were by Charles Level, himself a songwriter for Distel, Aznavour's daughter Seda, and Minouche Barelli, for whom Gainsbourg had written the Eurovision song *Boum-Badaboum*.

Prendre l'autoroute A1
(Take the A1 motorway)
Pour un petit voyage à deux
(For a little trip for two)
Et dans une auberge à Troyes
(And in a three-star inn in Troyes)
Étoiles, stopper pour dormir
(Just stop to have a rest)

Demain on va repartir
(Tomorrow we'll take the road again)
Dans la vieille Celta 4
(In the old Celta-4 automobile)
Qui roule à fond de train à cinq
(Driving its fastest at five)
A l'heure on est bien assis
(Miles an hour we're comfortably seated)
On prend le temps de rêver
(We have time for a dream)
On prend le temps pour s'aimer
(The time for loving)

Et moi je voyage blottie contre toi
(And I travel huddled against you)
Et j'apprends en roulant les plaines et les bois
(Learning as we're driving about valleys and woods)

Je sais la géographie du sud au nord
(I know geography from the North to the South)
Et beaucoup d'autres choses encore
(And so many more things now)
"L'Autoroute"

By the way, the city of "Troyes" is spelled just like "trios," the number three in French. Since its initial release in 1972, "L'Autoroute" has become a classic, re-issued on numerous compilations.

Jeanette

Jeanette was born in London to a Congolese father and a Spanish mother who had been raised in California, and was a real ray of sunshine in a country (Spain) under the strict military regime of the dictator Franco. In 1967, she joined Pic-Nic, a band of students from rebellious Barcelona. Soon, they had several number ones on the charts, but Jeanette, who wrote most of the material, decided to go solo and move to Madrid. In 1971, after a batch of successful singles, she put out her first album and, determined to "flood" the European market, decided to adapt her songs into its different languages: Italian, French, English, etc. It was nonetheless 1974's Spanish-sung "Porque Te Vas," from Carlos Saura's *Cria Cuervos* movie, that brought her international fame. In 1976, the French version of the LP comprised five songs adapted especially for French audiences: "Pourquoi Tu Vis," "Il Me Plaît Bien Ton Frère," "Amis, Amis," "L'Inconnu Qui M'Aimera" and "Je Suis Triste." Joe Dassin's lyricist Claude Lemesle had translated and rewritten them.

Hier au soir
    (Yesterday evening)
J'étais au square
    (I was in the park)
Assise avec Claudine
    (Sat with Claudine)
On entendait
    (We were hearing)
Le rire des
    (The laughter of)
Gamines
    (Young girls)
Il est passé
    (He passed us by)
D'un pas pressé
    (In a hurry)

Tout près du pont de pierre
    (Very near the stone bridge)
Je ne savais
    (I didn't know)
Pas que c'était
    (It was)
Ton frère
    (Your brother)
Il me plaît bien ton frère
    (I like him, your brother)
Il me plaît bien
    (I like him a lot)
Pourrai-je aussi lui plaire
    (Would he like me as well?)
Je n'en sais rien
    (I couldn't say)
Il me plaît bien ton frère
    (I like him, your brother)

Et plus que ça
    (And more than this)
Il me plaît bien ton frère
    (I like him a lot)
Ne lui dis pas
    (But don't tell him)
From "Il Me Plait Bien Ton Frère"

In 1977, Jeanette collaborated with André Popp on an LP sung entirely in French. Popp's originals "Le Temps De Mon Père" and "Jeremy" were highlights, as was a cover of (the also Popp-penned) "Manchester & Liverpool" (once sung by Marie Laforêt) and Nana Mouskouri's "Le Cœur Trop Tendre." Some of these carefree, harmony-laden jewels were later part of the *Popp Musique* compilation on Tricatel Records.

Viens me parler du temps de mon père
(Come tell me about the time of my father)
Dans la maison où je suis née
(In the house where I was born)
Viens me parler du temps de mon père
(Come tell me about the time of my father)
Dans la maison où j'ai tant aimé
(In the house I loved so much)
Viens me parler du temps de mon père
(Come tell me about the time of my father)
Dans la maison aux volets bleus
(In the house with the blue shutters)
Toi le plus grand et moi la dernière
(You were the taller and I, the youngest)
Je n'ai pas su qu'on était heureux
(I didn't know we were that happy)
From "Le Temps De Mon Père"

A song dating back to her Pic-Nic days, "Pequeña Preciosa" ("Precious Little") was a sure gem from the LP *Todo Es Nuevo*, which was also released with the French songs adapted by Carlos Luengo.

Claudine Longet

In America, Claudine Longet embodies French femininity. She sings in English with a delightful French accent, and in French with a touch of American one. She now lives in California with her husband Andy Williams.
    —Notes from the sleeve of the CBS 45
      Rien, Non Rien Au Monde

Along with Jeanette and Jane Birkin, Claudine Longet was one of those singers who whispered more than they actually sang. Born in 1942 in Paris, she had left for Vegas to try her luck as a dancer with the Folies Bergères group. Legend has it that she met crooner Andy Williams when both were involved in a car crash. They married in 1961, had children, and his own TV show to share their family happiness with

Peter Sellers and Claudine Longet in *The Party*

Mais n'oublie pas
  (But don't forget)
Si tout devait s'effondrer à tes côtés
  (If everything was to fall apart by your side)
Si tu n'as plus personne à qui parler
  (If you have no one to talk to)
Tu peux toujours m'appeler
  (You can always give me a call)
Et si tu voulais un jour
  (And if one day you wanted)
Un merveilleux jour
  (One marvelous day)

Rejouer le jeu de l'amour
  (To play the game of love again)
Et réapprendre à rêver
  (And learn how to dream again)
Ou si même tu me veux à tes côtés
  (Or even if you want me by your side)
Souviens-toi de ce que je t'ai dit
  (Remember what I told you)
Le jour où tu es parti
  (On the day you left)

the whole of America. Then, Longet's career took a new turn in 1968 when she played the lead opposite Peter Sellers in Blake Edwards' hilarious *The Party*. Despite being the archetype of the French ingenue to American eyes and ears, she was totally unknown in France, which would explain why she sang only two songs in her native language, noticeably the adapted "Rien, Non Rien Au Monde" ("Ain't No Mountain High Enough") in 1971. Since the death (murder? accident?) of her companion Spider Sabich in 1976, the year after she and Andy Williams divorced, she hasn't spoken to the press. (French writer Fabrice Gaignault recently published a book, *Aspen Terminus*, about the Sabich case.)

Joanna Shimkus

Born in Canada, Joanna Shimkus is unfortunately better known as Sidney Poitier's wife than as the great actress she was in the 1960s. Though she played for Hollywood (for instance with Richard Taylor and Elizabeth Burton in *Boom!*), it was in France that she had her most prominent roles, alongside actors such as Delon or Lino Ventura. She was also a *fille de la pop*, singing a cover of "Something Stupid" on the *Sacha Show*, just before meeting François De Roubaix. The latter wrote some of the most original scores of European cinema, being miles ahead in terms of home studio wizardry, and mingling organic, exotic instruments with electronics and keyboards to get totally inventive sounds, dynamics, and harmonies. He worked for experimental movies as well as blockbusters, documentaries, and children's programs (he died at the untimely age of thirty-six in a diving accident).

When Robert Enrico's *Les Aventuriers* was filmed in 1967, Joanna Shimkus was asked if she'd like to sing the theme song. She agreed, and her soft, "veiled" voice helped make the record very successful. Logically enough, she sang the beautiful "Le Monde Est Fou" on Enrico's following project, *Tante Zita*, in a sublime ode to peace on earth:

> *Le monde est fou, l'amour se meurt*
>   *(The world's crazy, love is dying out)*
> *La guerre tue tout*
>   *(War destroys everything)*
> *Et moi je pleure*
>   *(And I'm crying)*
> *Qui donc pourra me dire*
>   *(Who may tell me)*
> *Pourquoi sans toi*
>   *(Why without you)*
> *Tout est si noir*
>   *(Everything is so dark)*

10
FUNNY GIRLS

NOVELTY SONGS HAVE ALWAYS BEEN A PART OF French culture: think of Salvador and Vian, of Antoine and Dutronc, and remember how the French tried to deal with the angst of the immediate aftermath of WWII by wallowing in escapism—or how they tried at first to reject the Brit and Yank musical "invasion" with the artifice of tomfoolery. Before yé-yé girls such as Stella, "professional" comic singers occupied the scene. Annie Cordy is the first name that comes to mind; her repertoire was more accordion and "trad" (traditional) than pop, with two noticeable exceptions: "Pauvre Samouraï" (written by popster Bernard Chabert, it even featured sitar!) and "Je Vends Des Robes," a very R&B cover of Nino Ferrer. Suzanne Gabriello (for whom Brel wrote "Ne Me Quitte Pas"), the daughter of TV and cabaret star Raymond Souplex, was a true master in the parody of pop icons. She did so on "Z'avez Pas Lu Kafka" and "Votez Hein! Bon!" (Nino Ferrer's "Z'avez Pas Vu Mirza" and "O! Hé, Hein, Bon!"), two subtle exercises in pop inter-textuality. In essence, novelty songs were merely one-shots, and their singers, or at least the vast majority of them, have been long forgotten now.

Élizabeth

We owe to her the irresistibly catchy (and irresistibly dumb) "Je Suis Sublime," released in 1967 on Relax (for obscure labels such as the latter, comic songs were a way to get noticed):

J'aime le rodéo
  (I like rodeo)
J'aime le judo
  (I like judo)
Les robes de Paco Rabanne
  (Paco Rabanne's dresses)

Je suis sublime
  (I'm sublime)
J'aime le Coca le matin
  (I like Coke in the morning)
J'aime les croissants dans mon bain
  (I like croissants in my bath)
Mon nom, c'est Élisabeth
  (My name is Élisabeth)
Je suis sublime
  (I'm sublime)
J'aime le ma-jong
  (I like a game of mah-jongg)
Le tir aux pigeons
  (Shooting pigeons)
Le pétard de Steve McQueen
  (Steve McQueen's gun)
Je suis sublime
  (I'm sublime)

J'aime les motards
  (I like bikers)
J'aime me lever tard
  (I like to get up late)
Les solos de sitar hindou
  (Hindu sitar solos)
Je suis sublime
  (I'm sublime)

Élizabeth was a French dolly bird with a Mondrian dress, a comic-book character having a laugh at trendy girls of the time. French novelty pop or freakbeat bands were used to mocking such characters, though they belonged to the same field of expression. "Je Suis Sublime," with its harpsichord structures, its sitar and sound effects borrowed from film comedies, was archetypal of these songs, a cross between the Monkees and Tex Avery on acid. Except that *adults* were responsible for creating this music, not teenage acid freaks! People called it "Castel psych," and at the time, these exercises in mockery exasperated the purists. They are now highly sought after by collectors and hipsters.

Christie Laume

Christie Lamboukas was Théo Sarapo's sister (yes, the young man who married Edith Piaf in 1962, just a year before she died), and she liked to play at being the dumb blonde—which she wasn't, of course—a bit like Bardot when she started her career. Under her "Laume" stage name, imagined by Piaf, she released three 45s. In 1967, "Agathe ou Christie" established her sexy, witty repertoire, but it was "Rouge, Rouge," the following year, that became emblematic of the yé-yé girls' condition, both raging and shy, reserved and determined:

> *Quand un garçon vient me parler*
>   *(Whenever a boy comes to talk to me)*
> *J'ai peur de le faire sourire*
>   *(I'm afraid he'll laugh at me)*
> *Et si par hasard il me plaît*
>   *(And if by any chance I like him)*
> *Je m'affole et ça devient pireeeeeeeeeeeeeee*
>   *(I panic and it's woooooooorse!)*
> *Rouge, rouge*
>   *(Red, red)*
> *Je d'viens toute rouge, rouge*
>   *(I turn red-faced)*
>
> *Je me sens toute rouge, rouge*
>   *(I feel red-faced)*
> *Mais j'veux pas l'montrer*
>   *(But I don't want it to show)*
> *Mais j'veux pas l'montrer*
>   *(But I don't want it to show)*

In 1969, Christie left France and moved to New York with her soldier husband. When her brother died in 1970, she decided to put an end to her career and became a devout Christian.

Monique Thubert

She had her fifteen minutes of fame while imitating Bardot in what was perceived by some members of the public as sexy whispers from an idiot. 1968's "Avec Les Oreilles" and "Booff" were two bewitched twist songs that sounded utterly silly, and in which the pastiche was pushed to the limits (so bad it's good, you might say!):

Ton orchestre, qu'il est chouette!
  (Your band, wow, it's great!)
Qui c'est qu'a dit qu'on peut pas imiter les Anglais?
  (Who said we couldn't emulate the English?)
Oh dis donc, tu balances drôlement pour ton âge

  (Well, you sure swing at your young age!)
Et puis t'as un gimmick formidable. Oh terrible. J'en n'ai jamais vu de pareil
  (And you've got such a gimmick. Just terrific! I've never seen one like that)
Si j'avais ton disque, tu sais ce que j'en ferais?
  (If I had your record, you know what I'd do with it?)
Je le casserais pour en avoir un autre. Hihi.
  (I'd smash it down to get another one—giggles)
Tiens t'es comme moi, tu joues avec ton corps, tes hanches, ta bouche. Oh, du tonnerre.
  (Oh, you're just like me, playing with your body, hips, and mouth. Oh, so great!)
En somme, y'a qu'avec les oreilles que tu fais rien. Hihihi.
  (Actually, only your ears are worth nothing at all—giggles)

In the same absurdist-pop style, Quebec girl Anna Bell, a.k.a. Louise Lachnine, a child star aged only fifteen, had a hit with "La Moustache À Papa" (75,000 copies sold in 1971):

Elle me pique quand il essaie de m'embrasser
  (It stings when he tries to give me a kiss)
Elle me pique chaque fois qu'il veux me caresser
  (It stings each time he tries to stroke me)
Elle me pique les joues elle me pique le cou
  (It stings my cheeks, it stings my neck)
As tu vue maman la moustache à papa?
  (Have you seen, Mama, Daddy's moustache?)

Petite femme, tout en clin d'oeil, comme arrivant tout droit d'un film de Walt Disney: voici VETTY. Elle chante, mime, raconte et passe d'un personnage à un autre avec une déconcertante facilité.

Ses chansons, curieusement drôles, tendrement caustiques, sont une brillante caricature et un savoureux pastiche du petit monde de la chanson, celui du tube et de la rengaine.
Suivez VETTY, regardez-là, écoutez-la; je suis certain que vous l'applaudirez.

Vetty

Yvette Levis originated from Lyon. She started as an actress, playing cheeky characters, then met Jacques Martin (one of the most popular hosts and producers on French TV for decades) and Frédéric Botton, who wrote "Nicolas" for her. In the song she played a very convincing little vixen:

> *Faut plus que tu parles à Nicolas, c'est un faux-jeton!*
> *(You mustn't talk to Nicolas any longer: he's a hypocrite!)*
> *Il croit toujours qu'on ne l'voit pas copier ses leçons*
> *(He thinks we don't see him copying his neighbor's lesson)*
> *Et puis c'est lui qui tient la craie*
> *(And he's the one with the piece of chalk)*
> *Il salit tout, il fait exprès*
> *(Messing everything up with it on purpose)*
> *Pour qu'on ait tous des punitions*
> *(So that we'll all get punished)*

Natacha Snitkine

Her name will always be associated with the adaptation of "Music To Watch Girls By," which became "Le Jeu Du Téléphone":

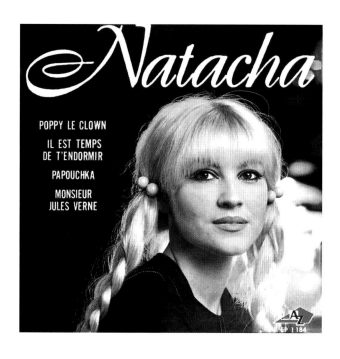

Les filles, les garçons
   (Girls and boys)
Les garçons et les filles
   (Boys and girls)
On ne pense qu'à chahuter
   (All we think about is making a racket)
C'est normal car on se réunit
   (That's normal, since we all gather)
Pour s'amuser
   (To have fun)

On joue ensemble à un jeu
   (We all play one game)
Qui n'est pas compliqué
   (Which is quite simple)
Le jeu du téléphone. Il suffit
   (The telephone game. All you have to do is)
D'appeler dans la nuit n'importe qui
   (Call anyone in the middle of the night)

Bonsoir c'est moi
   ("Hello it's me)
Devine qui je suis
   (Guess who I am)
Tu ne sais pas
   (You don't know)
Mais voyons réfléchis!
   (Well, just think about it!")

Et on invente des histoires
   (And we make up stories)
On raconte mille blagues
   (Telling a thousand jokes)
Ca n'a pas d'importance
   (It has no importance)
On s'amuse en restant dans le vague
   (We have fun remaining vague)
Quand on questionne
   (When questioned)
On appelle ça le jeu du téléphone
   (We call this the telephone game)

Caroline

This young girl's cover of David Bowie's "The Laughing Gnome" was particularly moving because of its charm and delightful naiveté:

Sur le chemin des écoliers
    (On my way to school)
J'ai rencontré par un beau matin
    (One fine morning I met)
Un bonhomme pas plus haut que trois pieds
    (A tiny little man)
–Hello!
Un petit lutin pas trop malin
    (A dwarf who was not too clever)
–Ah ah ah
En me voyant, il a bien ri
    (Upon seeing me he had a good laugh)
Je croyais qu'il se moquait de moi
    (I though he was laughing at me)
–Oh oh oh oh
J'aurais voulu partager sa joie
    (I would have liked to share his joy)
Et je l'ai pris entre mes doigts
    (And took him in my hands)

–Eh, petit bonhomme, t'as le fou rire?
    (Hey little man, you get the giggles?)
–C'est de voir ta tête!
    (It's because of your face)
Ah ah ah hi hi hi
Serais-tu le diable ou le Saint Esprit?
    (Are you the devil or the Holy Ghost?)
Ah ah ah hi hi hi

Es-tu la sagesse ou bien la folie?
    (Are you wisdom or pure madness?)
Dis, je t'en supplie
    (Please tell me)

The B-side, "Bach & Jerk," a good example of both high-energy teenage spirit and melancholy, is also worth a listen.

11
THREE OR FOUR 45s
I KNOW ABOUT HER

ON ONE EVENING IN DECEMBER 1973, CARINE LEFT without a trace. Just before Christmas, she had put some issues of *Mademoiselle Age Tendre* and *Salut Les Copains*, a bunch of 45s, and a notebook full of press cuttings of her favorite singers on her desk. She was a high school girl with no troubles at all, her boyfriend a nice guy planning to become a doctor. Her only craze was for *filles de la pop*. The list of the usual suspects was pretty long: France Gall, Françoise Hardy, Chantal Goya, Sylvie Vartan, Petula Clark, Sandie Shaw, Marianne Faithfull, Dani, Chantal Kelly, Gillian Hills, Marie Laforêt, Stella, Zouzou, Annie Philippe, Dominique Cozette, Stone, Pussy Cat, Françoise Deldick.

Her boyfriend Pierre couldn't help but shed a tear when he found the little notepad. The years passed by, though, and he got on with his life. A few years ago, one of his kids sold the records and the sketchbook full of pictures that he had found in the attic, gathering dust.

Eventually, the notepad and the records ended up at a car-boot sale, where I found them. They were perfect for someone who wanted to try and recreate the spirit of an era. Just like Carine, I wondered what had become of Aline after her *Censuré* single (produced by none other than Mickey Baker), which constantly used double entendres:

Quand on s'appelle ELSA... LAURENT

ELSA

Elsa Leroy

TRISTESSE

Paroles et musique : Elsa et Mevel.
Interprète : Elsa.

Là, tout autour de moi
Il y a garçons et filles
Ils pensent tous à toi
Ils ont les yeux qui brillent
Tu as quitté ce monde
La tristesse en nous gronde
On a tous le cœur gros
Et la gorge serrée
Ecoutant sans un mot
Ta guitare pleurer
Elle ne veut plus rien dire
Elle ne sait plus sourire
Alors pourquoi jouer
Jouer sur sa guitare
Il n'en sortira rien
Qu'un peu de mon cafard
La vie c'est long sans toi
Tu ne reviendras pas
Il y a garçons et filles
Tous ont les yeux qui brillent
Moi pendant tout ce temps
Je t'aime et je t'attends
Moi pendant tout ce temps
Je t'aime et je t'attends
Moi pendant tout ce temps
Je t'aime et je t'attends

Par autorisation des Editions Le Rideau Rouge.

... et elle admire Brel, Bécaud, Nana Mouskouri, Barbra Streisand... et Johnny pour des raisons diverses.

Pour "Nous Deux", un baiser, et un museau. Un sourire, et Merci. Avec mes amitiés, et celles de Raffatteuse.

Elsa Laurent, et....

ELSA - LEROY

Je vous pose une devinette
    (Let me ask you a riddle)
Quand le printemps est en fête
    (When the spring is blossoming)
Et qu'une fille et un garçon
    (And a girl and a boy)
Se trouvent seuls près d'un buisson
    (Are alone together near a bush)
Savez-vous ce qu'ils font?
    (Do you know what they're doing?)
Savez-vou-ous ce qu'ils font?
    (Do you-ou know what they're doing?)
Ils font...
    (They...)
Ils font...
    (They...)
Ils font...Censuré!
    (They...censored!)

Mais non, non, non
    (But no, no, no)
Ils font...
    (They...)
Ils font...
    (They...)
Des projets d'avenir
    (Have plans for the future)
Des projets d'avenir
    (Have plans for the future)
Un point c'est tout tout tout
    (End of the story, end of the story-y-y)
Y a pas de quoi censurer
    (Nothing worth censoring, you see!)

Carine must indeed have been a little fanciful if not kinky, and not as totally sentimental as she first appeared. In her stack of 45s, one by some girl named Piera caught my attention. The latter had only released one EP on Vogue in 1966, and nothing much is known about her. Her "Sucre Candy," though, was a true gem:

Il me donnait toujours
    (He'd always give me)
D'étranges noms d'amours
    (Strange loveable names)
Il m'appelait sucre candy
    (He'd call me sugar-coated candy)
Sur la table en satin
    (On the satin table)
Il grava un matin
    (He carved one morning)
Son nom tout à côté du mien
    (His name next to mine)
Oh baby, oh Betsy
    (Oh baby, oh Betsy)
M'a-t'il dit crois moi
    (He told me, believe me)
La route ne me reprendra pas
    (The road won't ever take me back)

Carine seemed to have a particular fondness for Vogue Records, as witnessed by Liz Sarian's *Pourtant Je T'aimais*, produced by Tenas, or the single Cosette released in 1967. Cosette, who I was able to talk to years later, told me that she was forbidden by her parents to cover Frankie Jordan's "Out Of Gas" because she was underage; that she met and befriended Salvador Dali in Port Lligat and Cadaquès; that she was much too young then to even think about keeping documents or taking notes; that she was lucky to have Filipacchi help her with her self-written "Idéalisation,"

"Les Cheveux Dans Les Yeux," "Ballade Pour Un Pour-quoi," and "Le Grand Chaperon Noir"—all sarcastic songs by a dillusioned but funny beatnik girl:

J'ai des cheveux dans les yeux
  (I've got my hair in my eyes)
Cette mèche qui m'empêche de te voir
  (This lock, preventing me from seeing you)
A failli briser notre amour
  (has almost killed our love)
Car je ne t'ai pas dit bonjour
  (Since I didn't say "hello" to you)

Cosette, already a feminist determined to assert herself, didn't agree with her backing band's arrange-ments, and her record flopped, Vogue suddenly not too intent on promoting it. She became a student, and had a small part in Jacques Tati's *Playtime*. She was very symbolic of these inexperienced girls with a pretty face who were suddenly at the mercy of producers or record company executives. After numerous changes in her life (with countless different jobs), Dominique Cozette (her real name) tried for a comeback in 2008 with "Toutes Les Filles De Mon Age En 60," a surprisingly optimistic account for women of her generation:

Toutes les filles de mon âge en 60
  (All the girls my age in 1960)
Ont comme moi soixante ans aujourd'hui
  (Are sixty today just like me)
Elle se promènent deux par deux dans la rue
  (They walk by in pairs in the streets)
Et se marrent en se racontant leur vie
  (And have a laugh telling about their lives)

Elles ont vécu tant de belles années
  (They had such great years)
Que leur visage est marqué
  (Their faces are full of wrinkles)
Oui mais leur cœur n'a pas vieilli d'un poil
  (Yes, but they're still young at heart)

Il a tant d'amour à donner
  (With so much love to give)

I like to think that just like Cosette, Carine had a life full of memorable adventures. She had good taste as a teen, that's a fact! To think that she could have purposely left on her desk the Vannier-arranged "Les Bottes De Caoutchouc" made her a classy female Tom Thumb in my eyes. The country-pop "Bottes" was a funny hymn to a lover's wellies by a woman clearly lapsing into fetishism:

J'avoue vraiment aimer tes bottes de caoutchouc
  (I confess liking your wellies very much)
Avec ton cache-nez, tes gants de pirou
  (With your scarf and your gloves)
Pour te garder ainsi, je passerai sur tout
  (To keep you like this I'd forget everything)
Et si t'en aimes une autre, y aura pas de jaloux
  (And if you love another one there'll be no jealous one)

On sera deux à bien aimer tes bottes en caoutchouc
  (We'll both like your wellies)
Deux à espérer de la pluie, de la boue
  (Both hope from the rain, from the mud)

→

Comment résister au charme que tu as
    (How can one resist your charm?)
Chaussé ainsi, on accepte tout de toi
    (When in boots like you are, you have
    everyone accept everything about you)

Carine did have a true sense of humor, as under-lined by French TV star Christine Delaroche's double 45 *L'Ascenseur/Vamp De Poche*, released in 1969:

Mon ascenseur s'est envolé
    (My elevator has flown away)
Il ne s'est pas arrêté
    (It didn't stop)
Au sixième étage
    (At the sixth floor)
Il a continué de monter
    (It kept going up)

Il en avait marre de grimper
    (It was fed up with climbing up)
Et de descendre dans sa cage
    (And down)
Comme un perroquet
    (Like a parrot)
Comme un bilboquet
    (Like a cup-and-ball game)

Mon ascenseur s'est envolé
    (My elevator has flown away)
S'est envolé tout à l'heure
    (Has just flown away)
Au paradis des ascenseurs
    (To the heavens of elevators)
Et des enfants non accompagnés
    (And unaccompanied children)

Hughes de Courson (later in folk band Malicorne) had penned the song, the arrangements were Roland Vincent's (who also wrote great melodies for Michel Delpech), and the whole thing was a baroque pop delight.

Jany L's one and only record was part of Carine's 45s too. Though totally unknown, the young Jany was described as a promising artist, rather emphatically, on the back of the record's sleeve. The lyrics described a woman selling the *New York Herald Tribune* on the Champs-Elysées, just like Jean Seberg's character in Godard's *Breathless*. Had Carine seen the film and been enticed to buy the single? I don't know. The tune was from the *saudade* of Brazilian or Portuguese music.

Marcel Mouloudji (1922-1994) was a figure of Left Bank *chanson*, which depended more on the strength

christine delaroche

■ UNE FLEUR

Paroles et musique de Johnny Rech et Bernard Ilous. Interprétée par Christine Delaroche.

Entre deux pages d'amour
Dans un vieux livre jauni
J'ai découvert l'autre jour
Le sourire d'une vie
Une fleur qui ressemblait au bonheur
Avait gardé ses couleurs
Pour s'accrocher à mon cœur
Une fleur qui ressemblait au bonheur
Avait gardé ses couleurs
Pour s'accrocher à mon cœur
De ce vieux livre jauni
J'ai appris tout en le refermant
Qu'il suffisait dans la vie
Pour être heureux simplement
D'une fleur pour retrouver le bonheur
Avec toutes ses couleurs
Pour s'accrocher à mon cœur
D'une fleur pour retrouver le bonheur
Avec toutes ses couleurs
Pour s'accrocher à mon cœur
D'une fleur pour retrouver le bonheur
Avec toutes ses couleurs
Pour s'accrocher à mon cœur
Par autorisation des éditions Agence musicale internationale.

Christine Delaroche

of the words than on the music. But at the end of the 1960s, he launched his own label and started to produce pop records. Christine Moncenis' *Sensation* was a period piece depicting the trends of the day, sung by one of the shooting stars of the time. Serge Franklin was responsible for the psych sound effects adorning it:

Quelle sensation, toi!
   (You what a sensation!)
Quelle illusion, toi!
   (You what an illusion!)
Quelle réaction, c'est bon!
   (What a reaction, that's so good!)

T'es mon jazz hot, toi!
   (You're my jazz hot, you are!)
Ma guitare pop, toi!
   (My pop guitar, you are!)
Mon cannibale, j'ai mal!
   (My man-eater, I hurt!)
Je vis dans un autre univers
   (I live in a different universe)

Tu aimes mes rêves à l'envers
   (You like my upside-down dreams)
Unis le paradis et l'enfer
   (Heaven and hell united)
Et brisé mon ciel d'ennui
   (And my sky of worries broken)
T'es mon Gainsbourg, toi!
   (You're my Gainsbourg, you are!)
Ma pomme d'amour, toi!
   (My apple of love you are!)
T'es mon poster, mystère
   (You're my mystery poster)

At the end of the day, what matters most is not the real Carine, but the dreamlike sensations her record collection brings. What would she tell me about all this now, anyway? Maybe nothing at all. Maybe she doesn't care anymore. Maybe it all belongs to the past, not to the people who like the songs any longer. In a few years, all the protagonists will be gone. These songs were meant to last only a season, sometimes one day. Singers would vanish, others appear, and themselves vanish in turn overnight—that was the rule of the game. Only their perfume remains, an essence of an era, encapsulated in a second. All I can do now is thank Carine, thank her for the music, for the traveling—and the vibe.

PAS DE TAXI

Interprète : Annie Phi-
lippe. Paroles et musique
de J. Schmitt et G. Bla-
ness.

Pourquoi m'a-t-il donné ce
rendez-vous
A six heures du soir
Dans le métro il y a un
monde fou
Et je vais être en retard
Et pas de taxi
Pour me sauver la vie
Et pas de taxi
Pour m'emmener jusqu'à lui
Je ne peux plus rester sur ce
trottoir
Des vieux messieurs m'en-
nuient
Je marche un peu en cher-
chant au hasard
Tiens ! manquait plus que la
pluie
Une voiture roule à côté de
moi
Son chauffeur n'est pas beau
Il peut sourire je ne répondrai
pas
Pourtant mes souliers pren-
nent l'eau
Mais j'ai si froid que
Je vais, j'en ai peur,
Sourire à mon suiveur
Moralité : quand on n'est pas
très beau
Il faut avoir une auto
Soudain un taxi
Enfin me sauve la vie
Soudain un taxi
Peut m'emmener jusqu'à lui
Soudain un taxi
Enfin me sauve la vie
Soudain un taxi
Peut m'emmener jusqu'à lui.

Par autorisation des Nou-
velles Editions Barclay.
France.R.

17 DÉCEMBRE (Née le)
ANNIE PHILIPPE
21, RUE LESUEUR,
PARIS-16e

■ CŒUR BRISE CŒUR EN FETE

Musique de Christian Gaubert.
Paroles de Pierre-André Doucet.
Interprétée par Annie Philippe.

Cœur brisé cœur en fête
Qu'on soit fille ou qu'on soit garçon
Cœur brisé cœur en fête
C'est toujours la même chanson
Aujourd'hui le ciel est bleu mais le
    [voilà qui se couvre
Une porte s'est fermée mais bientôt
    [une autre s'ouvre
Cœur brisé cœur en fête
Qu'on soit fille ou qu'on soit garçon
Cœur brisé cœur en fête
C'est toujours la même chanson
On rêvait d'un grand voyage mais on
    [reste sur la rive
Un ami s'en est allé mais déjà un
    [autre arrive
Cœur brisé cœur en fête
Qu'on soit fille ou qu'on soit garçon
Cœur brisé cœur en fête
C'est toujours la même chanson
Les ennuis et les chagrins toutes les
    [joies et les peines
Un jour seront effacés par ce garçon
    [que l'on aime
Cœur brisé cœur en fête
Qu'on soit fille ou qu'on soit garçon
Cœur brisé cœur en fête
C'est toujours la même chanson.
Cœur brisé cœur en fête
Qu'on soit fille ou qu'on soit garçon
Cœur brisé cœur en fête
C'est toujours la même chanson.

Par autorisation des éditions Tutti.

DELIZIA ADAMO

B ELSA. LEROY

Katty Line:

PUISQUE TU DORS, J'OSE TE DIRE

Paroles et musique de Bruhn, Loose, Noël Deschamps. Interprétée par Katty Line.

Puisque tu dors, j'ose te dire
Sans craindre encore de te
voir rire
Que la fillette avec qui tu
jouais
A bien grandi
Les poupées, vois-tu, ne m'amusent plus
Puisque tu dors et que je
t'aime
Je veux bien encore t'avouer
même
Parfois au fond de mon cœur
Je suis triste et j'ai très peur
Je sais déjà que tu t'en iras
J'ai vraiment tout essayé pour
t'obliger
A remarquer que j'existais
Mis des talons, couper mes
nattes à regret
Mais jamais, jamais rien n'y
a fait
Puisque tu dors, pardonne-moi
Si j'insiste encore c'est malgré
moi
Je suis sotte et ne veux croire
Que la folle et belle histoire
Bâtie par nous deux ne sera
qu'un jeu
Je suis sotte et ne veux croire
Que la folle et belle histoire
Bâtie par nous deux ne sera
qu'un jeu
Puisque tu dors, j'ose te le
dire
Puisque tu dors, j'ose te le
dire.

■ LES GARÇONS

Paroles anglaises et musique de Barry Mason et Graham Bonney.

Paroles françaises de Michel Dumontier.

Interprétée par Katty Line.

Hey les garçons ! Hey hey
Mais qu'est-ce que vous avez
Ça ne peux plus durer
Il faudrait vous remuer
Hey les garçons ! Hey hey
C'est bien beau de danser
De jouer les blasés
Et de nous oublier
Les filles ça vous embête
Avec vous pas d'amour
Alors chacun son tour
De nos cœurs vous n'êtes plus les
[maîtres
Hey les garçons ! Hey hey
Nous voulons autre chose
Faut savoir nous parler
Nous aimons ceux qui osent
D'accord pour la coiffure
Les tenues dernier cri
Mais ce n'est qu'un vernis
Que reste-t-il sans la parure
Hey les garçons ! Hey hey
Malgré nos mini-jupes
Nous ne seront jamais dupes
Il faut vous réveiller

Par autorisation des Editions Chappell.

KATTY LINE

Anne Vandelove

Nicole Croisille

Vicky LÉANDROS

Stone

STONE

France GALL

Maïté LAFORET

■ LE JOUR LA NUIT

Paroles et musique de Lennon et Mc Cartney.
Paroles françaises de Brian Mu.
Interprétée par Stone.

Chanter ça me plaît
Le jour la nuit
Chanter ça me plaît
Le jour la nuit
J'aime autant chanter
A midi qu'à minuit
Chanter ça me plaît
Le jour la nuit
Le jour la nuit
M'amuser me plaît
Le jour la nuit
M'amuser me plaît
Le jour la nuit
J'aime autant m'amuser
A midi qu'à minuit
M'amuser me plait
Le jour la nuit
Le jour la nuit
Je fais ce que je veux
Ce que je désire
Je fais ce que je veux
Ce à quoi j'aspire
La vie ça me plaît
Le jour la nuit
La vie ça me plaît
Le jour la nuit
J'aime autant la vie
A midi qu'à minuit
La vie ça me plaît
Le jour la nuit
Le jour la nuit — yeah

Par autorisation des Ed. Northern Songs France.

NOTRE GENERATION

Paroles et musique de Eric Charden.
Interprétée par Stone.

Notre génération
Est dans la nuit
Notre génération
Est dans l'ennui
Nous ne la voulons pas comme telle
Le droit d'aimer, de le prouver librement
La liberté de s'exprimer, nous la voulons
Notre génération
Est dans la nuit
Notre génération
Est dans l'ennui
Nous ne la voulons pas comme telle
Nous n'aimons pas la comédie de ces gens
Qui sous prétexte de sécurité freinent le temps
Notre génération
Est dans la nuit
Notre génération
Est dans l'ennui
Nous ne la voulons pas comme telle
Oh non jamais nous ne la vivrons comme telle

Par autorisation des Editions Agence Musicale Internationale.

DANI

"H" comme hippies
petit taureau ☆ *dring dring*
les artichauts

photo benjamin auger (S.I.C.)

Pathé

EMI
LA PLUS GRANDE COMPAGNIE
MONDIALE DE DISQUES

12
CLOSE ENCOUNTERS OF THE POP KIND

Dani

What were your first musical emotions?

I was raised in the southeast of France, in Perpignan. My father liked songs you could hear in variety shows, like Mistinguett's, as well as people such as Charles Trenet or Maurice Chevalier—also Edith Piaf. There was one single record shop then, this is where I discovered Elvis and Paul Anka, the soundtrack to all the parties I had when I was sixteen. Then I came to hear French rock: Johnny, Les Chaussettes Noires, Vince Taylor—I loved all things a bit dark. I got rebellious as a teen, I remember there was this band, Bad Boys, with two black men, which was quite unusual at the time. When I left for Paris, I was already a fan of the Stones (we belonged to the same generation). I went to London many times after I had started as a model (my husband was a photographer for *SLC*). I saw Hendrix there, the Doors—and the first audition I ever did was on a song by the Kinks.

You came to be an artist yourself and meet your idols quite soon, then?

Life is crazy, you know. As I was also fond of variety shows (which I still am today, it's always a good laugh), I was delighted to star at the Alcazar in 1969. Jean-Marie Rivière was a sort of cabaret equivalent for pop songs. What we sang was very French—some typical chansons written by Frédéric Botton. It was a bit different from what I was used to, but I didn't mind: rock is more of an attitude to me. I know bakers who are very rock!

Your repertoire has always been mixing rock numbers such as "Sans Astérisque" or "La Fille A La Moto" and more typically French things, anyway.

Even "La Machine," which the Stranglers enjoy playing live today (I sang it with them too!). Frédéric Botton had a chanted, almost *rap* way of writing. That's the main reason why his songs are not outmoded, people still like hearing them onstage. He had a knack for finding the right syllable or word on the right note.

Are you surprised at the young generation being so infatuated with your songs?

When I started singing, Sylvie Vartan, Françoise Hardy, and France Gall were already at their top. They'd sing many covers, apart from Françoise, who wrote her own songs. Like her, I was into singer-songwriters. I met Jacques Datin and Maurice Vidalin, who probably got inspired by me. I always recorded things I liked, without thinking about career plans or having a hit, or getting on the covers of magazines. That would explain why my repertoire has not aged that much.

Are artists more independent in their choices now than they used to be?

Freedom is such a big word. The important thing was to follow one's heart, and attract good record companies. I was rather ill at ease when it came to negotiating, so I had occasional periods of silence waiting for A&R men to come back to me.

Was there more male chauvinism then?

No, there wasn't. Women of my generation could claim their right to sing, dance, act, or pose naked—to have an autonomy and different emotions from those of men. Today, it's not happening that much in the world of show business—and women are still less paid than men. The status of women has improved a lot, but there'll always be a gap.

Any anecdotes about the Alcazar cabaret? It was the place to be in Paris for a while.

People came there from all over the world! I was singing a song by Jean-Jacques Debout, "Darling Dollar," for which there was a change in the scenery. I was dressed in a Paco Rabanne T-shirt with coins, golden tights, and high heels, performing walking on the tables, almost stepping on people's plates. At the end, Jean-Marie Rivière would give me his wallet and some guy his trousers which I'd give him back for the finale. One evening, I cut all the guys' trousers into pieces, because I was mad with rage, for some reason. From then on, all the men from the cast started to take their trousers off before climbing onstage, just for fear I might ruin them (laughs).

Let's talk about the movies: you had a great working relationship with Truffaut.

He was a friend of mine. Along with Pascal Jardin (a famous scriptwriter and novelist), Truffaut was like an artistic father to me. I met François through my children, who went to school in the same street where he had his production company, Les Films du Carrosse. The first time I ever played in a film though was with Jean-Marie Périer, who was working with my husband Benjamin Auger at *SLC*. Critics really liked his *Tumuc Humac* (directed in 1970) but the public didn't care. Filmmakers

171

"Three Hairstyles to Follow," *Mademoiselle Age Tendre*, No. 24, October 1966

fascinate me. Making movies is a very difficult job, you've got to learn the technique, to be focused and not afraid of anything.

Do you still need to recharge your batteries in Perpignan?

Your place of birth always leaves marks: you've grown up there, you've gone to school there. I rediscovered Perpignan's exceptional light after some years away. Many painters went to the area to try and capture the blue of the sky and the color of the wind. As a girl from the province, I came to know Paris quite well—better than some Parisians who can't care less about visiting tourist places or leaving their own district. I still discover things in Paris today.

Your latest LP is a love letter to the city.

Yes, even if everything is not always that simple. *Paris is said to be less and less popular, the working classes being forced to move out to the suburbs.*

Some areas are still popular. When they were building the Beaubourg Arts Centre, I thought that was horrible: they were destroying the Halles, which was an extraordinary place. I've changed my mind about Beaubourg now. One has to get accustomed to new things, that's all—the same goes for the Louvre Pyramid: some architects are just visionaries. I feel I am privileged: I earn some money, on and off, and am satisfied doing my music and growing my roses. One has to remain curious about everything.

Paris may evolve, just like the rest of the world!

Yes, it's impossible to drive or park your car in Paris nowadays! You have to take the Underground (which I used to do just for the sake of getting to a place I wasn't familiar with). I still do it today—don't misunderstand me: I'm no bourgeois pretending to act working-class!

How did you happen to envision this album about Paris?

I've got a contract with AZ, whose producer is a man I really like, Valery Zeitoun, who suggested I make a new record. I asked for the concept. He had planned a duet LP, but I had already done "Boomerang" with Etienne Daho. Then there was talk of recording old Paris songs, but I found the idea outmoded. I decided to ask my closest friends for a song dealing with the theme of Paris: Jacques Duvall, Alain Chamfort, François Bernheim, and Jean Fauque, they all thought it'd be better to have the same songwriter on the whole album. I didn't

agree, and asked different people to contribute. The first to answer was Bruno Cali, a friend from Perpignan I've known for ages. I ended up with twenty-five songs from different writers, and we had to cruelly select only eleven. I think I should record the others on a different album one day.

What lessons have you learned from show business?
   This is a very violent milieu. Very, very harsh for human beings. One is either up there or down there, there's no balance. There's a lot of hypocrisy too, with people coming to see you only when you've had recent success.

How come you're so fond of roses?
   The first time I saw one was in my grandma's garden. My sister and I used to go have lunch with her, and she'd give us a rose each time we were about to leave and go back home. Time passes, one becomes more focused on boys, clothes, lipstick, and so on. But I never forgot roses. And I happen to have been offered many in my whole career! Thirty years ago, I met a rose grower named Jean-Claude Boucreu who's been helping me since with my flowerbeds. A rose is unique, just like a person: it can be sublimated or put inside a jewel box.

Zouzou

Danièle "Zouzou" Ciarlet was born in Algeria before moving to the working-class Bastille area of Paris in 1945. An archetypal Parisian girl, her career evolved as she met the most important artists of the 1960s. She had considerable highs and lows before her work got some recognition in the 2000s.
   While still a teenager studying at the École d'Arts Appliqués, she befriended Jean-Paul Goude, who decided to completely reinvent her. The son of a Broadway dancer who had settled in France, he was still a student himself, but on his way to a prodigious career in fashion and arts. He had Danièle change haircut, clothes, and attitudes, and be photographed and filmed for different ads. The two had an affair that didn't last for very long, and went their separate ways. But Goude had been very influential for Zouzou. In the 1970s, he'd become artistic director for *Esquire*; in the 1980s he launched his new muse, Grace Jones, and at the end of that same decade, he was in charge of the celebrations for the bicentennial of the 1789 French Revolution—among many other achievements.
   Zouzou discovered twist music in 1961 and became a regular at the Drugstore, Chez Castel, and so on. She moved out to go and live in London with lover Brian Jones of the Rolling Stones, and was literally snatched up by the music industry: a still-unknown Dutronc wrote her first EP in 1966 (she wrote the lyrics herself, which was uncommon). The highlight was "Il Est Parti Comme Il Était Venu":

Il s'est enfui sans se retourner
   (He ran away without turning back)
Pour ne pas me montrer qu'il pleurait
   (So as not to show he was crying)
Il s'est enfui sans rien demander
   (He ran away not asking for anything)
Pour ne pas me montrer qu'il m'aimait
   (So as not to show he loved me)
Il a fui sans savoir où aller
   (He ran away without knowing where to go)
Tout simplement pour oublier
   (Just to forget)
Que sa vie s'est juste un peu brisée
   (That his life had just been broken)

Lorsque de lui je me suis moquée
   (When I laughed at him)
Il parti comme il était venu
   (He left as he had come)
Et pour toujours il a disparu
   (And disappeared forever)

Zouzou's romantic way of singing and acting live made her seem very similar to Nico and Marianne Faithfull. As fate would have it, she became one of Marianne's best friends of that period (they could be seen in one episode of the *Tom Jones Show* having a laugh at the Welsh singer filling his trousers with cotton to conform to his manly legend!). She also hung around with George Harrison, Pattie Boyd, and Donovan, whose "Young Girl Blues" she turned into "Ce Samedi Soir" on her second EP in 1967. The latter flopped, and she left Vogue. The post-May '68 blues left a deep scar on her; Robert Crumb once published an autobiographical comic book that illustrated the sensation pretty well, the impression that

you're sailing on a "yellow submarine" full of fascinating people, then are left alone on a desert island.

In 1969, with the band Calcium and her new partner Stéphane Vilar (who played the guitar in Marc'O's *Les Idoles*), Zouzou released one last 45, much heavier in its sound and mood. She then decided to travel the world, gaining a reputation as a totally unpredictable artist—she never told her agent where she was, and could disappear overnight without anybody knowing her whereabouts. In 1972, she played Chloe, the female lead in Eric Rohmer's *L'Amour L'Après-Midi*, about a desperate woman who destroys the life of a married family man. Hollywood got interested; she said "no" to Warren Beatty, had dinner with Andy Warhol, and posed for star photographer Richard Avedon. In 1974, she accepted Irvin Kershner's proposal to play in the comedy *S*P*Y*S* opposite Elliott Gould and Donald Sutherland. She then had lots of professional offers to continue inside the American studios, but she turned them all down (she's more proud now of meeting Jack Nicholson, still a good friend of hers today).

Zouzou then fell into hard drugs (like her old friend Faithfull), but miraculously survived, getting through such unhappy and exhausting experiences with a touch of class, self-derision, and humor. Her vitality and clear-sightedness today seem like life lessons that every one of us should learn.

Chance has been a very important factor all through your whole life, hasn't it?
Journalist Frédéric Taddeï once said to me I was a true magnet. People have kept coming to me, without me doing anything particular: for instance,

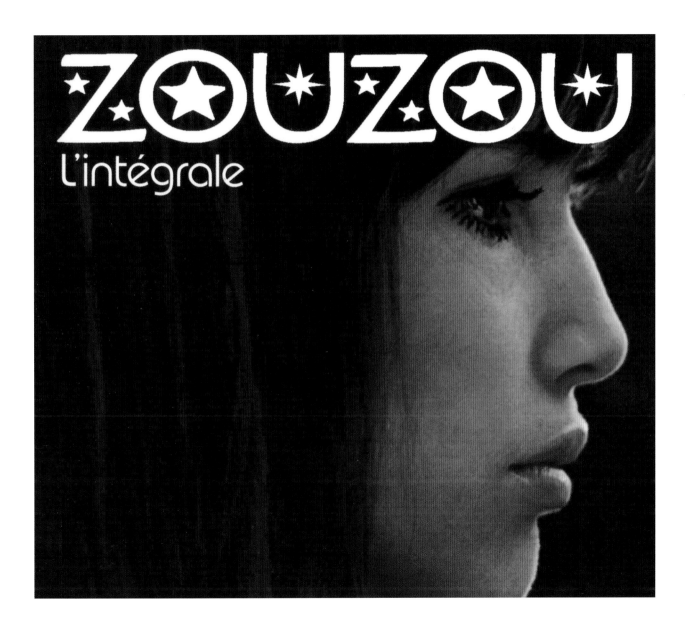

Wolfsohn signed me after he had seen me joking with (famous journalist) Pierre Bénichou at the Flore café—he liked me but hadn't even heard me sing! As for the fashion photos, I thought I was too short. The same goes with Brian Jones: I hadn't even heard of him since I only loved the Beatles and found the Stones so repulsive. I had to have dinner at the Bilboquet before I found Brian so charming! Donovan, Nicholson, and Dylan I met by pure chance too. Jean-Paul Goude freaked out because of this carefree attitude of mine: I could have done so much more—but I didn't give a damn.

Was it a typical 1960s thing?

Totally: only feelings and emotions were important, nothing was planned for me. I turned down many interesting roles at the cinema simply because I didn't like the director—I even said "no" to Kubrick! Somebody had told me he kept shouting at his actors, especially women, so I refused to go through it myself—even the money I could get wasn't important (Garrel's films had nothing to do with Hollywood in terms of one's wages—but I did them anyway). It all had to be funny, entertaining for me. I'd work for months, get enough to live decently, and then vanish—I'd go out, have parties, etc.

Such unprofessional behavior would be impossible today.

I couldn't tell you, since I've got no friends in show business now. I'd probably be unable to accept being marketed as models and actresses are today. Helmut Newton was really horrible with me whenever he was shooting fashion photographs—and adorable when he had to choose between Catherine Deneuve, Jacqueline Bisset, and me for a *Vogue* cover. Simply because, as he told me, I was really a pain as a model, always moving during work, never on time—but for *Vogue*, I'd become an actress, and an actress was allowed to move!

Jacques Wolfsohn was another figure that counted.

He was bigger than life! He was raving mad, I loved him for that! He had a portable sauna installed in his office, all you could see when coming in was his head! When musicians hit a wrong note in the studio, he'd shoot in the air with a gun—and laughed! He was always ready for a good joke, it could be a nightmare for technicians and artists. My recording sessions were a joyful mess.

To understand Dutronc then, one had to know Wolfsohn.

Dutronc was his assistant in the first place, he was supposed to be an A&R man, not a singer. I asked Dutronc why he didn't start a career, given that he could play the guitar and sing—and

Wolfsohn had had Lanzmann's lyrics in his drawers somewhere for ages. We had such a laugh, Dutronc, his bunch of pals and me: we did things that were really shocking, I'm a bit ashamed of them now—Françoise Hardy was very funny too, which I had no idea about before I met her.

People like Wolfsohn would sign artists on the spot, just because they liked them.

Yes, which could have completely blown it, actually. He may have found me pretty and funny, or simply affable. Or he saw that I wasn't a go-getter of some sort. I had a fight with him in recent years, since I discovered that he had "forgotten" to declare copyrights at the SACEM: I've only gotten some money from them since 2004…almost forty years later!

Annie Philippe

The *filles de la pop* could easily be divided into two categories: on the one side, the mysterious ones (Zouzou, Françoise Hardy, Marie Laforêt), on the other, the funny ones (Stella or popular baby-dolls such as France Gall). Annie Philippe would belong to the second category. She was a girl-next-door pinup type, in a way, but the smiling neighbor become a pop star.

Born in the Ménilmontant area of Paris, she started at seventeen as a DJ at Club 21, before releasing her first single "Une Rose" in 1964 (it was a cover of Elvis' "Love Me Tender"). Until the beginning of the 1970s, she'd record twelve EPs and one LP. In 1965, her version of the Supremes'

"Baby Love" and the "Ticket De Quai" ballad got huge airplay. The catchy "C'est La Mode" of 1966 probably best summed up Annie Philippe's hedonistic spirit, a certain *joie de vivre* in a consumer society that enabled access to so many different things. But the more cynical decades that followed put a stop to her career: the oil crisis, the fear of losing one's job, of nuclear arms, of terrorism, had people not wanting to listen to that carefree, Mary Poppins-esque music any longer.

Moi je porte sans complexes
     (I wear with no complex)
Des bas rouges et des chaussettes
     (Red tights and socks)

C'est la mode
     (That's fashion)
C'est la vie
     (That's life)
C'est la mode
     (That's fashion)
Je la suis
     (I'm just up to date)

Je fais comme les autres filles
     (I'm doing like other girls)
Je me promène en blue-jean
     (I hang around in my jeans)

C'est la mode
     (That's fashion)
C'est la vie
     (That's life)

→

C'est la mode
   (That's fashion)
Je la suis
   (I'm just up to date)

Dans les magazines au fil des saisons
   (In the magazines, as time passes by)
Je vois autant de modèles
   (I see as many models)
Que j'entends, que j'entends de chansons
   (As I'm hearing, hearing songs)
Acheter tous les gadgets
   (Let's just buy all kinds of gadgets)
Et ne voyager qu'en jet
   (And only travel with jets)

Light songs such as Papa John Phillips' "Go Where You Wanna Go" were ideal for Philippe, as were more dramatic ones ("Pour Qui, Pour Quoi"), since the listener always had the impression that she was more of a healer than a depressed singer anyway. An icon of French rock from the 1980s to the 2000s, Alain Bashung, wrote "Quarante Maringouins," a delirious psych pop ditty for Annie, as well as "Une Petite Croix" (the latter a paean to dead love):

Une petite croix sur un amour
   (A little cross on a love)
Un amour qui s'est fâné
   (A love that has withered)
Une fenêtre sur la cour
   (A rear window)
Qu'on vient juste de fermer
   (That has just been shut)
Une petite croix comme un écueil
   (A little cross on a reef)

Sur une mer déchaînée
   (On a raging sea)
Et puis voilà mon cœur en deuil
   (And here's my heart grieving)
On a fini de s'aimer
   (We've ceased to love each other)

Une petite croix qu'on a plantée
   (A little cross that's been planted)
En plein milieu du mois de mai
   (In the middle of May)

Tous les deux
   (The both of us have done it)
Une petite croix comme tant d'autres
   (A little cross like so many others)
Et qui nous rend l'un comme l'autre
   (Making us both)
Malheureux
   (Unhappy)

Frédéric Botton offered "Le Flingue" in 1968, which passed unnoticed because of the May events–people suddenly needed more politically-committed singers. Annie signed with Flèche, which was owned by her former lover Claude François. She had always been seen as some sort of "sex bomb," thanks to her Scandinavian looks: she even appeared in nude photos for *Lui* magazine, and had affairs with some of the most attractive men in show business (notably film director and actor Jean Yanne, who was very fond of her).

In 1978, she tried vainly for a comeback with a disco song, and had to wait until the general revival of the 2000s to triumph live onstage with singers of her own generation.

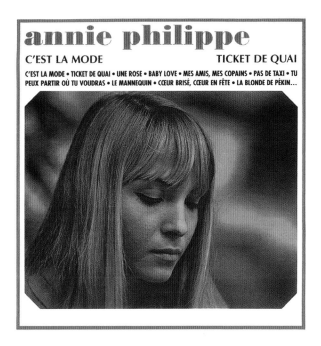

How did your career start?

I was sixteen, was DJing and working in a record shop and thought I sang really well. One day, conductor and arranger Paul Mauriat came to see my boss—totally out of the blue, I asked him if I could have an audition. He gave me three songs to learn and asked me to go and see him at his home. I was rather wary, because I was so young. The songs were Marie Laforêt's "Les Vendanges De l'Amour," France Gall's "Laisse Tomber Les Filles," and a Leny Escudéro composition called "A Malypense." Mauriat played the piano as I was singing, recording the whole of the session, then he said I should have singing lessons. When I heard the tape, I was horrified! So I took lessons and came back to see him, and he then told me he'd produce me.

It all went pretty fast, then, including performing live!

Yes, the first song, "Vous Pouvez Me Dire" didn't sell. But "Baby Love" did, mainly thanks to RMC's American DJ Rosko, who kept playing it.

I toured with Claude François as a supporting act, then with Jacques Dutronc, and I was sometimes topping the bill. I had an affair with Claude, who was dating France Gall at the time. He wanted to marry me; it was rather hot with him, but he had too much personality for anyone to live with him, he was too demanding. I left him in the middle of the tour, just to avoid making our little drama even worse. I saw him one week before he died, we went to the pictures to see *The Island Of Doctor Moreau*, then we had dinner with his musicians. I went to Switzerland, he was supposed to call me when I returned, then he had this accident, getting electrocuted in his bathroom.

ANNIE
philippe

LETTRE POUR ANNIE • POUR LA GLOIRE
DE CE COTÉ DE LA RIVIÈRE • CŒUR BRISÉ, CŒUR EN FÊTE

Ⓜ 437.344 BE

PHILIPS

PHILIPS

Did he have that many groupies?

Oh, yes, amazing! Girls would faint when seeing him. He had to call the police and take their Black Maria to escape from fans.

What about Dutronc? How was he with you?

Very nice. Jacques was always mucking around, except when Françoise was there, when it was completely different. He had nicknamed me the "best breast of French pop." I remember him getting into my room as I was sleeping one night, just to tell me that "you know, Annie, I'll really have to…you one day," and then leaving, laughing his head off. His musicians were so great: Alain Chamfort on keyboards, Christian Padovan on bass, Michel Pelay on drums, Krapou and Jean-Pierre Alarcen on guitars. They had this fantastic band called Le Système Crapoutchik, and had written the superb "Bonjour, Bonsoir Et Au Revoir" for me.

You changed labels a couple of times.

Yes, Riviera, then Philips, and eventually Decca for a song by Jean-Jacques Debout. I left Flèche after I broke up with Claude François.

Were you fond of Anglo-Saxon bands, even when you started DJing?

Yes, I liked many things. And I still do; I think that even in very bad albums there is sometimes one little gem that one shouldn't neglect.

Who decided on your covering "Baby Love"?

Paul Mauriat did, but that was fine with me: I loved the Supremes and had bought their records. Richard Anthony turned "Ticket de Quai" down, because he'd had a hit with "J'Entends Siffler Le Train" and said, "oh no, not trains again!"—I thank him for this whenever I see him, [since] I sold 1,200,000 of "Ticket."

Was it easy for you in a business ruled by men?

Sheila, Sylvie Vartan, Françoise Hardy, and France Gall were already there. But I had to establish myself, anyway. *SLC* helped me a lot (though one had to please them to be promoted), and *MAT* took many pictures of me.

How do you react to people getting interested in your songs again today?

The fans who created my official website and MySpace are thirty. I'm not surprised at people wanting to discover more about the 1960s, because there was that special soulful vibe and good songs. But all this about me in particular came as a shock. What I find interesting is how wide my audience is: kids aged ten and grandmothers, this is really moving.

Christine Pilzer

Christine "Pilzer" Van Den Haute was born in Nice and raised in the upper-class Paris district of Neuilly. With sister Violaine, Christine was used to buying American records and seeing musicals on TV. She'd go to the American military base in Fontainebleau to get every American object she could, then started to hang out with the Drugstore group on the Champs-Elysées.

Her friends were "minets" (French mods) into the Small Faces and Sam & Dave, among them future pop and rock stars Ronnie Bird and Zouzou,

Formula One driver Jacques Laffite, concert organizer and record-shop owner Marc Zermati, *Bouton Rouge* producer Michel Taittinger, lyricist Boris Bergman, and singer Gérard Manset. While Christine was hired by José Artur on the radio, her sister Violaine was the first to sign a contract as a singer-songwriter, in 1966. A regular at the Golf Drouot, Violaine was a purist, not too indulgent with the yé-yés.

Violaine's first EP comprised "Cessez La Guerre," a song destined to bring peace in the conflict between early rockers like Hallyday and newish popsters such as Antoine. Wearing her trademark cap on the cover, she paid tribute to Donovan with "Il N'y A Que Des Chansons" and "J'ai Des Problèmes Décidemment," the latter about parent-child problems. Sponsored by Ford, Vio was offered a chance to play at the Olympia, but refused to sell out, couldn't bear the pressure, and quit! To this day she refuses to mention her aborted career, still feeling acrimonious about the music biz.

Far less tormented, Christine knew how to seize opportunities. She liked to have fun, to listen to colorful pop songs and go see horror movies with friends. Her first 1966 EP, with "Dracula," "Ils Pataugent," "Non, Tu N'es Pas Seul," and "L'Horloge De Mon Grand-Père" was a delight. Vogue set up a tour with Antoine, which was very successful. The second record, *Mon P'tit Homme Spatial*, co-written with Bernard Jamet, included an impossibly catchy tune that has now become a classic:

Mon meilleur ami
    (My best friend)
Il vit loin d'ici
    (Lives far away from here)
Dans un monde sans lumière
    (In a world without lights)
Mon meilleur ami
    (My best friend)
N'est pas de Paris
    (Is not from Paris)
Il vit sur Jupiter
    (He lives on Jupiter)
C'est un extra-terrestre
    (He's an extraterrestrial)
Un p'tit homme spécial
    (A peculiar little man)
C'est un extra-terrestre
    (He's an extraterrestrial)
Mon p'tit homme spatial
    (My little man from space)
Il prend son spoutnik
    (He takes his sputnik)
Sur rayon cosmique
    (On cosmic rays)
Pour me voir chaque soir
    (To see me each night)
Ou bien il m'appelle
    (Or he just calls me)
Me donne des nouvelles
    (To give me news)
Par bigophone-radar
    (By radar-blower)
C'est un extra-terrestre
    (He's an extraterrestrial)
Un p'tit homme spécial
    (A peculiar little man)
C'est un extra-terrestre
    (He's an extraterrestrial)
Mon p'tit homme spatial
    (My little man from space)

CHRISTINE PILZER

disques vogue

VOGUE INTERNATIONAL INDUSTRIES

CAFE CREME

MON P'TIT HOMME SPATIAL

CHAMPS ELYSEES

AH-HEM-HO-UH-ERRR...

With "Ah-Hem-Ho-Uh-Errr" (spelling out A.M.O.U.R.), "Café Crème," and "Champs-Élysées," Pilzer offered three lovingly funny, baroque-meets-jerk-music songs. She definitely preferred the chrome of American cars, Courrèges dresses and boots, and chewing bubble gum to philosophical and political questioning! At least that's how superficial she pretended to be: she was much more subtle in mocking what surrounded her than people realized at first.

Once she had reached the top of the charts, Pilzer got bored with music, going back to being a designer and stylist. That is, until 2001 and the *Wizzz* compilation, which had her play with the young band Les Terribles, and saw April March cover her songs on an American tour with Air.

How did it all begin?

I used to be an announcer at the Maison de la Radio when Michel Delancray, who thought I was the funny type, suggested I record a demo. As I knew people working for Vogue (and with José Artur pushing me), it all happened very fast, really. Vogue people didn't want other labels to sign me, so they had me record on the spot, then pressed me to tour—I ended up singing in front of thousands of people in the Nimes Roman arena without having ever taken singing lessons or rehearsed the songs. That was great, though, thanks to Antoine's backing band Les Problèmes, who kept cracking jokes and making fools of themselves. But the tour was exhausting due to the time schedule and the fact there were so many of us singing: me, Sullivan, Karine, Bernard Laferaud, Cédric, and Cléo. I wished I could have had private singing lessons as Sheila had. I did several TV shows, in which most of the audience came to throw rotten tomatoes at young, new singers—a real mess!

How come you had such a good spirit for jokes and fun?

I've always been that kind of girl, even at school. I was always making a fool of myself, annoying people as much I could—my mom could have told you stories about all this…

Dracula *was a reference to your fondness for horror movies.*

We all loved being frightened: we'd go to cemeteries at night, just like teenagers getting rid of their fear of death. I remember that film with Audrey Hepburn, *A Shot In The Dark*, with a scene during which every spectator screams their heads off. I did too—I ended up under my chair, in fact.

What about "Mon P'tit Homme Spatial"?

It was after I had bought this book about the U.S. space conquest. I loved all things modern. My stage suit was a kind of space suit, with a golden, lamé miniskirt. I loved Courréges and La Gaminerie, who designed my costumes. I was crazy about Jean-Paul Goude too, who'd only wear white boots—I've always liked people with white boots (my brother used to go to the Molitor ice rink in the 16th District, wearing white skates). Goude I first heard of from the Drugstore. The young people there were loaded upper-class kids, nicknamed "the golden jackets" by their rivals. They were all very handsome, girls and boys alike, tall, with long Vidal Sassoon locks. We spent the whole day getting dressed before going out in the evening. We crashed parties, looking sublime and acting vulgar! Zouzou was a master of that craft. I was very pure and naive, for most of the parties ended pretty badly. Carlos was my guardian angel, others knew when to leave before things turned sour. We were happy to escape from our parents, that's all.

Let's talk about your experience at the radio.
I was the host on a cultural program, *Les Arts d'Hugo*, with Frédéric Chapus, as well as for *Table Ouverte* with José Artur. He was such a good laugh! He even asked me to marry him once, one minute before we were on air—I never knew if he was joking or not.

Your career was very short.
Two EPs, and two tours! I was into this relationship with a boy I didn't love anymore, so

I ran away from the music business and resumed working as a stylist, drawing things for *MAT*, Carrita, Orlane, and Pierre Cardin. Then I designed pullovers, quite successfully actually—in Wim Wenders' *Wings of Desire*, you can see an angel fly, wearing one of my creations—I was so proud! I loved going to catwalks, discovering new artists such as Yohji Yamamoto or Jean-Paul Gaultier.

Laura Ulmer

Even though Laura Ulmer was the daughter of famous 1950s singer Georges Ulmer, she got involved in the world of pop music by chance. Her career lasted from 1963 to 1966, with three EPs and one Canadian LP—plus some appearances on television movies.

> *La la la la la*
> *La la la la la*
> *J' suis un' affiche bleue*
>   (I'm a blue poster)
> *Qui a un amoureux*
>   (With a lover)
> *Blonds sont ses cheveux*
>   (Blond is his hair)
> *Bleus sont ses deux yeux*
>   (Blue his eyes)
> *Chaque jour, il passe*
>   (Everyday he passes me by)
> *Le long de mes rues*
>   (Along the streets)
> *Où j' pose avec grâce*
>   (Where I pose with grace)

Presque à demi-nue
  (Half-naked)

La la la la la
La la la la la
Petite gaine en tricotine
  (Little knitted girdle)
Petite fille en capeline
  (Little girl in wide-brimmed hat)
Je sais bien que je te fascine
  (I know I fascinate you)
Voyons, qu'est-ce que tu imagines?
  (Well, what do you have in mind?)

Her most remarkable title was "Amoureux D'Une Affiche" (lyics above), which evoked the new eroticism in advertising and the fetishism for bodies exposed on the walls of the cities. Laura Ulmer didn't feel singing was a necessity for her; she became a cult figure against her own will.

Laura Ulmer

How did you get interested in music in the first place?

My dad Georges was a singer-songwriter. I was contacted by one Léo Missir from Barclay when I was only thirteen and a half, but since I was attending a religious school, I wasn't allowed to record anything. It didn't matter to me, it wasn't vocational anyway. Then Eddie Barclay himself heard me sing to accompany a neighbor in my mom's restaurant, and he wanted to sign me straightaway. I was sixteen, and my parents accepted. It enabled me not to go back to that horrendous sisters' school, so that was perfect for me. Needless to say I was very surprised to see myself on the front page of *SLC*, let alone on TV! Especially after five years in a monastery.

It only took one 45 to launch you?

I did a lot of TV shows, which I liked—apart from the stress of singing live. The papers got interested only because I was so young and pretty, I think. The second record sold less, I had to move back with my parents, which was not as cool as the life I'd had for a few months—my dad kept telling me my songs were rubbish. I toured with him though, even duetting live, but he was appalled by all these teens running after our car or asking for a lock of my hair. Shows took place on villages' main squares, they were free, spectators dared to do things they wouldn't have done under different circumstances—I got hit by a rotten tomato once, which hurt but made me laugh: I had become a star, then, getting rotten vegetables thrown at me! For the third single, Barclay's photographer Alain Marouani took pictures of me, and I was able to choose one title—"Jean-Paul"—which was simply the name of one guy who had once kissed me on the head—and also one cover: "Jimmy Attends-Moi."

Your career was very brief.
    Yes, from 1963 to 1966.

You were very popular in Canada.
    Yes, surprisingly enough. I had quit singing, I was hanging around with my mum who was MD at the Monte Carlo Casino club, and I suddenly got a call from Barclay saying I was number one in Canada! I took the first plane to sing at the Arena Saint-Paul in front of five thousand screaming people who didn't even listen to me but were apparently delighted with just being there. So an album was rush-released but I went back to France, then moved to the States, where I auditioned in front of juries that were totally laughing their heads off, thinking I was very funny—but I wasn't on purpose, you see! Maurice Chevalier thought the same about me: he was a friend of my parents' and insisted I started a career as a comedian. But I was young, I wanted to travel a bit, I went to Morocco where I lived the hippie life, and eventually came back to work for Air France as an air hostess. I only sang to make passengers laugh aboard the planes, when imitating (MOR singer) Mireille Mathieu. I wouldn't have wanted to become as famous as she is, though.

Françoise Deldick

Françoise Deldick, born in Saint-Maur-des-Fossés, had always been a theatre buff: she took lessons at the prestigious school Le Cours Simon, and played roles on television while she was very young (mostly, as a mock ingénue actually less innocent than expected). Married to the bass player in rock pioneers Danny Logan & Les Pirates, she was an announcer at the Olympia, introducing bands. From 1966 to the early 1970s, she was also a recording artist. Her first 45 was *Hum!, Hum!*, a cover of "Love Is Strange" arranged and produced by Mickey Baker, in which she displayed a bad girl image that was fairly different from her so-called innocent rivals in the world of girly pop.

    Such a deliberately inflammatory image was an obstacle to greater success, which would explain why she quit the business and led a totally different life with her second husband, a soccer player (they eventually bought and worked in a restaurant). Then one day she had a terrible road accident, which left her in a coma for a long time and thus put an end to her acting career, which she had tried to re-launch. After she recovered, she dedicated her life to help beginning actors with their art (her son Aurélien Wiik, now famous, has been one of them).

What was the starting point of your singing career? Were you brought up in a music-loving family?
    My dad was a very religious man who only liked Gregorian chant, so I was able to listen to the choir at church when I was a little girl. It was beautiful, I still like listening to this now. I used to listen to the

radio, to hear people singing on holiday [summer] camps, but nothing was that special to me.

I started acting when I was twenty. And then when I had this announcing job at the Olympia and was living with a musician, I was able to listen to many different people of varied musical backgrounds, of course: Brel, for instance, but also, obviously enough, the tons of yé-yé girls and boys who were starting their career. Coming from where I was coming (a little, provincial town, going to the church every Sunday), that made a difference!

How did you come to be a recording artist?

I shot a film with Bourvil and Paul Meurisse, with Bourvil rehearsing for an operetta written for him and Annie Cordy, and he asked me to fill in for a small part. I couldn't sing, tried not to on

stage (I was just humming, in fact), but a producer noticed me nonetheless, and attempted to make me record an EP with Pathé Marconi, but it didn't work. So I ended up on small label Monte Carlo. Someone translated the songs, I learned them phonetically and started an Italian tour, backed by Radio Monte Carlo (RMC), the single "Je Recherche Un Garçon" getting incredible airplay.

When I came back, I resumed working with Bourvil for the operetta *Ouah! Ouah!*, and we had a six-month tour in France. A Belgian A&R man offered me the chance to record two songs he had, "Le Diable De Près" and "Joue Avec Moi," one thing led to another, suddenly I was on different Belgian TV shows, then I fell in love with a boy who eventually introduced me to Mickey Baker. I had two jobs: as an actress and as a singer, and didn't want to choose between them.

How did people react to this?

They were OK. Some songs were rather confidential, but we had fun going to England to record there, because musicians were great. I remember that for "Toute Nue Avec Les Mains Dans Les Poches," I sang as if I were totally out of my mind, the English technicians didn't get a word of it, but they would take part in it anyway. "Pleasure" was the most important word, while having a career, being ambitious was out of the question. What I liked was the interaction between the vocals and the arrangements in the manner the English were working.

Mickey Baker worked with Chantal Goya, among many others. He must have had a hectic working schedule!

He also used to sing, covering standards, because he had a great voice. He was such a nice man! You know, his "Love is Strange" was itself a standard, but he had to leave the States: he couldn't bear being segregated that much any longer—just like many jazz musicians did, he took refuge in France.

What about touring? Do you remember any particular anecdotes?

I remember many things about being a comedian, but much less about my experience as a singer, since that wasn't as important to me. There were many young singers trying to be a success—it's the same for comedians now, they all want to have their own stand-up show and become the new thing.

I started playing at the theatre in 1959, I had three lines. Jean Marais was heading the bill, he was such a star, on tour, the cities we'd visit would rave about him being there. I had many cameos afterwards, and people were not that enthusiastic about me being an actress. So I did television films: at the time, they were shot live, you couldn't ask for several takes, all you could do was work very hard, learn your lines and rehearse over and over again.

It was nevertheless a great period, directors would pop in on the set and ask you to play in their next thing. Viewers started to act as "regular customers" of such and such a program or series.

It was indeed the first time television had been that important in people's households.

Yes, and as there was only one channel they would all watch the same things. I remember this woman in the subway telling me, "Oh, I saw you on TV the other day!"—I was proud, that was the privilege of having no competition in this domain.

Any memorable encounters in the acting business?

At the same time as the operetta with Bourvil, I featured in the *Salvatore Adamo Show*, in which people would sing, dance and play—good memories.

I met Jean Gabin too, I played with him in *Le Président* in 1961. Everybody had told me he was going to treat me as a little girl and be a real pain—but no, on the contrary, he was such a nice and polite man, really adorable!

I was also part of a play by Fellini's scriptwriter Tullio Pinelli at the Comédie des Champs Elysées. Fellini came to see me as I was playing the female leading role, he wanted to make a film of it, but the play didn't work—it was too harsh, in a way. My part was a little bitch that was always telling men what nobody dared to tell them at the time—I mean, telling them how cowardly they are sometimes. And people didn't like it. It wasn't *bourgeois* theatre, you understand me, do you? It was the first serious role for the young starlet I was. Such a shame, indeed.

Pussy Cat

Born in 1947, Evelyne Courtois started with band Les Petites Souris. A fan of Tom Jones, she adopted the stage name "Pussy Cat" just before she signed with RCA (the label Jones was on). Her musical style was closer to the Who's, though, as shown by her first EP in 1966, *Ce N'Est Pas Une Vie*. The record was very mod indeed (the song was actually a cover of the Small Faces' "Sha La La La Lee"). The EP also included The Moody Blues' "Stop," and "Les Temps Ont Changé," a brilliant adaptation of the Spokesmen's "Have Courage, Be Careful."

"Les Temps Ont Changé" was anticipating the Women's Lib movement by a few years:

> *Ces garçons, ils sont bien tous les mêmes*
> (These boys are all the same)
> *Ils prennent leurs désirs pour des réalités*
> (They took their wishes for granted)
> *Ces garçons, ils sont bien tous les mêmes*
> (These boys are all the same)
> *Ils espèrent toujours pouvoir nous*
> *faire marcher*
> (They hope we'll obey them)
> *Car ils oublient que les temps ont changé*
> (They're forgetting times have changed)
> *Aujourd'hui c'est aux filles de décider*
> (Today girls are deciding for themselves)

On her second EP, Pussy Cat offered originals, one penned by Alain Bashung, and the energetic "La, La, Lu." She'd be invited to numerous TV shows (sometimes playing the drums as well as singing), and even toured with Chuck Berry. Her next record had her cover the Hollies' "Bus Stop" and "Have You Ever Loved Somebody" (the very convincing "Arrêt d'Autobus" and "Si Vous Avez Déjà Aimé"). After a brief break, Pussy Cat changed looks: she dyed her hair blonde, with long, curly locks. Her 1968 single, "Aucune Fille Au Monde," was a heavy-psych killer, and "Dans Ce Monde Fou" a groovy, catchy pop song. On her last EP, released in 1969, she covered the Zombies' "She's Not There" ("Te Voilà"), and wrote the other three numbers, which proved how gifted she was, and how she could have lasted longer as a songwriter.

What kind of social and artistic backgrounds did you have?

I was born in Paris, in a working-class family: my dad was a mechanic and my mom a housewife with

four children to bring up. Les Chaussettes Noires or Les Pirates were very influential: I saw them in one Milk Shake Show at the Olympia, and it led me to want to do the same—with girls. I had friends who accepted, I soon learned two or three chords on a guitar, then there was this song contest that we won. Pathé Marconi wanted to sign me as a solo artist; I refused, because I believed in this girl band concept. So we carried on rehearsing, with a drummer now joining, and after the odd gig here and there, one day Gérard Hugé came in, taught us new chords, new rhythmic patterns, and signed us. One of the guitarists lost her mom, and we had to replace her. We chose to hire a keyboard player instead, the drummer then left after quarreling with me, and I had to replace her myself for a concert, and, as it had gone well, I decided to carry on with it. Then we had live dates supporting Tom Jones, and the record company suddenly asked me to go solo and release what we had been working on as a band under the "Pussy Cat" name.

You sang many covers, as was the habit of the time.

We were a small group of artists at RCA: Noël Deschamps, Ronnie Bird, Tom & Jerry, Stella, Bashung, and we all had to do French adaptations of hits—publishing companies would establish a list of things to sing, and another one of people to sing them.

I was quite lost after the Petites Souris split. I turned to Gérard, who became like a mentor for me (and later, my husband), and I loved working in the studio with him—double-tracking vocal tracks, for instance.

In '68, Gérard signed guitarist Patrick Dietch, who became the leader of Martin Circus Mk 1. Original songs were more acceptable then, so I was able to write my own lyrics on music Patrick had composed. I was finding my inner self, that was why I changed looks, probably.

It was pretty rare for a female singer not to have a whole army of writers-arrangers-managers-technicians behind her then.

Gérard had one very solid team: the same musicians, sound engineers, press attachés, just like a family or a bunch of friends who were accustomed to work with and for each other. I started to be more interested in writing than singing live or touring.

What became of you when your career ended?

I started as a model, and did many photo sessions or fashion shows—but I carried on writing for other artists, such as Christopher Laird or Martin Circus, even for the Mirapolis amusement park (I wrote children's songs for them). When Gérard died in 1992, I didn't want to see anyone from the music business any longer—until about six years ago, when I was asked for an interview about Noël Deschamps. I even played some live dates, also as a backing vocalist for Annie Philippe. I'm a happy grandma taking care of her granddaughter, too.

What do you think of all these young fans you have now?

I think it's fantastic. I just take the necessary bit of glory from it—the rest belongs to Gérard, to his genius.

Stella

Born Stella Zelcer in 1950 in Paris to a family of Polish immigrants, she stood in a field of her own among the *filles de la pop*. When her first 45 was released by Vogue in 1963, she was only thirteen, and was completely against the current of yé-yé girls. "Pourquoi Pas Moi" was a clear assault on the teenage idols' inadequacies as singers and stars:

Moi je trouve
   (I think)
Que j'ai tout pour faire une idole
   (I've got all it takes to make a cult)
De mes chansons
   (Of my songs)
J'écris musique et paroles
   (I write all the words and music)
Je devrais déjà gagner
   (I should already earn)
Des sommes folles
   (Huge amounts)
Oui mais voilà pour l'instant
   (Yes, but as for now)
J'n'ai pas un sou
   (I'm penniless)

Pourquoi pas moi (yé-yé-yé yé-yé)
   (Why not me?)
Je fais très bien (wo-wo-wo-wo wowo)
   (I'm doing "wow wow wow" so well)
Pourquoi pas moi (yé-yé-yé yé-yé)
   (Why not me?)
Je fais très bien (yé-yé-yé yé-yé)
   (I'm doing "yé yé yé" so well)

J'ai tout pour plaire
   (I've got everything to please)
Je chante comme une casserole
   (I sing completely out of tune)
J'ai 14 ans
   (I'm fourteen)
Je vais encore à l'école
   (I still go to school)
J'ai le regard cloué
   (My stare is blank)
La tête un peu molle
   (My brain is soft)
Oui mais seulement
   (Yes, but the only thing is)
J'connais pas trois Manitous
   (I don't know any mogul at all)

The song (unfortunately enough?) could match every period of pop music (Mareva Galanter covered it on *Ukuyéyé* in 2006). Now working for RCA, Stella carried on with a batch of incredibly groovy as well as very witty titles: "J'achète Des Disques Américains" was poking fun at the fact that all things U.S. were automatically deemed superior by youngsters, in the same way that "Le Folklore Auvergnat" parodied Sheila's "Le Folklore Américain" in its quotations of Dylan, when French teenagers understood precious little (if anything) of his lyrics. Funnily enough, Stella was accused of "imposing segregative views about the Auvergnats" (Auvergne being a very traditional district in the centre of France)!

Undeterred, she went on with "Si Vous Connaissez Quelque Chose De Pire Qu'un Vampire," pretending to protest against the new craze of horror films, and "Cauchemar Auto-Protestateur" (a spoof of protest singers!). She also recorded "Beatniks D'occasion," which was akin to the Kinks' "Dedicated Follower of Fashion" and foreshadowed what would happen after May 1968, when phony rebels would conform to the norms of yesteryear and renounce revolutionary ideals:

Beatniks d'occasion
  (Second-hand beatniks)
Révoltés de carton-pâte
  (Pasteboard rebels)
Qui portent cheveux longs
  (Wearing long hair)
Mais roulent en TR4
  (Driving in TR4)
S'ils regardent le monde d'un œil désabusé
  (If they look at the world with a blasé eye)

C'est que par leur tignasse le deuxième est caché
  (It's because the second one is hidden by their mop of hair)

Beatniks d'occasion
  (Second-hand beatniks)
Révoltés de carton-pâte
  (Pasteboard rebels)
Qui portent cheveux longs
  (Wearing long hair)
Mais roulent en TR4
  (Driving in TR4)

Ils veulent la pilule
  (They want the pill)
Et refusent la bombe
  (And refuse the bomb)
Heureusement qu'ils sont là pour refaire le monde
  (We're lucky to have them imagine a different world)
Depuis quelques temps ils se sont mis à penser
  (For some time, they've started to think it over)
Ils ne devraient pas ça pourrait les fatiguer
  (They shouldn't, they're gonna get tired)
Ils chantent sous les ponts
  (They're singing under bridges)
Mais habitent le XIème
  (But live in the 11th district)
Ils changent de chemises sales
  (They change dirty shirts)
Sept fois par semaine
  (Seven times a week)

→

*Quand ils en auront marre de la bohème en
blue jean*
  *(When they get tired of the bohemian life
  wearing jeans)*
Demanderont à père une place dans son usine
  *(They'll ask Father for a good job in his
  factory)*

In 1967, "Le Silence" was a nightmare for radio
DJs: it featured several ten-second intervals of silence
within the song, to rightfully insist on how noisy the
world was becoming, with people incapable of
listening to each other (predating what we all live
today). After one single in '67, and three in 1968,
Stella started to grow tired of the vanity of show business, and of the emptiness of the relationships she
had with people immersed in this milieu. She ended

her career with "L'Idole Des Jaunes" and "Trempe
Tes Pieds Dans Le Gange," which ridiculed Mao's
fans and hippie travellers to India. In 1967, she married Magma's drummer and singer Christian Vander,
whose prog-jazz band was singing in Kobaian, a new-
ly-coined language for an invented, sci-fi universe, all
miles apart from where she came from. For a good
while, Stella Vander refused to evoke her "original
sins" as a yé-yé singer, then gradually became aware
of the musical quality and political incorrectness of
her tunes, which were the French equivalent of what
Mad magazine was doing in the States.

*What were your first musical emotions? What
sort of music did you listen to as a kid?*
  I recorded Jean-Claude Darnal's "Le Tour Du
Monde" in a "self-service" recording booth when
I was seven or eight, with my uncle Maurice. You
got a floppy disc at the end of the session. With
the school's choir, I noticed the sound was tighter
when I was part of it than when I wasn't.

*What is your most remarkable memory of
the 1960s?*
  I've got a thousand! One word sums up the
whole period though: carefreeness.

*How influential was your uncle in the
sharpness of your lyrics?*
  Of course, he wrote all the songs. But we really
shared the views that were expressed in them—the
humor, the sometimes harsh criticism.

*What were your pet songs—and pet peeves—in
French music then?*
  I found all French youth pathetic—apart from

Françoise Hardy. I loved more mature singers such as Brassens, Brel, Nougaro. Apart from them, I'd listen to American jazz, all the Tamla, Motown and Stax bands.

In retrospect, what do you think of SLMC, MAT, or the yé-yés now?

It was no more pathetic than today's musical TV reality shows. And the gossip press is much worse nowadays.

Why did you stop your career in the late 1960s?

I was looking for something different, musically speaking. And I was really fed up with show business.

How did you discover Magma? How did you connect to Christian Vander's music?

I saw him at the Rock 'n' Roll Circus in early September 1969. He had the same tastes and energy as I had. It took me a week to find the studio where he used to rehearse. It wasn't already Magma then, he was looking for musicians to work with. We instantly clicked, although our couple has evolved into a brother-sister relationship since.

Are you surprised at the incredible popularity your 1960s songs have gained as time passed by? The original records are being exchanged for huge sums!

Of course I was flattered, and I must admit now that they were pretty good, actually. With updated arrangements, they'd be very listenable even today!

How did you react when people used to compare you to Dutronc? Were you flattered or irritated?

Neither. I liked him a lot, anyway.

How did you feel as a young girl inside the music industry?

That wasn't too easy. Women were not treated better than in the rest of society. But as I had a very strong character (I could be very opinionated), I always managed to get what I wanted.

What are your plans for the very near future?

Magma, of course, but also side projects, such as a double-sided solo album with Pierre-Michel Sivadier. My son Marcus' band, too: Marcus & the Music. I think they're very original, I'd like to help them if I can—though Marcus doesn't need me to succeed in music, to tell you the truth.

victoire scott

461 163 M

DECCA

13
PSYCH & FOLK GIRLS

WITH MAY 1968 AS A RELEASE MECHANISM, French pop evolved a lot in the late 1960s/early 1970s. A new generation of singers was appearing, with less naiveté about the system, and influences like the Americans Karen Dalton and Carole King, women who could write their own material. Folk rock, psych rock, and political awareness about aesthetics and sound were prominent, so much so that French labels had to sign artists in accordance with this new demand.

Victoire Scott

A strange light ball has just crashed down at my feet, and from all this broken glass a golden butterfly goes out, landing on my hand mistaking me for a rose, telling me it likes my perfume. And suddenly the sky gets light, and I'm hearing a symphony, it's being played on an anvil by a child smiling at me. And it's so, so nice!
—Extract from "4ème Dimension"

Even the people who met her, such as Boris Bergman (a famous French lyricist who wrote "Rain & Tears" for Aphrodite's Child) or Alain Turban (a cabaret singer), have lost trace of her. It was in April 1968 that Scott released her first record. On the black-and-white photo adorning the sleeve, she looked like a heroine from a documentary about the beatniks—a beatnik wearing only black. The music was outstanding: "4ème Dimension" is a baroque pop masterpiece, a Paris Existentialism-meets-American psych rock kind of thing. Its string arrangements, atmosphere, and texture created a unique vision.

On August 25, 1968, Victoire Scott was featured on *Au Risque De Vous Plaire*, one of the rare TV shows in color, which was directed by Jean-Christophe Averty. Stella and Annie Philippe were also invited to perform. In the show, Scott was filmed with Paul Delvaux's paintings superimposed in the background. In September 1968, she guest hosted on another episode to present a second single, "Une Fleur Dans Le Cœur." The Boris Bergman-written "Un garçon, Une fille" was a beautiful psych-pop ballad, while "Sophie" and "La Licorne d'Or" were touched by a gracious melancholy. Her adaptations into French mostly sounded as good as the originals: for example, The Web's "Baby, Won't You Leave Me Alone" as "Le Petit Train De Sasfé." On the same 45, "Contestation" was a major song, full of Beatlesque brass instruments:

Toi ah ah — tu m'as traitée d'analphabète stop
   (You, ah ah, call me an illiterate)
Moi ah ah — je t'ai lancé à la tête
   (Me, ah ah, I threw at your head)
Mon bouquin, mon coussin, mon bonbon
et le chien
   (My book, my cushion, my candy, and
   my dog)
Tu as ri, puis pâli, puis dit blanc comme
un pape
   (You laughed, then turned pale and said,
   white as the Pope)
Attends que je t'attrape
   ("Wait 'til I catch you")
C'est la contestation
   (This is protest)

Moi ah ah barricadée dans la cuisine stop
   (Me, ah ah, locked up in the kitchen stop)
Toi ah ah mal abrité sous une bassine stop
   (You, ah ah, badly sheltered under a
   basin stop)

J'ai jeté le café la farine et le thé
   (I threw coffee, flour, and tea)
Tu pensais iouh! résister oh!
   (You thought, hey, you were going to resist)
J'ai fait parler la poudre avec le sucre
en poudre
   (I had powder do the talking in the form of
   caster sugar)
C'est la révolution
   (This is revolution)

In 1970, Scott released her last single, with a rockier and groovier sound that was as attractive as the previous ones. Then, nothing: Victoire Scott left us, with only fourteen tracks in her catalogue, becoming like a faded dream, a sort of mythical figure of French pop.

Véronique Sanson

Everybody knows Véronique Sanson in France, and some Americans may remember she was once married to Stephen Stills—but how many of them have ever heard the wonderful things she did at the very beginning of her career? Born in 1949, she was the daughter of two great figures of the French Resistance against the Nazis. Having been taught the piano from her parents at a very early age, she formed her first band at eighteen with sister Violaine and composer François Bernheim: Les Roche Martin. She then met Michel Berger (recommended by the Pathé Marconi MD), who became her partner and wrote for her.

Soon, though, she'd excel in writing songs on her own. "Maria De Tusha" was the first prominent song she published, which was both moody and sensual. She also wrote for other people: Isabelle de Funès (the hugely popular actor Louis' niece) was granted "Mon Voisin," a gorgeous bossa nova ballad:

Ils sont rentrés
    (They have come back in)
J'entends le bruit sur le palier
    (I'm hearing a noise on the landing)
Peut-être ils vont jouer du piano
    (Maybe they're about to play the piano)
Alors il arrivera
    (Then he'll come)
Dira bonjour, les embrassera
    (Say hello and kiss them)
Et j'entendrai son pas
    (And I'll hear his footstep)
Je devinerai où il va
    (I'll guess where he's going)

Je devinerai où il va
    (I'll guess where he's going)

Ils sont rentrés
    (They have come back in)
Le piano a cessé de jouer
    (The piano has stopped)
Je crois que sa chambre est au fond
    (I think his bedroom is at the back)
Je suis triste s'il y va
    (I'm sad if he goes there)
Parce qu'alors je ne l'entends pas
    (Because I can't hear him then)
Mais si j'entends sa voix
    (But if I hear his voice)
Je devinerai où il va
    (I'll guess where he's going)
Je devinerai où il va
    (I'll guess where he's going)

Mais je ne veux plus y penser
    (But I don't want to think about it anymore)
Mais je ne veux plus écouter
    (But I don't want to listen anymore)
Je vais bientôt aller me coucher
    (I'll soon get to bed)
Et je ne veux plus y penser
    (And I don't want to think about it anymore)

For de Funès, Sanson composed two other magical songs: "Jusqu'A La Tombée Du Jour" and "Une Odeur De Neige." She would then disappear from view, after one more EP and the film *Baba Yaga*, shot in 1973, which was an adaptation of Guido Crepax's comic book.

She had been involved in an all-consuming love relationship with Michel Berger, who gave her the beautiful "Le Printemps Est Là" and "Le Feu Du Ciel" in 1969. It was nevertheless only a trial run before her masterpiece, 1972's LP *Amoureuse*, which equaled in its beauty even Françoise Hardy's best work. "Dis-Lui De Revenir," "Amoureuse," and especially "Besoin De Personne," an instant classic, were just a few of the gems on the album. Being signed by an American label, Sanson had the honor of having four of her songs adapted into English.

Following her breakup with Berger, she released the average "De L'Autre Côté De Mon Rêve" the following year, then left for the U.S. to live with Stephen Stills. There, she met with many of her hero musicians, and had considerably more means to produce her music. Logically enough, her songs were less interesting: she could only but duplicate herself, sounding "gimmicky," in a way. Véronique is still a huge star in France, but she's only released MOR music for too many years.

Catherine Lara

Born in 1945, Catherine "Lara" Bodet was a young violin prodigy who earned a prize at the age of five at the prestigious Conservatoire de Paris. She played in chamber music orchestras, then accompanied the stars of pop music for the odd concert, before she decided to release her own album, *Ad Libitum*, in 1972. Though grandiloquent and pompous at times, it was nonetheless a successful attempt at offering skilled progressive pop, with arrangements by Jean Musy. In April 1972, Lara was invited to play on

Discorama: she gave heartbreaking renditions of "Morituri," a Gothic pop gem with Gregorian chant, and "Dis-Moi," a lovely acoustic ballad. When interviewed about her lyricist Daniel Boublil, she said that he "was able to find things to say about me I didn't know of myself." The show ended with the title track "Ad Libitum," which was a very ambitious work with many chord changes and hooks. Sadly, as the years went on Lara would sink into the quicksand of mediocre MOR music, just like her friend Sanson had done.

Other Psych, Folk, and Pop Late '60s/Early '70s Girls

Julie Saget

She was first noticed for adapting Jean Genet's *Querelle de Brest* into a sort of musical. In 1970, out of the blue, she released the extraordinary "La Robe En Plexiglas," an ode to modern women delivered in impeccably cold, psych style and with arrangements by Christian Chevallier (a master of library music).

> *J'aimerais une robe en plexiglas*
> *(I'd like a Plexiglas dress)*
> *Ça plisse pas, ça tient en place.*
> *(It creases, it doesn't fit)*
> *C'est transparent, c'est comme la glace*
> *(It's transparent, it's like ice)*
> *Ça glisse pas quand on s'enlace*
> *(It doesn't slip when we embrace)*
> *Ça reste fixe de toute une face*
> *(It stays fixed to a face)*

> *J'aimerais une robe en plexiglas*
> *(I'd like a Plexiglas dress)*
> *Si c'est pas flexible, je m'en passe*
> *(If it's not flexible, I'll do without it)*
> *Si c'est rigide, ça f'ra cuirasse*
> *(If it's stiff, I'll wear it as a breastplate)*
> *Pour qu'on s'y glisse, faudra de l'audace*
> *(To slide ourselves in we'll need boldness)*

Julie looked as if she were straight out of a Biba catalogue, singing about the "Machine Electronique" in a TV program introducing scientist Jacques Bergier, a figure who believed in all-out exploration of psychological and imaginary boundaries, and whose closest associate was writer Louis Pauwels. In mainstream TV *variétés* shows, Julie sang "La Nuit Noire Et Blanche," another incredible song, though more accessible that

time, then she tried to become a full-time successful actress—in vain.

Brigitte Fontaine

At seventeen, Brigitte Fontaine left her native Brittany to go to Paris and work in the theatre. She played Ionesco, then in the infamous "café théâtre" post-'68 style, and had quite a success with the *Maman J'ai Peur* play, with actors Rufus and Jacques Higelin. In 1965, she moved on to chanson, releasing an LP on Jacques Canetti's label (Canetti had launched Boris Vian and Jeanne Moreau, among many others). Being very involved in leftist militancy, both Canetti and Fontaine viewed everything that came from the U.S.

with a great wariness (they deemed rock 'n' roll badly played sub-jazz). Then, in 1968, Brigitte signed with Pierre Barouh's Saravah label (Barouh himself was more a jazz or Brazilian music fan). Unexpectedly, the LP she made was a fantastic pop record, called *Brigitte Fontaine Est…Folle!*, which Jean-Claude Vannier arranged and which was mostly written by Olivier Bloch-Lainé. The sleeve was a pastiche of a Jerome Bosch painting, and the palette of songs was itself very rich. "Le Beau Cancer" was a bittersweet ode to life, "Une Fois Mais Pas Deux" could have been included on *Melody Nelson*, while "Comme Rimbaud" and "L'homme-Objet" were among the best songs ever written by a female artist about being a female artist.

> *Que ferais-je de vous, mon homme-objet?*
>   *(What would I do with you, my sex-object man?)*
> *Que ferais-je de tout ce beau palais?*
>   *(What would I do with this huge palace?)*
> *De grands muscles si doux et si parfaits*
>   *(Such big, sweet, perfect muscles)*
> *Que ferais-je de vous, mon homme-objet?*
>   *(What would I do with you, my sex-object man?)*
> *Vous mettrais-je debout, à mon chevet?*
>   *(Would I have you stand at my bedside table?)*
> *Pour voir luire vos genoux hardiment faits*
>   *(To see your boldly-made knees shine)*
> *Vous garderais-je couché à mes pieds?*
>   *(Would I keep you lying at my feet?)*
> *Pour vous frôler du bout de mon soulier*
>   *(To brush against you with my shoe)*

Couperais-je vos joues de mon stylet?
  (Would I cut your cheeks with my stiletto?)
Pour connaître le goût de vos attraits
  (To discover the taste of your charms)
Vous placerais-je tout le jour d'après
  (Would I place you on the following day)
Dans la serre pour vous les fleurs mourraient
  *(In the greenhouse where flowers would die
  for you?)*

After many meanderings in folk-trad-world music with her companion Areski Belkacem, Brigitte recorded, against all odds, the EP *Caliméro* with Stereolab in 2000, adding a modern touch to her classic sound of the late 1960s, and bridging the gap between fans of the past and present.

Claude Lombard

With her soft, fresh, and dancing voice, Claude Lombard sets up her own art: design, colors, sounds. The lush orchestrations, scattered over with glittering electronics, the rich harmonies spiraling around the voice; then the literary texts, so far away from the usual routine of lyrics: all this forms a whole that goes way beyond the sentimentalism of chanson, in a sort of "personal eloquence" in deep resonance with the best tendencies of today's music.
  —Jacques Stehman, a professor at the
    Conservatoire Royal de Bruxelles, and a
    journalist for *Le Soir*

French audiences know Claude Lombard thanks to all the cartoon theme tunes she recorded and the children's programs she sang on. A whole generation of thirty-somethings still know the songs by heart. Even today, she's still working for Disney France.

Born in Belgium in a family of musicians, she released her first LP in 1969 on Jacques Canetti's label. It was remarkable because of the surreal words in songs such as "Polychrome," "Sleep Well," "L'arbre Et L'Oiseau," and "Petit Frère." The music sounded like pure sunshine pop, and Lombard's voice was angelic, of course.

Dessous l'écorce
  (Underneath the bark)
Polychromée
  (Polychrome)
Il y a un tronc
  (There is a trunk)

Lisse et gonflé
  (All smooth and swollen)
De sa laitance
  (With soft roe)
Dessous la mer
  (Underneath the sea)
Polychromée
  (Polychrome)
Y a les poissons
  (There are fish)
Lisse et gonflés
  (All smooth and swollen)
De leur laitance
  (With soft roe)

Dans les églises
  (In the churches)
Polychromées
  (Polychrome)
Il y a les troncs
  (There are collection boxes)
Toujours gonflés
  (Always swollen)
De complaisance
  (With complacency)

Sophie Makhno

She was the Left Bank singer Barbara's secretary and businesswoman, and on a more global level, a woman acting in the shadow for the benefit of French *chanson*. Between 1966 and 1970, she was A&R for CBS, where she favored music more traditional than yé-yé. But that didn't prevent her from recording a 45 on her own in 1968, *Obsessions 68*, a duet with Colin Verdier. The album depicted daily life in a universe little by little being invaded by concrete—the suburban areas outside Paris—and the wish young people had to escape from it, by whatever means necesary:

Ce que je veux c'est du sérieux
  (What I want is something solid)
C'est pas de l'herbe de banlieue
  (It's not suburban weed)
C'est pas du pavot domestique
  (It's not homemade poppy)
Ce que je veux c'est du sérieux
  (What I want is something solid)
Viens dormir dans mon hamac
  (Come sleep in my hammock)
Viens dans mon grand lit tout blanc
  (Climb into my big white bed)
Pas besoin d'aphrodisiaques
  (No aphrodisiac needed)
Pas besoin de stupéfiants
  (No narcotics needed)
Stupéfiants
  (Narcotics)
Ce que je veux c'est du solide
  (What I want is something solid)

De la mécanique du rapide
  (Mechanical and fast)
Ce que je veux c'est du bolide
  (What I want is something of a hot rod)
Ce que je veux c'est du sérieux
  (What I want is something solid)
Du sérieux, du sérieux
  (Solid, solid)

Léonie

Léonie Lousseau recorded a fantastic, joyful pop LP in 1968 that was arranged by Jean-Claude Vannier. Her sexy, audacious vocals strengthened her deliberately light, funny lyrics. Her persona perfectly suited the era: she was both accessible and underground, which led avant-garde directors to ask her to play in their films. She thus featured in *Paul,* shot by Bernadette Lafont's husband Diourka Medvecky, alongside Jean-Pierre Léaud, Bernadette Lafont, and Jean-Pierre Kalfon.

In 1971, thanks to maverick singer Christophe, she signed with Francis Dreyfus from Disques Motors (Dreyfus had introduced France to the likes of David Bowie, Cat Stevens, Pink Floyd, and T. Rex, as well as being Jean-Michel Jarre's producer). Her first single on Motors was a very strong move toward a completely different musical direction. With Vannier still on board, she had lyricist extraordinaire Etienne Roda-Gil write for her. "La Fille De La Véranda," in particular, was a marvel:

Et si jamais je vous disais
  (What if I told you)
Ce qui fait tous mes regrets
  (What my regrets are made of)
Mes regrets
  (My regrets)
Le désespoir de mes nuits
  (My despair at night)
Et le vide de ma vie
  (The void in my life)
De ma vie
  (My life)

De ma pauvre vie...
  (My miserable life)

La fille de la véranda
  (The girl in the veranda)
Que je n'ai vue qu'une fois
  (That I only saw once)
La fille de la véranda
  (The girl in the veranda)
Que je n'ai vue qu'une fois
  (That I only saw once)
Comment peut-on être amoureux
  (How can one be in love)
D'une ombre blanche aux yeux bleus?
  (With one blue-eyed white shadow?)
Aux yeux bleus
  (Blue-eyed)
Je donnerais le paradis
  (I'd give the heavens)
Pour ne pas trouver l'oubli
  (So as not to face oblivion)
Et l'oubli
  (Oblivion)
Dans ma pauvre vie
  (In my miserable life)
La fille de la véranda
  (The girl in the veranda)
Que je n'ai vue qu'une fois
  (That I only saw once)
La fille de la véranda
  (The girl in the veranda)
Que je n'ai vue qu'une fois
  (That I only saw once)

"Le Jardin Anglais" and "Mozart" were also precious, with Léonie's crystalline voice sounding even more

léonie

fragile and captivating. Her following singles, "En Alabama," "Wahala Manitou," and "Lennon," all written by Christophe, were even better.

> Lennon, John Lennon
> Lennon c'est pour toi
>   (Lennon, this is for you)
> Pour toi
>   (For you)
> Lennon, John Lennon
> Écoute-moi
>   (Listen to me)
> Écoute
>   (Listen)
> John Lennon
> John Lennon
> John
> Si je fredonne Lennon
>   (If I'm humming Lennon)
> C'est pour toi
>   (This is for you)
> You are not the only one
> I dream of you
> I love you
> You are not the only one
> I dream of you
> I love you

Repetitive, hypnotic, and sung almost in a whisper, the song was attractive and frightening, like a stalker explaining the origin of her obsession. The A-side of the *Lilith* LP, written by Léonie and Karl-Heinz Schäfer, would have perfectly fit the pagan-folk film *The Wicker Man*. Schäfer wrote the score for the film *Les Gants Blancs Du Diable*, on which Léonie sang "Couleurs," which none other than François Truffaut raved about.

In 1975, Léonie vanished after an unremarkable record for RCA, before coming back with a song for an Eram shoes commercial. She took one last stab at fame in 1979, in the shape of "Y' À Rien À Faire Avec Les Hommes," a blend of disco and new wave that could have been a hit had it been released on Michel Esteban's ZE Records.

Ann Sorel

Ann Sorel was a post-yé-yé singer who caused a scandal when she released a soft-porn hymn to debauchery in 1972, "L'Amour A Plusieurs." The song had been written by Frédéric Botton and arranged by Jean-Claude Vannier, whose Eastern-oriented strings are instantly recognizable here:

> Des amis sont venus prendre un verre, une heure
>> (Some friends have come for a drink, for an hour)
> Et nous avons fait l'amour à plusieurs.
>> (And we had sex altogether)
> Sans chercher pourquoi, sans autres raisons
>> (Without asking ourselves questions, with any or no reason)
> Que d'aimer un peu à la déraison
>> (But to love a little senseless)

> L'amour à plusieurs , c'est bon pour le cœur
>> (Love with several people is good for your heart)

> Sur le canapé, j'étais près de toi
>> (On the couch I was next to you)
> Oui mais dans mes bras, ça n'était pas toi
>> (Yes, but in my arms, it wasn't you)
> Quand tu t'es penché pour me regarder
>> (When you leaned on me just to have a look)
> Juste à cet instant, je t'ai désiré
>> (On that very moment I wanted you)

> L'amour à plusieurs , est-ce bon pour le cœur?
>> (Love with several people, is it good for your heart?)

> Puis tu t'es glissé tout contre mon corps
>> (Then your body slid against mine)

> Et je sens ta peau qui me brûle encore
>> (And I still feel your burning flesh)
> Ainsi, j'ai compris n'aimer plus que toi
>> (Thus I understood you were the only one I loved)
> Et que nous faisions là n'importe quoi
>> (And that what we were all doing there was nonsense)

> L'amour à plusieurs , c'est pas bon pour le cœur
>> (Love with several people isn't good for your heart)

Anna St. Clair

Born Nicole Rudent in 1948, Anna St. Clair was the symbol of the flower child, although she had a hard time succeeding in the music business. She traveled across Europe (even getting expelled from England because she had played in the streets without the mandatory authorization), before she signed on Fontana in 1967 and made an EP arranged by Jean-Claude Vannier, with the song "Les Corbeaux" getting regular airplay. Her repertoire was that of her generation: pacifist, socialist numbers such as "L'Amour À Travers Et À Tort" or "Les Caméléons," in which she mocked the way female pop stars constant changed their hairstyles just to have the press talk about them. Released in November 1968, "L'Amour Par Quatre Chemins" was a dreamy ballad and "C'est Que Tu N'es Pas Loin" a killer with very dynamic arrangements. She had managed to escape her producer Lee Hallyday's grasp and let her creativity blossom.

He had her record more mundane covers of Tom Jones, Simon & Garfunkel ("El Condor Pasa" became "Sur Les Chemin Des Andes"), and Huayno de la Roca in the following years, though. With her black boots, black suit, gold medal, and white cloche hat, Anna St. Clair was simply ahead of the pack of grayish men that surrounded her.

Louise Forestier

Louise Forestier was born in 1943 in Shawinigan, French Canada. She started in the theatre, then moved to traditional chanson and eventually ventured into pop territories after meeting Robert Charlebois. In 1969, her "From Santa To America" was a psych-folk rant against the army, criticizing "American imperialism." On the album *Lindbergh,* clearly influenced by Zappa, the title track was an instant classic of French-language pop:

Des hélices
   (Propellers)
Astrojet, Whisperjet, Clipperjet, Turbo
À propos chu pas rendu chez Sophie
   (By the way, I ain't arrived at Sophie's)
Qui a pris l'avion St-Esprit de Duplessis
   (Who took the St. Esprit de Duplessis plane)
Sans m'avertir
   (Without telling me)

Alors chu r'parti
   (Then I've jus' gone back)
Sur Quebec Air
   (On Quebec Air)

Transworld, Nord-East, Eastern, Western
Puis Pan-American
   (Then Pan-American)
Mais ché pu où chu rendu
   (But dunno where I am now)

J'ai été
   (I've been)

Au sud du sud au soleil bleu blanc rouge
   (To the southernmost south with blue, white, and red sun)
Les palmiers et les cocotiers glacés
   (Palm trees and frozen coconuts)
Dans les pôles aux esquimaux bronzés
   (Down the poles with suntanned Eskimos)
Qui tricotent des ceintures flêchés farcies
   (Who knit belts and stuffed arrows)
Et toujours ma Sophie qui venait de partir
   (And my Sophie who'd just gone)

Partie sur Quebec Air
   (Gone on Quebec Air)
Transworld, Nord-East, Eastern, Western
Puis Pan-American
   (Then Pan-American)
Mais ché pu où chu rendu
   (But dunno where I am now)

In 1972, Louise Forestier took part in *IXE-13*, a musical that was a parody of a detective story. Directed by Jacques Godbout with music by François Dompierre, it was a sketch-turned-political-satire. Alongside Louise Forestier, stars from 1970s Quebec—such as Carole Laure—were also featured. The film remains as a vibrant testimony

LOUISE FORESTIER

FROM SANTA TO AMERICA

STÉRÉO + MON

GAMM

to the nonconformist and independent spirit of the country then.

Charlotte Leslie

Born Rosetta Aiello in Tunisia to Italian parents, Charlotte Leslie began as a swinging mademoiselle with the single "Les Filles C'est Fait." In 1970, she paid tribute to the Beatles with "Monsieur Harrison," written by François Bernheim. The song is a simple, soft pop address to the "quiet one":

Midi sonne, monsieur Harrison
    (It's noon, Mr. Harrison)
Vous dormez, il faut vous lever
    (You're sleeping, you've got to get up)
Midi sonne, monsieur Harrison
    (It's noon, Mr. Harrison)
Levez-vous et dépêchez-vous!
    (Get up and hurry up!)

Prenez vite votre guitare
    (Pick up your guitar)
Rejoignez le studio!
    (Go to the studio!)
Vous allez être en retard
    (You're going to be late)
Pour faire votre solo!
    (For your solo!)
Ils sont déjà là-bas
    (They're already there)
Ils vous attendent tous
    (All waiting for you)

Et vous êtes encore dans votre lit
    (And you're still in bed)
Et il est déjà mi-di, midi, midi, midi, midi, midi, midi
    (And it's noon, noon, noon, noon, noon)
Montez dans votre Rolls blanche
    (Get in your white Rolls-Royce)
Avec votre chauffeur
    (With chauffeur)

Regardez Londres en ce dimanche
    (Have a look at London: it's Sunday)
Il y a même des fleurs!
    (There are even flowers!)
Et vous devez jouer
    (And you're supposed to play)
Et vous devez chanter
    (And you're supposed to sing)
Mais vous êtes encore dans votre lit
    (But you're still in your bed)
Et il est déjà mi-di, midi, midi, midi, midi, midi, midi
    (And it's noon, noon, noon, noon, noon)

Uta

Uta Taeger, born in 1940 in Germany, was an actress who played in *Aimez-Vous Brahms?* alongside Ingrid Bergman and Anthony Perkins, in Claude Lelouch's *Vivre Pour Vivre*, and in Gérard Pirès' *Erotissimo*. In 1969, she released a 45 with a cover of the Shan-gri-Las' "Past, Present, and Future" ("Hier, Aujourd'hui, Demain") and "Baudelaire," a wonderful heavy-psych tune by Pierre Groscolas, which used the poem "Recueillement" from *Les Fleurs Du Mal* for lyrics:

Sois sage, ô ma Douleur, et tiens-toi plus tranquille.
   (Be quiet and more discreet, O my Grief.)
Tu réclamais le Soir, il descend; le voici:
   (You cried out for the Evening; even now it falls:)
Une atmosphère obscure enveloppe la ville,
   (A gloomy atmosphere envelops the city,)
Aux uns portant la paix, aux autres le souci.
   (Bringing peace to some, anxiety to others.)
Pendant que des mortels la multitude vile,
   (While the vulgar herd of mortals, under the scourge)
Sous le fouet du Plaisir, ce bourreau sans merci,
   (Of Pleasure, that merciless torturer)
Va cueillir des remords dans la fête servile,
   (Goes to gather remorse in the servile festival)
Ma Douleur, donne-moi la main ; viens par ici.
   (My Grief, give me your hand; come this way)

Élisa

In some '72-'73 TV shows, Élisa was still seen wearing her Yankee pullover, carrying a little schoolbag, and adopting a very timid attitude. She then completely disappeared from the public eye, until a comeback in recent years under another stage name, performing a completely different sort of music. Even today, she doesn't want people to know about her past as a pop singer. Being an admirer and a nice person, I'll respect her wish and just add that she was discovered in the French version of *Hair*, that her first 45 (*La Fille En Jeans/Les Pirates Convalescents*) was written by Guy Bonnet, and that the second (*En Stop/Les Pensionnaires Du Carmel Des Citrons Verts*) reinforced her image as a nice family girl playing at being naughty:

Je vais comme ça en stop à Port-Grimaud
    (This is how I'm going hitch-hiking to Port-Grimaud)
Avec mon vieux chapeau de paille brûlée
    (With my old burnt-out straw hat)
Une jupe à clochettes
    (A bell-shaped skirt)
Un collier des bracelets
    (A necklace and bracelets)
Et mes chaussettes qui baillent sur mes baskets
    (And my socks gaping wide on my tennis shoes)

Alors décide-toi
    (So make up your mind)
Je voudrais bien partir avec toi
    (I'd like to go with you)

Avec toi
    (With you)
Avec toi
    (With you)

Je vais comme ça en stop à Port-Grimaud
    (This is how I'm going hitch-hiking to Port-Grimaud)
Ma brosse à dents ma carte d'identité
    (My toothbrush, my ID)
Avec la photo où je ne suis pas très belle
    (With the photo on which I'm not too good-looking)
J'ai même un peu de sous à une ficelle
    (I even have some money attached to a string)

Je suivrai le chemin
    (I'll follow the road)
Qui me prend par la main
    (Taking me by the hand)
En copain
    (Like a friend)

Ellen Le Roy

In very psych-pop style, full of wah-wah guitars and a declamatory grandeur that was close to agit-prop, Ellen Le Roy released "Amérique, Appelle-Moi" in 1970, on the Riviera label. The song was pretty harsh on U.S. policy, something that probably pleased post-1968 students very much:

> *Amérique*
> *(America)*
> *Amérique*
> *(America)*
>
> *Quand tu auras fini de baver sur ta serviette*
> *(Once you have finished drooling on your napkin)*
> *Quand tu auras fini de bouffer du Viet*
> *(Once you have finished saying bad things about the Vietnamese)*
>
> *Appelle-moi*
> *(Call me)*
> *Amérique (America)*
>
> *Quand tu auras fini de broyer du noir*
> *(Once you have finished feeling blue)*
> *Quand tu n'auras plus de verres à boire*
> *(Once you've finished your last drink)*
>
> *Appelle-moi*
> *(Call me)*
> *Amérique*
> *(America)*

> *Quand tu n'auras tué plus de Kennedy*
> *(Once you have killed the last of the Kennedys)*
> *Quand la mort t'aura cané, dis*
> *(Once life has got you, hey)*
>
> *Appelle-moi*
> *(Call me)*
> *Amérique*
> *(America)*
> *Quand tu auras bouffé tous tes ice-creams*
> *(Once you have finished your ice cream)*
> *Quand tu auras accomplis tous tes crimes*
> *(Once you have committed all your crimes)*
>
> *Appelle-moi*
> *(Call me)*
> *Amérique*
> *(America)*
> *Quand tu auras fini ton cauchemar*
> *(Once you have dreamed all your nightmares)*
> *Quand tu auras refait ton plumard*
> *(Once you have refurbished your bed)*
>
> *Appelle-moi (je me couche tard)*
> *(Call me) (I'm going to bed quite late)*
> *Amérique (tard)*
> *(America) (Late)*

Geneviève Ferreri

Another one of these obscure singers, Geneviève Ferreri nonetheless recorded the very powerful "L'arc En Ciel" in 1970, with romantic leanings close to Procol Harum or Aphrodite's Child. Ferreri wrote the lyrics based on a melody penned by Michel Bernholc (composer for Alain Chamfort and Véronique Sanson, among many others):

> *Je suis comme un arbre mort*
> *(I'm like a dead tree)*
> *Mes larmes se sont fanées*
> *(My tears have wilted)*
> *Le sourire qui m'abreuvait*
> *(The smile I drank from)*
> *Cristallisé à jamais*
> *(Crystallized forever)*
> *Aucune autre source ne pourra me donner*
> *(No other spring could ever give me)*
> *Ce philtre enchanteur qui me faisait rêver*
> *(This enchanting potion that made me dream)*
> *Par un soir d'été, je viendrai te chercher*
> *(By a summer night I'd come and fetch you)*
> *Et dans l'arc-en-ciel, nous irons nous cacher*
> *(And by the rainbow we'll hide)*
>
> *La rosée du matin a noyé dans tes yeux*
> *(The morning dew has drowned your eyes)*
>
> *Les petites flammes bleues qui réchauffent ma vie*
> *(The little blue flames that warm my life)*

Par un souffle de pluie mes doigts se sont figés
(With a touch of rain my fingers have frozen)
Caressants les cheveux qui leur servaient de nid
(Stroking the hair that served as a nest)

Charlotte Walters

The repertoire of the *filles de la pop* in the 1968–73 period was very different compared to 1961–67: drugs, sexual freedom, the Women's Lib movement, and political protests were all in the air after '68. The look of the singers had evolved too—the chic-hippie style had become the norm. Charlotte Walters' "Fleurs De Pavots Bleus" in 1969 corresponded to it all: an oriental pop song musically, its lyrics had been written by Etienne Roda Gil, in a mock surreal style that would be massively copied in the nascent 1970s:

> *Fleurs de pavots bleus*
> *(Blue poppy flowers)*
> *Au cœur de nos villes*
> *(In the heart of the cities)*
> *Fleurs de pavots bleus*
> *(Blue poppy flowers)*
> *Au cœur de nos villes*
> *(In the heart of the cities)*
>
> *Chardons venimeux*
> *(Venomous thistles)*
> *Au sein des principes*
> *(At the heart of principles)*

Chardons vénéneux
   (Venomous thistles)
Dans nos républiques
   (In our republics)
Républiques
   (Republics)

Jodie Foster

Of course Jodie Foster doesn't need an introduction to the American public. Still, few people know that she speaks—and can sing—perfect French. In 1977, one year after *Taxi Driver*, she played with Jean-Yanne and Bernard Giraudeau in the romantic comedy *Moi Fleur Bleue*, in which she sang a ballad full of Moog synths, "La vie C'est Chouette":

La vie c'est chouette
   (Life is fine)
Quand on a une amourette
   (When you're in love)
Quand la vie veut dans une île
   (When life wants an island)
Quand la vie va dans la ville
   (When life goes to the city)
La vie c'est chouette
   (Life is fine)
Quand on a une amourette
   (When you're in love)

Y a tant de jours où c'est l'ennui
   (There are so many days of boredom)
Tant de réveils aux matins gris
   (So many gray mornings when you wake up)

Et l'on rêve d'un amour
   (And you dream of a love)
Que l'on vivrait un jour
   (That you'd be living one day)
Toute une nuit
   (A whole night)
Mais avec qui?
   (But who with?)
Mais avec qui?
   (But who with?)

La vie c'est chouette
   (Life is fine)
Quand on a une amourette
   (When you're in love)
Que l'on soit côté fleur des champs ou côté violence
   (Whether you are on the flower child or violent side)
Un enfant vous dirait que la vie c'est chouette
   (A child would tell that life is fine)
Quand on a une amourette
   (When you're in love)

JE T'ATTENDS DEPUIS LA NUIT DES TEMPS

MUSIQUE DU FILM

moi, fleur bleue

VERSION
FRANÇAISE

Jodie Foster

Marcy Music

MUSIQUE DE FRANÇOIS D'AIME

CARRERE

14
EIGHTIES GIRLS (AND ONE MAN)

Lio

IN THE WAKE OF THE PUNK AND NEW WAVE MOVE-ments, a revolution was happening on the radios. In the second half of the 1970s, *filles de la pop* had disappeared—there were leftist protest songwriters on one side, and *variétés* singers on the other.

Wanda Maria Ribeiro Furtado Tavares was born at the beginning of the 1960s in Portugal, then her family had to leave for Brussels, Belgium, running away from the Salazar régime. Thanks to Eric Dierks-Hagen (a.k.a. Jacques Duvall) and Jay Alanski, Wanda became Lio, as a tribute to a character from Jean-Claude Forest's *Barbarella*, and in accordance with the young girl's love for the world of comics. Ariola would release the trio's "Banana Split" in 1979, which was a smash hit: two million singles sold in a few months, Lio being invited on every possible radio or television show, and becoming a favorite of rock musicians (Debbie Harry and the Cramps demanded to meet her when they played Brussels).

Ca me déplairait pas que tu m'embrasses
  (I'd quite like it if you kissed me)
NA NA NA
Mais faut saisir ta chance avant qu'elle passe
  (But you have to seize the opportunity before it passes you by)
NA NA NA
Si tu cherches un truc pour briser la glace
  (If you're looking for something to break the ice)
BANANA BANANA BANANA

C'est le dessert
  (It's the dessert)

Que sert
  (Served by)
L'abominable homme des neiges
  (The abominable snowman)
A l'abominable enfant teenage
  (To the abominable teenage snowgirl)
Un amour de dessert
  (A real love of a dessert)
BANANA NA NA NA NA BANANA SPLIT
Les cerises confites sont des lipsticks
  (Crystallized cherries are lipsticks)
NA NA NA
Qui laissent des marques rouges sur
l'antarctique
  (Leaving red marks on the Antarctic)
NA NA NA
Et pour le faire fondre une tactique
  (And to have him melt, the right tactics are)
BANANA BANANA BANANA

Lio turned into a pop icon in 1980 with Jacno's "Amoureux Solitaires," then recorded *Suite Sixtine* with the Sparks in 1982, a whole LP in English. *Amour Toujours* in 1983 and *Pop Model* in 1986 (featuring hit single "Les Brunes Comptent Pas Pour Des Prunes") sold very well, establishing her as a modern grown-up Lolita who combined glamour and feminism.

Tout le monde
  (Everybody)
Répète en chœur que les hommes préfèrent
les blondes
  (Keeps repeating that gentlemen
  prefer blondes)
Qu'ils fondent
  (That they can't resist)

Pour une décolorée en moins d'une seconde
  (A dyed blonde, not more than a second)
J'ai l'impression qu'ils confondent
  (Seems to me that they're making a
  mistake)
Et la Joconde, à moins qu'on la tonde
  (And the Mona Lisa, unless they shave
  her hair)
C'est quand même bien une brune
  (Is definitely a brunette)
Les brunes comptent pas pour des prunes
  (Brunettes are not worth nothing)

Certaines brunettes se font appeler
  (Some brunettes have people call them)
Des blondes vénitiennes
  (Venetian blondes)
Vilaines
  (Naughty girls)
Menteuses, elles trichent, et puis à quoi ça
les mène
  (Liars, they cheat, and what's the
  point anyway?)
Il faudrait qu'on les prévienne
  (Someone should tell them)
Sophia Loren
  (Sophia Loren)
J'suis pas daltonienne
  (I'm not color-blind)
C'est quand même bien une brune
  (She's brown-haired, isn't she?)
Les brunes comptent pas pour des prunes
  (Brunettes are not worth nothing)

On a du caractère, et dans nos artères
  (We've got character and in our veins)

C'est du sang chaud qui coule
    (Hot blood is flowing)
On la joue pas cool
    (We're not that cool)
Attention aux brunes
    (Beware of the brunettes)
Les brunes comptent pas pour des prunes
    (Brunettes are not worth nothing)

In 1988, the album *Can Can* paid homage to graphic novel creator Hugo Pratt (father of the *Corto Maltese* series), before Lio took a break, mostly to become a film actress. *Des Fleurs Pour Un Caméléon* marked a return to form in 1991, which was confirmed by *Wandatta*, a true masterpiece in the form of a concept album created with lyricist Boris Bergman, with

a cover by Guy Peellaert. Sadly enough, the public was bewildered by its darker sides and it was close to being a flop, despite the quality of songs like "Cruauté Menthol" or an adaptation of Presley's "In The Ghetto."

Coupe-moi le son je veux bien être dans le noir
    (Turn the volume off, I'd rather be in
    the dark)
Histoire de m' déshabiller du regard
    (So that you'll undress me with your eyes)
Pour se mettre à nu avant la crise
    (To get naked before the crisis happens)
J'croyais qu'y avait que le strip-tease
    (I thought there only was strip-tease)
J'enlève le haut par modestie
    (I'm undoing my top, being modest)
Un bas filé pas vu épris
    (A hole in a pair of stockings, unnoticed, not
    in love with it)
Chute de bretelle pour elle c'est dur
    (A bra strap falling, pretty hard for her)
Chauffeur dérouté p'tite ceinture
    (The road has been detoured, small belt)

Ça vient d'sortir
    (It's just been on)
Ça a du style
    (There's some style to it)
T'appelles ça cruauté menthol
    (You call that menthol cruelty)
Quand les âmes perdues vont toucher le sol
    (When lost souls have touched the ground)
Qui me dit que tu vas bouger d'un cil
    (Who knows if you're going to move at all?)

Rather unexpectedly, Lio also released an album with some poems by French poet Jacques Prévert (2000), then went to Sweden to record *Dites Au Prince Charmant* with indie-pop guitarist Peter Von Poehl (2006). In 2009, on the Freaksville label (aided by prolific musician Benjamin "Miam Monster Miam" Shoos), she worked with Duvall again, for an album with the band Phantom.

Lio has always had a tendency to escape categories, suddenly disappearing from view to reappear where least expected. She's the essence of pop: rare, precious, evanescent.

I'd like to start with your career at the movies. Which of the films you made were the most remarkable ones?

The first two ones, of course, were important to me: *Elsa Elsa* by Didier Haudepin, in which I replaced the late Pascale Ogier, which was first of all named *Tendre Belvédère*. I loved the name, and I loved Pascale and her mum, Bulle.

Then I worked with Chantal Ackerman, whose universe was totally different from mine. My parents had told me to "at least try and go see her movies," which I did. It had nothing to do at all with the "Lio" thing—that's why I agreed to do the film, in a kind of survival instinct move.

A casting against type, in a way.

Maybe not, but Ackerman was millions of light-years away from the perception people had of me, the way my image was bi-dimensional, squashed by pressure, if I may say so, there were less dimensions than in that sort of movie. I didn't know if I'd be able to do that, but I wanted to escape the *SLC* thing and talk with new words, with different people.

To show the world that Wanda existed behind Lio.

Yes, to show I was a real person, not just a magazine creature. It was through another imaginary world that I wanted to exist and claim I was for real.

Then I was asked to play in *L'Été Meurtrier* and *Mauvais Sang*, but I turned them down, for whatever reasons. The *auteurs* cinema got interested in me—mainly because I'd become bankable, I think. I was supposed to be at the beginning of the whole thing (financing, etc.).

As I was extremely popular, I thought I could play in popular comedies, but since my first films were deemed intellectual, I was categorized (something the French adore above all). It took me a long time to play in TV series, for instance. Now I have access to both types of cinema—and I like it.

How do you view the French cinema today?

The problem is we are torn between blockbusters with no artistic ambition at all, and very, very small budget productions. An author should have the time to mature, his/her ideas should be allowed to blossom after three or four films. I'm not sure producers are ready to be patient now. The most difficult situation being for the directors who are in between very avant-garde things and the mainstream, what director Pascale Ferran called *"les films du milieu"* (the in-between movies).

A bit like the middle class having difficulties surviving, paradoxically.

Yes, except that you once had films out of the mainstream with a budget that was big enough to develop many different characters and roles—the same goes for pop music.

What about television? Are the French still way behind the U.S.?

Very far away still. Themes are becoming more interesting than they used to be—but their presentation clearly lacks audacity, the character development hasn't got the same finesse. In the U.S., you've got huge teams working on the scripts, when in France it's still the old Left Bank thing of "this is my own script, my own project, my own little baby." Hitchcock's movies had very precise storyboarding, everything was planned months and months before even starting to shoot, but it was creative too. In France, one tends to think that planning things ruins them, that it isn't pure creation—and so not really worth it. But we're making some progress with this notion.

The same goes for musicals: some years ago, they were simply appalling. It's much better now: *Nine* was a total flop at the Folies Bergères seventeen years ago though it was pure Broadway, today *Cabaret* is pure genius—even better than the American one.

What are your plans musically—I was about to say, "as a pop icon"?

Pop icons…well, France Gall was one for a start—her 1960s songs were especially fantastic. Hardy is also a favorite of mine, she had that elegiac quality. Marie Laforêt, too. I'm not too fond of the yé-yé movement, generally speaking: I think they were all part of an era, that's all. As for men, I love people who came later, such as Jacno or Christophe: they were borderline, a bit tragic, real dandies.

Do you plan to make another record?

Why not? It's a bit difficult to offer a projection of oneself as one grows older. *Dites Au Prince Charmant* was really the conclusion of something for me. It took five years to make—and I like things to be immediate, light as a feather, I don't like to spend ages on things. I've been working with a musician recently, at a distance, through the Internet. I've got four songs that might end up on vinyl, or on a downloading site. My dream when I started was to meet people and understand how things were made—I can't read the music, I had so many hang-ups, you see.

This you did on Wandatta, *didn't you?*

I did, I was always next to the mixing desk, asking questions, doing the counterpart instruments vocally for the producer Philippe Dry to understand what I wanted. The sound engineer, Mitch, who was very open to new things, accepted that I tried many different options, in the way I sung for instance.

I think there were great songs on that album: "Garde À Vue," for instance. *Wandatta* enabled me to get rid of many of my fears—I remember I didn't dare record or arrange backing vocals before, for example.

Jacques Duvall

Nobody ever served the *filles de la pop* as well as Jacques Duvall: he was much more than a Pygmalion for Lio, whom he helped to discover her own, beautiful personality, and was a precious right-hand man at some point or another for Jane Birkin, Marie France, Dani, and Helena Noguerra. He's the only songwriter to rival Serge Gainsbourg's talent at his peak. His inclusion in this book dedicated to female singers is thus perfectly understandable. And he had been a little girl once—or at least, that's what he pretended to be when he sent his song "Little Sister" to Kim Fowley, who bore no grudge, and included it on the Runaways' *Waiting For The Night* album!

Who are the female icons of French pop from the 1960s to today?

I don't think there are any icons. "Cult" singers such as Nico or Barbra tend to bore me stiff, you know. I much prefer underrated people: I'd rather have Annie Philippe than France Gall, Gillian Hills than Bardot. That's for the 1960s. As for today's artists, I have a fondness for Pascale Borel, that wonderful Japanese girl Kahimi Karie—and even very mainstream *filles* such as Mylène Farmer,

© P. Schyns – Sofam

Elodie Frégé, or Chimène Badi give me strong emotions. I'm not always a snob, you see—but still, I have a taste for forgotten ones, France Flory, Myriam Mézières, Mallaury Nataf—all of them fantasies, the physique counts, I must admit. I like when artists do the job for me: they create, suffer—and I cry.

The songs Serge Gainsbourg wrote for the yé-yé girls were exercises in style for him, bringing him more fame and money than his own records. How would you explain why they have lasted until today?

Probably because he expressed his originality through them all, not in his previous Left Bank songs. He was the first in France to move between the yin of the art, and the yang of the entertainment—something writers in Broadway used to do way before (Gainsbourg "borrowed" that from Cole Porter). The fact his songs lasted is called the very paradoxical essence of pop, don't you think? Burt Bacharach, now much revered, was laughed at by critics at the moment when he was writing all his great classics. There's no major or minor art, contrary to what Gainsbourg once bitterly pretended.

You wrote for Jane Birkin, with Alain Chamfort. How did you escape from being too much influenced by Gainsbourg then?

Alain Chamfort wrote the music for *Les Clefs Du Paradis*, and Jane agreed to sing it out of her friendship for him—I don't think she had ever heard of me. I'm just one those people under Serge's influence, whether I admit it or not. But I'm not complaining: we're all unique anyway. To try and get away from your influences is still living under their yoke. I've since long decided to put an end to such lost-before-it's-even-begun type of battles within myself.

How would you describe Lio to someone who hasn't heard of her?

(Laughs) Are you kidding me? That's impossible! I wouldn't even try. An artistic relationship is like a love affair, it can be a marriage made in heaven. Lio is someone so special…well, I'd just mention a few of the people she worked with, that says it all: Sparks, Hugo Pratt, the Stinky Toys, Doisneau, John Cale, Telex, Chamfort, Boris Bergman. Speaking of the exceptional singers I had the good fortune to write for, I could mention Marie-France too—who herself worked with Rita Mitsouko, Frédéric de Botton, Chrissie Hynde, Marc Almond. Or Helena Noguerra: Rezvani, Katerine, Doriand. And Dani: Truffaut, Daniel Darc, Daho. Not forgetting Elisa Point or Charline Rose, Arabian divas Amina and Biyouna. And Ann Luu, Nathalie Gabay, Coralie Clément, Claudia Barton, who I wrote for in English. I loved them all!

How come the Brits and the Americans are so fond of French yé-yés now, when such music was totally unknown outside of French-speaking territories in the 1960s?

Yé-yés were often criticized for being mere copycats aping th e Anglo-Saxons. The musicians playing on their records were very often seasoned jazzmen, though, who were much more gifted than the original musicians had been: they brought a certain elegance in, to compensate for a lack of rock 'n' roll savagery. One must also bear in mind that what the Anglo-Saxons do or did, getting interested in people like Gainsbourg, is not different from us French buying Italian records made by Celentano, Bobby Solo, Patty Pravo, or Ornella Vanoni, who was a yé-yé girl but in a more intellectual manner.

What might the French female star singer of the future look like?

I really don't know. I'm going to answer backward if I may, and praise singers who were there *before* the yé-yé movement. So I love Jacqueline Danno for her sense of drama, Magali Noël for her sensuality, Lucienne Delyle for her veiled voice, Arletty for her cheeky humour, Annie Cordy because she's Belgian like me, smart Suzy Delair and enigmatic Suzy Solidor. And I adore their heiresses, of course: Marie Möör who revisited old songs with Barney Wilen, Simone Tassimot who brought Gainsbourg back to cabaret, Hermine Demoriane singing Roy Orbison as if it were Kurt Weill, Julie Depardieu redoing *La Villette*. And the one who transcends it all, making traditions sound hyper-modern: Ingrid Caven.

Any contemporary fille de la pop *you'd recommend?*

I discovered quite a few on MySpace, some years ago: Florence Denou, Salomé Califano, Mauve a.k.a. Alka, Ana Pankratoff—who released a good album that went nowhere, and is working on a better one even—that's the everlasting story of pop, isn't it?

Marie-France

Marie-France has been considered a glamorous underground icon in very different scenarios, from Marguerite Duras' plays to punk, pop, cabaret, and 1970s queer militancy. She was born in Oran, Algeria, and after arriving in Paris she was immediately attracted to stars such as Anita Pallenberg, Nico (with whom she shared a flat), and Amanda Lear. Like them, she always tried to be one craze above the rest of the

© Clément Boulland

flock: when Paris was all Indian dresses and hippieish boots, she had already adopted the androgynous decadent look that would be the number-one trend at the Palace or the Bains Douches ten years afterward. Even before she became a star in the world of show business, she was one in her everyday life. It was pretty normal that she'd connect with eccentrics, then. In 1967, she met Gainsbourg for France Gall's *Dents De Lait, Dents De Loup* TV show:

> *I was a dancer there, with an orange miniskirt and long hair. I clearly saw he was attracted to me. He asked me out, and we went for dinner at the Entresol in the Marais district. We ended up in his room at the Cité des Arts, he played the piano for me, very charmingly. The next morning, we listened to Anna Karina's album, which he had just received by the post.*

Marie-France was the informal leader of Gazolines, a group of Amazons of the third-sex kind, who liked to disturb post-1968 demonstrations with slogans like "makeup is a way of life," "proletarians of all countries, unite and fondle each other!" or "now's the time for champ, coke, and fripperies!" She used to sing at the Alcazar, inspiring artists like Arrabal and Jay Alanski, who made her record "Déréglée" and "Daisy" in 1977:

Ta petite chérie
   (Your little darling)
Ne veut pas ce soir
   (Doesn't want to do it tonight)
Parce qu'elle est réglée
   (Because she's got her period)
Alors tu viens me voir
   (So you come and see me)

Tu sais que je ne suis
   (You know that I am)
Qu'une déréglée
   (Only but deranged)

Je suis gentille, je suce des réglisses
   (I'm nice, I suck licorice sticks)
Je suis méchante, je prends des raclées
   (I'm bad, I get beaten up)

Comment vous me considérez glisse
   (How you envision me, pass)
Sur mon indifférence: j'suis déréglée
   (On my indifference, I'm deranged)

Tous les mâles le savent
   (All the males know of it)
Ils connaissent le chemin
   (They know the way)
Et ils ont la clé
   (And have the key)
Pour eux c'est pas grave
   (To them that's nothing serious)
Après tout je suis rien
   (After all I'm only)
Qu'une déréglée
   (Deranged)

Alors n'aie pas peur
   (So don't be afraid)
Monte me voir un quart d'heure
   (Come see me for a quarter of an hour)
Et tu seras comblé
   (Eventually you'll have what you needed)
Tu sais qu'j'suis ton amie
   (You know I'm your friend)

→

Du moment que t'oublies
   (As long as you do not forget)
Pas de me régler
   (To pay)

The record was a five-hundred-copy limited edition on the small Romantik label, but left a mark on history (Nouvelle Vague covered "Déréglée» in 2010). 1981's *39 De Fièvre*, written with young pop prodigies Bijou, was more rocking. It featured a cover of Gillian Hills' "Avec Toi" and successful adaptations ("Shakin' All Over" became "Le Diable En Personne") as well as strong originals: "Chez Moi À Paris" and "Comme Les Autres," with lyrics by Jean-William Thoury. The following year, Jay Alanski and Jacques Duvall wrote the hilarious "Je Ne Me Quitterai Jamais" for her (the sleeve was a Pierre & Gilles' effort), and Lio slightly modified its words for her own 1986 hit, "Je Casse Tout C'Que J'Touche."

She published her memoirs, *Elle Était Une Fois*, in 2003, but her career wasn't over. This was proven by 2008's *Marie-Antoinette* (with contemporary music artist Jac Berrocal), a show about Bardot in 2009, and a pure rock 'n' roll LP in 2010 (*Kiss*), featuring Jacques Duvall and Miam Monster Miam—there was even a duet with longtime fan Chrissie Hynde.

Les Calamités

Caroline Augier (vocals, bass), Isabelle Petit (vocals, guitar), Odile Repolt (vocals, guitar), and Mike Stephens (drums): they were one of the best French power-pop bands in the 1980s. In 1983, the three girls, bored with their lives in the countryside and inspired by '60s girls groups and the newish Paisley Sound, formed a band that they wanted to be miles apart from the mundane realities of rock combos—an anti-Runaways stance, so to speak. Their songs were to be positive and fresh: their first single "Les Calamités" and album *À Bride Abattue* (on legendary New Rose label) succeeded in that respect. The Calamités even carried on with their studies while touring and recording beauties like "Pas La Peine" or "Toutes Les Nuits" (lyrics below), which became hymns for the youth of the time.

Tous deux égarés dans ce cauchemar
   (Lost in this nightmare)
Nous cherchions en vain à sortir du trou noir
   (We both try to find a way out of the
   black hole)
Soudain sous nos pieds le sol s'est dérobé
   (Suddenly the ground falls away under
   our feet)
Alors j'ai crié je me suis réveillée
   (So I cried out and woke up)
Ne serrant dans mes bras qu'un oreiller
   (Only hugging a pillow against me)
À la place de mon fiancé
   (Instead of my boyfriend)
J'ai beau secouer le gros édredon
   (I shake the old eiderdown)
Soulever le matelas je ne te trouve pas
   (Look underneath the mattress, but I can't
   find you)
Soudain je comprends: tu as recommencé
   (Then I understand: you did it again)
Car j'entends des pas là-haut sur les toits
   (For I hear footsteps up there on
   the rooftops)

→

Tu marches la nuit mais tu ne le sais pas
  (You're a sleepwalker but you don't know it)
Tu te promènes sans savoir où tu vas
  (You're taking a walk not knowing where
  you're going)
Chaque fois poussé par un je-ne-sais-quoi
  (Each time led by a je-ne-sais-quoi)
Tel un zombie tu vas hanter les toits
  (Like a zombie you're haunting the rooftops)
(Oh non!)
  (Oh no!)
Lyrics from "Toutes Les Nuits"

The Calamités were a French Bananarama or the Bangles: in between rock and pop, no mere parodies though wearing their influences on their sleeves, ready to sing in their native language or to cover international standards ("Nicolas," "Le Supermarché," "The Kids Are Alright," "Teach Me How To Shimmy," "You Can't Sit Down," and "With A Boy Like You"). This innocence and honesty were rewarded when authentic rock icons such as the Dogs' Dominique Laboubée came to play on their records ("Pas La Peine," "C'Est Embêtant," "Boy From New York City"). Their favorite themes were boys becoming too insistent at parties, insomnia after drinking too much champagne, and wild exploits downtown with girlfriends: a middle-class way of life under the influence of American movies.

The group split up after just a few years, then Odile and Isabelle came back for a duet and hit it big with *Vélomoteur*, which was produced by Daniel Chenevez of the band Niagara and sold 350,000 copies in 1987. Their sound was now poppier, and definitely more radio-friendly, though they still looked like mid-1960s secretaries (which certainly influenced the fact that they were so popular with children and parents alike). Odile and Isabelle soon grew tired of promotion (for six months, they had followed an almost press-junket-a-day rhythm), split the band a second time, and decided to go on with their family lives ("the royalties? Well, we each bought a huge house for us to live in, with our husbands and kids—what would you have done?")

Je revois notre voiture rouge
  (I remember our red car)
Filant à toute allure sur les routes
  (Driving at full speed on the roads)
Moi, les cheveux dans le vent
  (And I, my hair in the wind)
Tu regardes au loin, droit devant
  (You staring in the distance ahead)
Tant de choses auraient pu se passer
  (So many things could have happened)
Que je n'aurai pas regrettées
  (That I wouldn't have regretted)
(Oh non!)
  (Oh no!)
Mais tu es toujours trop pressé
  (But you're always in such a haste)
Et on ne s'est même pas arrêté
  (And we didn't even stop)
Je t'assure que je n'ai pas peur
  (I can say I'm not afraid)
Je n'ai pas non plus mal au cœur
  (I'm not even feeling sick)
Je n'suis même pas de méchante humeur
  (I'm not even in a bad mood)
Mais je préfère les vélomoteurs
  (But I prefer motorbikes)

→

LES CALAMITES

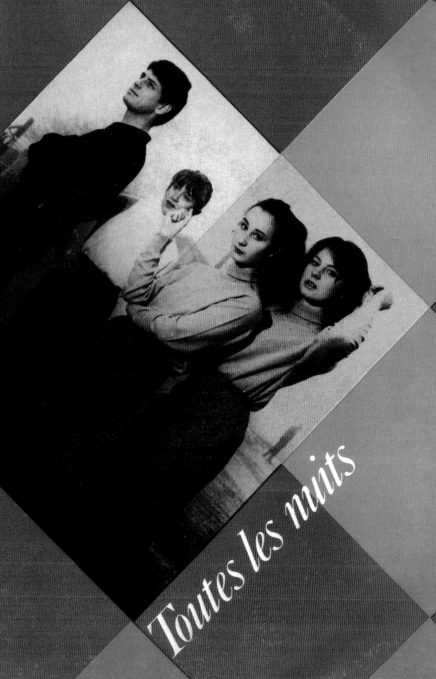

Toutes les nuits

Qui font: pa pa pa pa pa…
  (That go: pa pa pa pa pa!)
Pa pa pa pa pa pa pa
Pa pa pa pa pa pa pa

Niagara

In 1982, Muriel "Moreno" Laporte met Daniel Chenevez in Brittany's Rennes, where new wave bands and cultural figures such as Marquis de Sade, Arnold Turboust, and Etienne Daho had originated. Muriel and Daniel formed the cold-wave group L'Ombre Jaune, which lasted for two years, then adopted a more pop-oriented approach and became Niagara. The band found immediate success with "Tchiki Boom" and then had a string of hits: one, "L'Amour À La Plage," was emblematic of the country's desire to escape the grim reality of the economic crisis of the mid-1980s:

Ce soir j'irai danser le mambo
  (Tonight I'm going to dance mambo)
Au Royal Casino sous les lambris rococo
  (At the Royal Casino under rococo lights)

La pluie viendra me faire oublier
  (Rain will come and have me forget)
Tu me feras rêver comme dans les chansons d'été
  (You'll make me dream as in summer songs)

C'est l'amour à la plage (ah-ouh cha-cha-cha)
  (It's love on the beach)

Et mes yeux dans tes yeux (ah-ouh ah-ouh)
  (And my eyes into yours)
Baisers et coquillages (ah-ouh cha-cha-cha)
  (Kisses and seashells)
Entre toi et l'eau bleue (ah-ouh ah-ouh)
  (Between you and the ocean blue)

1986's LP *Encore Un Dernier Baiser* was filled to the brim with catchy pop songs, though hindered in its clinical production, contrary to 1988's *Quel Enfer!*, which was much more rocking, and showed in-depth thinking about the state of the world around them. Though Muriel was still the sexy French Barbarella she had always appeared to be on TV shows, the lyrics reflected this new maturity of theirs, and the production values were miles apart from their beginnings. Pessimistic singles "Flammes de l'Enfer," "Assez!," and "Soleil d'Hiver" all climbed up the charts, but it was "J'Ai Vu," an apocalyptic song about war, that said it the best:

J'ai vu Berlin, Bucarest et Pékin comme si j'y étais
  (I saw Berlin, Bucharest, and Beijing as if I were there)
Matin et soir le nez dans la télé, c'est encore plus vrai
  (From morning 'til the evening in front of my TV, it's truer than true)
J'étais de tous les combats, collée devant l'écran
  (I was into all the fights, just in front of my screen)
À la fois à Soweto, en Chine et au Liban
  (At the same time in Soweto, China, or Lebanon)

*Lancer des pierres au bord de Gaza, je ne
regrette pas*
  (Throwing stones in Gaza I don't regret)
*Des religieux, au nom de leur foi, m'ont lancé
une fatwa*
  *(Religious people have started a fatwa
  against me because of their faith)*

*J'ai vu la guerre, la victoire était au bout de
leur fusils*
  (I saw war, victory depended on their guns)
*J'ai vu le sang sur ma peau, j'ai vu la fureur et
les cris*
  *(I saw blood on my skin, I saw fury
  and screams)*
*Et j'ai prié, j'ai prié tous ceux qui se
sont sacrifiés*
  *(And I prayed, yes I prayed for all those who
  sacrified themselves)*
*J'ai vu la mort se marrer et ramasser ceux
qui restaient*
  *(I saw death have a laugh and pick up the
  ones who had stayed)*
Et j'ai vu...
  (And I saw...)

When *La Vérité* came out in 1992, the couple had separated, but the fans were still there: it was a gold record, despite its darker and darker atmosphere. The single "Un Million d'Années" sold immensely well, and concerts were packed. But the duo split for good the following year, Muriel turning to electro and Daniel to film scores.

Mikado/Pascale Borel

Pascale Borel would be Edwige Belmore's antithesis: her personality and style were indeed much warmer. As Mikado, she and percussionist-keyboard player Gregory Czerkinsky released their first 45 in 1983, on Belgian label Les Disques du Crépuscule, created by Michel Duval and Annik Honoré (who was once Ian Curtis of Joy Division's lover). "Ce Garçon-Là" and "Par Hasard" established Mikado's style: kitsch, mockingly naive, with an on-edge sensitivity. In 1985, the band met stylist Fifi Chachnil and photographers Pierre & Gilles, who'd contribute to their image and help define the quintessence of 1980s pop (even on the commercial they did for La Sardine—whose visuals have been so influential since).

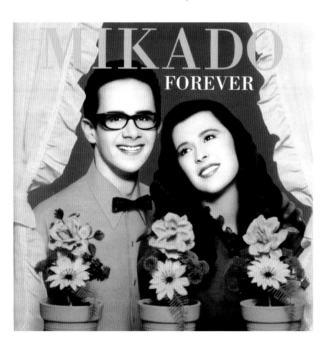

The same year, Vogue would put out their first album, with a cover of Gainsbourg-penned France Gall's "Attends Ou Vas-T'en" and originals with lyrics by Pascal Mounet, who would later write for April March and Burgalat. "Naufrage En Hiver" was a great single, with double-entendre lyrics and an era-defining music video:

Un jour d'hiver tu as décidé
(One winter day you decided)
De m'emmener dans une maison cachée
(To bring me to a hidden house)
Je ne voulais pas t'accompagner
(I didn't want to come along)
Au bord de cette mer enchantée
(To this enchanting sea)

Mais tu m'as dit que mes yeux brillaient
(But you told me my eyes were shining)
Juste comme deux belles pierres oubliées
(Just like two forgotten gems)
J'avais écrit ton nom sur le sable
(I had written your name on the sand)
Quand la mer a tout effacé
(When the sea erased it all)
J'ai roulé dans tes doigts des colliers de varech
(I rolled in your fingers the kelp necklaces)
Où la nacre et le sel unissaient leur parfum
(In which mother-of-pearl and salt united
their scents)

J'ai surpris ton reflet changeant
(I saw your changing reflection)
Dans les lames de l'océan
(In the waves of the ocean)

Dans l'écho de ta voix sucrée
  (In the echo of your sugary voice)
J'ai bien cru que tout basculait
  (I thought everything was toppling over)
L'océan emporte ton nom
  (The ocean is taking your name away)
Au hasard des vents et marées
  (To winds and tide changes)
Dans les brumes de mes pensées
  (In the mist of my thoughts)

Ton beau visage s'est effacé
  (Your beautiful face has been erased)

Japan soon became a new homeland for Mikado: they did three tours there and sold by the ton. 1987's single *La Fille Du Soleil* (on CBS) was a last shot at fame before Pascale and Gregory went their separate ways. Borel collaborated with Etienne Charry (Oui Oui), Louis Philippe, and Towa Teï (ex-Deee-Lite). Then in 2001, she met Jérémie Lefebvre, which led to "Oserai-Je T'aimer" four years later. Mikado's style had evolved into a more mature product, with less pastiche. The song "Alicante" was a gem of sensual groovy pop, as was a cover of Madonna's "Into the Groove." In 2008, Pascale duetted with artist Valérie Lemercier on the charming "J'ai Un Mari," and got a few TV spots to promote the song. 2012's *Moyennement Amoureuse* album sounds like her best work so far: political sharpness, psychological accuracy, and humor are her best assets.

Elli & Jacno/Elli Medeiros

Born in 1956 in Montevideo, Uruguay, Elli Medeiros came to France when she was fourteen. Still in high school, she met Denis "Jacno," who was just doing nothing at all, with great nonchalance and style, not too confident in the nascent punk nor the fading hippie dream—he was simply a sort of aristocratic iconoclast and a dandy, at a very early age. In 1976, the Stinky Toys played punkish music but proclaimed their love of France Gall and Françoise Hardy—not exactly a sign of rock credibility. Invited by the Pistols manager Malcolm McLaren to play the 100 Club in London, they made an impression with their looks and attitude and were put on the front page of *Melody Maker*, a totally unheard-of privilege for a foreign band. But Jacno wasn't that impressed: he called the Pistols "a boy's band"!

The Toys released two LPs before Elli and Jacno split the band to start a duo (Jacno had scored a

Elli Medeiros

massive solo hit with the Kraftwerk-meets-yé-yé instrumental "Rectangle". Elli & Jacno were an enchanted parenthesis in French pop and rock: the marriage between the melancholy, sometimes gritty lyrics of the singer and the minimalistic, synthetic tunes of her partner was made in heaven. Journalist Yves Adrien would write:

Elli was criminally gorgeous, perfecting her dance moves in trendy Prince of Wales clothes on the Wednesday afternoon music video show Platine 45: *emotions, only emotions, et moi, émoi!*

Elli saved the French pop of the 1980s from mediocrity and easy recipes. At a time when the term "postmodern" hadn't been invented, she created a whole universe, drawing from the Atomic Style of Hergé or *Spirou* as well as a futuristic dreamland. She was young and proud to be alive, as demonstrated during parties at the Rose Bonbon or the Palace, in interviews with *Façade* magazine (illustrated by graphic designers Bazooka), or later when she and Jacno scored the soundtrack to Eric Rohmer's *Full Moon in Paris*. The duo split when the couple became estranged, which was echoed in some of their songs:

Je regarde tes yeux ça me fait pleurer
    *(I'm looking at your eyes and it makes
    me cry)*
Ne fais pas cette tête, je ne veux pas te blesser
    *(Don't make such a face, I don't want to hurt
    you)*
Je t'aime tant je t'aime tant
    (I love you so much, I love you so much)

Aujourd'hui je pars je reviendrai demain
    (Today I'm leaving, I'll be back tomorrow)
C'est pas toi et moi, toi et moi ça ne fait qu'un
    *(It's not you and me, you and me are
    only one)*
Je t'aime tant je t'aime tant
    (I love you so much, I love you so much)

Dès que je ne suis plus là
    (As soon as I'm not there anymore)
Tu dis elle ne m'aime pas
    (You say "she doesn't love me")
Ouvre les yeux regarde-moi
    (Open your eyes, look at me)
Ma vie serait vide sans toi
    (My life would be empty without you)

Nos erreurs appartiennent au passé
    (Our mistakes belong to the past)
Elles sont rayées annulées oubliées
    (They are crossed, called off, forgotten)
Je t'aime tant je t'aime tant
    (I love you so much, I love you so much)

Les choses trop belles doivent être préservées
    *(Things that are too beautiful shall be
    preserved)*
Si c'est cassé nous allons réparer
    (If it's broken, we're going to mend it)
Je t'aime tant je t'aime tant
    (I love you so much, I love you so much)

In 1980, Lio recorded "Amoureux Solitaires," an electro-pop remake of the Stinky Toys' "Lonely Lovers." Jacques Duvall actually rewrote the lyrics, considerably improving on them—but Elli got the copyright, which was a bit of a shame, to be honest.

Eh toi dis-moi que tu m'aimes
   (Hey you, tell me you love me)
Même si c'est un mensonge et qu'on n'a pas une chance
   (Even if it's a lie and we don't stand a chance)
La vie est si triste, dis-moi que tu m'aimes
   (Life is so sad, tell me you love me)
Tous les jours sont les mêmes, j'ai besoin de romance
   (Everyday looks the same, I need romance)

Un peu de beauté plastique pour effacer nos cernes
   (A little plastic beauty to erase the bags under our eyes)
De plaisir chimique pour nos cerveaux trop ternes
   (Some chemical pleasure for our dull brains)
Que nos vies aient l'air d'un film parfait
   (Let our lives look like a perfect film)
Eh toi dis-moi que tu m'aimes
   (Hey you, tell me you love me)
Même si c'est un mensonge puisque je sais que tu mens
   (Even if it's a lie, since I know you're lying to me)
La vie est si triste, dis-moi que tu m'aimes
   (Life is so sad, tell me you love me)

Oublions tout, nous-mêmes, ce que nous sommes vraiment
   (Let's forget everything, ourselves, what we really are)

On May 5, 1987, television show *Les Enfants Du Rock* featured a long segment on Elli Medeiros, in the wake of her "Toi, Toi, Mon Toi" hit song, written by her new partner Ramuntcho Matta, which sounded much more Latin-flavored than her work with Jacno. One year before, actress Pauline Lafont (daughter of Bernadette Lafont, one of the Nouvelle Vague icons, and Jacno's new girlfriend) had covered Elli & Jacno's "Oh, La, La." Elli demonstrated how multitalented she was (discussing her roles as a singer, songwriter, and stylist), while Jacno told journalist Alain Maneval that he and Elli "had met when smashing up shop windows during students riots," and how regrettable it was (for him? her?) that she was now doing things on her own.

The year after the story appeared, Elli released another LP, before a fifteen-year hiatus that ended with 2006's *EM*, produced by Etienne Daho. She had focused on an acting career, her best move being playing in Olivier Assayas' *Fin Août, Début Septembre* in 1988. People who read gossip magazines know she also became Brian de Palma's lover, and got involved in *Femme Fatale*.

April March

- Chick Habit
- Laisse Tomber Les Filles
- Tu Mens
- Le Temps De L'Amour
- La Chanson De Prévert
- + bonus tracks

15
MODERN DAYS

FROM THE SECOND HALF OF THE 1990S UNTIL today, a whole new generation of *filles de la pop* has emerged. The break with the past has a name: globalization. The exchanges have become numerous, singing in a foreign language seems natural, and crossing the Atlantic to collaborate with different artists is easier and easier. New links with the past have been discovered and new alliances founded. Girls don't need Pygmalions anymore, which doesn't prevent them from having references and influences, if not mentors.

But a majority of female singers are now songwriters who are able to depict their own universe and feelings. More and more, they also come from varied backgrounds: comedy and the cinema (Valérie Lemercier), design and graphic arts (April March), fashion (Fifi Chachnil), modeling and television (Helena Noguerra). Keen to pay a deserved tribute to their comrades from the past, they are determined to have their say, here and now, and that's the main reason why we have loved (and still love) them so much.

April March

April March is a multifaceted diamond who, like a cat, must have already lived several lives. A graphic designer who studied at the prestigious CalArts school, she worked for Pee Wee Herman, Spümcø (*Ren & Stimpy*), Madonna (the credits of the *Who's That Girl* film), Archie Comics, Steve Ditko (Spiderman), and even the mythical Harry Smith. She was a member of girl group the Pussywillows (Ronnie

Spector was a huge fan), then turned punk with the Shitbirds, and sang songs for animated cartoons. A Francophile from an early age, she enabled a wide, international audience to at long last discover Gainsbourg, Hardy, Stella, Dani, Pilzer, and countless others. Bertrand Burgalat became her French Phil Spector (as talented, though less interested in guns).

It's no wonder April was noticed by Quentin Tarantino (remember "Chick Habit" in *Death Proof*), Brian Wilson, Jonathan Richman, Los Cincos, Steve Hanft, or the Dust Brothers. Now, after a stint with

© Isabel Asha Penzlein

filmmaker Marie Losier, March is going back to her experimental roots, working with Aquaserge. More eccentric than Lady Gaga, way cooler than Katy Perry, it's up to you to discover her.

What was your first musical revelation? Your pop epiphany, so to speak?

I had a reel-to-reel tape recorder when I was four or five. I noticed that when I sang into it, it seemed like it recorded the room and my dolls and [my] stuffed animals extra in my voice that I didn't hear in my head, so it was a bit like having a mirror sing to me, which I found very funny and comforting at the same time. The first pop song that excited me was hearing "Porque Te Vas" when I was eight or nine in the movie theater.

What makes '60s French girls in pop so different from their U.S. counterparts?

Who knows, maybe their bras are tighter?

As compared to the USA, what do you think of the status of women in the French music industry?

I don't know anything about the French or the U.S. music industry, to be honest. It's a great big black hole to me.

Some people say one shouldn't meet their heroes. What was your reaction when you finally met some of yours?

Some were super, and some were witchy.

Tell us about your collaboration with Bertrand Burgalat: what did you learn from him?

I keep learning every time I work with him.

It seems that your meeting, subsequent friendship and artistic collaboration with Marie Losier brought to light another side of your personality: more people will be aware of your links to experimental arts. Like other women in pop before, do you think that people are inclined to put artists in "little boxes"?

Yes, if they're not very intelligent, but I wouldn't generalize.

Tell me about your fine arts heroes and models.

I like Francis Alys, Alain Cavalier, Werner Herzog, Chong Gon Byun.

What did your collaboration with Julien Gasc and Aquaserge bring to the April March "sound," and more generally, craft?

I don't analyze what I do so I can't really say. I think it just brought another album that I can be proud of. I always pick people to work with that I feel like I can stretch with. After I've made my choice, I let go of the result.

Some time ago the Time *magazine headlines were about the "death of French culture" and the end of France as an important creative nation. What is your opinion on this debate?*

That seems like headline idiocy to me. I don't believe in creative national identities. There are important artists everywhere. "Headlines shmeadlines," as we say here in April March land!

What do you like (and why) about French modern culture? Some of your fellow countrymen and women seem to only quote '60s creations (like Godard, Gainsbourg, Brigitte Bardot). They were very important, but this attitude seems to hide the current creative forces, and say to us "this was your heyday, now your time is gone!" I 'd love to know what your view is on these transatlantic relations!

Well, I think the fact that I remain interested in working with primarily French artists who are all alive and well kind of says it all. It does seem that the French have become more self-deprecating regarding their culture lately, as opposed to pedantic. I think it's best to just not be so defensive artistically, that's a recipe for disaster, in fact, in all areas of life.

What do you think of French politics as compared to the U.S. politics?

I see very little difference, frankly. The socialist structure in France seems more and more like a hoax to me.

Helena Noguerra

Even though her first single as LNA, "Lunettes Noires," was "imposed on her" as she now says, it was nevertheless a true cornerstone of French pop—magnified by its Pierre et Gilles video—and a sign that a great singer was born. Helena Noguerra has confirmed these promises since then, with the single "Rivière Des Anges" (1992) and her work in numerous projects, such as the group Ollano in 1996, and Olivier Libaux's albums *L'héroïne Au Bain* in 2003 and *Imbécile* in 2007. Of course, she has also released five solo albums, which should all be on top of your buying list: the cinematographic *Projet: Bikini* (1999), bossa nova *Azul* (2001), introspective *Née Dans La Nature* (2004), postmodern country-rock *Dillinger Girl & Baby Face Nelson* with Federico Pellegrini, and a Serge Rezvani's cover songbook, *Fraise Vanille* (2007). Helena has also published novels and is a successful actress, having played in many comedies—she's something like the daughter Peter Sellers and Raquel Welch never had.

Whether it's risky projects (Artus de Penguern's *La Clinique de L'Amour*) or more commercial films (*Heartbreaker*), Helena can play everything with disconcerting ease. She is also a director: *Peep Show Hero* in 2008 was strange avant-garde porn, while *Strip Burlesque: Ou La Philosophie du Corset* in 2011 was an impressive documentary about go-go dancers. She is a *fille de la pop* who has drawn from a vast field of European cultural horizons (including America: she's about to take part in the Joe Dante-produced *Theatre of Bizarre 2*).

In April 2013, Helena went one step further by writing her own songs for her new album *Année Zero*. The wondrous artist decided to reinterpret herself and the result is one of the best *fille de la pop* albums I have ever heard. In *Année Zero* Helena brings along her sister Lio, her son (the talented musician Tanel), and the cult actress Anna Mouglalis (who played Juliette Greco in the recent Gainsbourg biopic). With this new

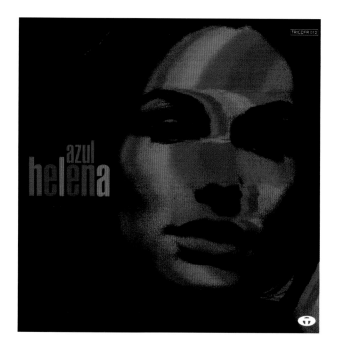

opus, Helena shows that she is a modern woman, with her doubts but also with an incredible will to bring happiness to the world. It's like she has learnt from all the previous *filles de la pop*, not to copy them but to drive her ship in new directions. Evolution is the key word in this! *Année Zero* is also a direct link to Helena's life experience, showing she is no longer a teenager she was when she first started but an accomplished artist. Last but not least, the little films she directed are the proof that the modern spiritual daughter of Jean-Luc Godard is very much well and alive and living in Paris.

Who were your chanson and pop icons?

Blondie, in the first place: I liked Debbie's energy, voice, blending of sounds. I thought she was beautiful. France Gall and her sugary songs too, her sweet high-pitched voice, her looks in the '60s. Bardot as a singer: her voice sounded very peculiar, very free.

How do you consider LNA and Lunettes Noires in retrospect?

I didn't know what I was doing. I wanted to become an actress, but my sister Lio and Michel Esteban, her companion at the time, thought I sang well and wanted me to record something. So here goes…I was eighteen, a model, waiting for parts in films, getting none, so it was pure entertainment for me to be a recording artist. I had no idea what would follow.

Who have been the most important people you have met in your different careers?

People crazy enough to believe in me. Bertrand Burgalat, who signed me on Tricatel for my second album. Daniel Richard at Universal Jazz who did the same for *Dillinger Girl*. Dominique Farrugia, who forced me to write for the theatre with Barbara Dalessandri. Olivier Rubinstein and Florence Robert at Denoel who liked my novels and published them. And so on…all the people who gave me self-confidence, actually: Anna da Palma, who I made two films with, Federico Pellegrini who helped me feel free when singing, Serge Rezvani, a master in freedom of the mind, precisely. Katerine, of course—another free individual.

Would you say the status of women has evolved in the world of entertainment? How?

Girls have had their chance since the 1960s: they have turned from mere objects to real subjects. I don't feel there's that much male chauvinism any longer, even though it's still difficult for aging women at the cinema. More than for a singer: Patti Smith *et al.* still produce good records and [have] success.

Would you like to do everything yourself on a whole album: writing, singing, producing—just like Carole King or Kate Bush?

No, I don't need to control everything, I like to have collaborators, to be confronted [by] other people's problems. They give me fresh air. This is why I like concerts so much: this communication with the musicians. Doing everything on my own would be like wanting to be the master of the universe—not my thing.

Any anecdotes about touring the USA with Nouvelle Vague?

I'm useless for anecdotes. All I can say is it was a

great tour, a joyful dream come true: packed venues, enthusiastic audiences, mythical places. My best traveling experience ever. And the most formative one. As a singer within a band, my persona as LNA had vanished—and a certain shyness too. I had the others call me Martine, I was very at ease on stage, dancing, telling jokes, having simple fun.

Stereo Total/ Françoise Cactus

Stereo Total was born following the meeting in Berlin of German boy Brezel Göring and French girl Françoise Cactus, formerly a punky Lolita for the 1980s. She drew inspiration from older models of *filles de la pop*, with a good dose of derision and a love of blending antagonistic tastes: disco, punk, garage rock, power pop, the yé-yé sound, and electro. A total postmodernist in that way, Cactus has sung in French, German, Japanese, Turkish…and English, of course!

On her first album *Oh Ah!*, released in 1995, she paid tribute, playing with the rough sounds of her suburban accent, to Vartan's "Comme Un Garçon" and Bardot's "Moi Je Joue," not forgetting the odd Gainsbourg or Johnny Hallyday cover. The originals she had written with her partner, such as "Miau, Miau" or "Morose," didn't spoil that long, glorious tradition. *Monokini* (1997), *Juke Box Alarm* (1998), and *My Melody* (1999) carried on with an exploration of the European patrimony, while "L'Amour," an extract from the *Musique Automatique* LP in 2001, had them reach a much wider audience in unlikely places such

as Sweden or Argentina, thanks to its inclusion on the soundtrack of a commercial. The song was a direct reference to Ann Sorel's *L'Amour À Plusieurs*, itself released in 1973:

Moi ce que j'aime
　(Me, what I like)
C'est faire l'amour
　(Is making love)

Spécialement à trois
　(Especially a threesome)
Je sais c'est démodé
　(I know it's old-fashioned)
Ça fait hippie complet
　(It sounds so hippie-ish)
Mais je le crie sur les toits
　(But I like to say it aloud)
J'aime l'amour à trois
　(I like a threesome)

Moi ce que j'adore
　(What I enjoy most)
C'est les petites
　(Are little)
Caresses à 4 mains
　(Caresses with four hands)
Si l'un des 2 s'endort
　(If one of them falls asleep)
L'autre s'occupe de moi
　(The other one takes care of me)
Ouh! voila l'amour à trois
　(Ooh, here's a threesome!)

Oooouuuh, j'aime l'amour à trois
　(Ooooooohhhhh, I like a threesome)

In 2005, Françoise Cactus collaborated with Jacno on her "Do The Bambi" and his "Tant De Temps," for the single "Mars Rendez-Vous," a song with tones of desperate romanticism bathed in electronics. The osmosis between the "pop dandy" and the Berlin duet was only natural, all of them being (grand-) children of the 1960s French sound.

Stereo Total continued with *Paris-Berlin* in 2007, *No Controles* in 2009, and *Baby Ouh!* in 2010. Françoise Cactus is a kind of Stella 2.0, and her *Cactus Vs. Brezel*, due for release on American label Kill Rock Stars, is eagerly awaited.

© P. Schyns – Sofam

Bertrand Burgalat

The head of Tricatel (the best of the current French labels), Bertrand Burgalat is a talented songwriter, musician, singer, producer, and arranger—as well as a ladies' man. By that I mean that he has continued to help women release records and have a go in the music business: April March's *Chrominance Decoder* (1999) and *Triggers* (2003) are two of the most convincing examples, both in a retro-futuristic way, paying tribute to glories from the past while offering suggestions for modern pop. Valérie Lemercier, Helena Noguerra, and Natacha Lejeune (from AS Dragon) are also worth noticing, and now there are Showgirls, a house music-meets-pop band with gorgeous Estelle Chardac as a frontwoman, and La Classe, a jazz-pop sensation whose Paulette is an exuberant leader.

Which female pop icons were the most outstanding as you grew up?

Stella and Chantal Goya. Christine Pilzer and Jacqueline Taïeb too, for the quality and sharpness of their words. Obviously Françoise Hardy, for everything she did. Mireille Darc for the song "Hélicoptère." Nancy Holloway for "Hurt So Bad" and "Sand & Rain." Martine Clémenceau for "Tu Viendras Mon Amour." Lio. Mylène Farmer's first two singles, noticeably "On Est Tous Des Imbéciles." Corynne Charby. And Amanda Lear.

What have the singers you worked with brought to you, both personally and on an artistic level?

I had been so traumatized by all these "full-lung" singers of the 1990s that I kept looking for counterparts. That's why most of the women I worked with weren't actually considering themselves singers. I was very much influenced by labels such as ZTT and él Records, and bands like the Would Be Goods or Bad Dream Fancy Dress, who insisted on the "microphone always just noticed us by pure chance" side of things.

What are the records you're the most proud of?

Triggers, because I was trying at the time to have April March move away from her 1960s influences and adopt a more futuristic approach. I think I went as far as I could in that direction. She'd like us to record another album now, but I can't really see the point, insofar as the LP flopped. Why bother to re-do one when no one cared about the first?

Was Serge Gainsbourg too much of an influence on generations of songwriters and producers acting like Pygmalions with their Galatée singers?

He favored the charm and personality of his singers, and rightfully so. Bardot was often laughed at, but she was a very good singer, just like Birkin in her own, particular style. The same songs sung by other women would have been boring.

How would you explain this new trend and taste for Gallic female singers, especially for the ones who worked with him then?

Conformity and nonconformity keep replacing one another. There's been a tendency to like all things Gainsbourg for some years now. As for me, I'm not cool enough to decide what is cool or is not.

Would you establish a parallel between the evolution of filles de la pop *and the status of women in everyday life?*

Female singers are in no way different from the rest of the population. Today the luxury industry is manufacturing creatures who slavishly copy the icons from the past. It's just the usual phony rock 'n' roll circus.

Can you imagine what the new French woman pop icon would be like—whether she's working for Tricatel or not?

I've always wanted to focus on original people who didn't fit, and that led to us at the label being broke. Since the early 1990s and the success of Britpop, the media and the bands have tried to hide their real influences, which is the best way to never get rid of them. I know it's pretty smart now to sneer at Lana Del Rey, but to me, "Video Games" was very good. When I wrote "The Life Of The Party" for April March twelve years ago, it was akin to this, though in a more tortuous way.

Which female artist would you like to work with—or would have liked to?

Mina.

Mareva Galenter

Mareva Galenter is a Tahitian girl who became a star in France when she won the Miss France title of 1999. Shepherded through French society by designer boyfriend Jean-Charles de Castelbajac, Mareva became associated with pop culture, recording the album *Ukuyéyé* in 2006, in which she covers yé-yé classics such as Jacqueline Taïeb's "7 Heure du Matin," Anna Karina's "Ne Dit Rien," Stella's & Nino Ferrer's "Les Cornichons," (and like April March), sings France Gall's "Laisse Tomber Les Filles." In her videos, Galenter resembles the actress Jessica Paré, who sung the Gillian Hills' classic, "Zou Bisou Bisou," on the popular TV program *Mad Men*.

CONCLUSION

I HOPE THIS BOOK HAS BEEN INFORMATIVE IN showing that beyond Françoise Hardy and Sylvie Vartan, the concept of French *filles de la pop* has existed across time and space, continents and eras. Behind the songs, behind the human adventures and the evolution of the condition of women, there lies what Guy Debord called the "the society of the spectacle": a society where everything and everybody are for sale, and the life of modern French pop girls is even more available for everybody to scrutinize. Our post-reality TV world was predicted by Debord decades ago.

There doesn't seem to be any specifically French approach to female pop music nowadays, due to increased globalization, with Japanese girls able to collect the latest item in Lady Gaga's huge catalogue of by-products, or taste a savory French baguette freshly imported from a trendy Parisian bakery. Well, that's only partially true: some modern French artists, like Helena Noguerra, Fifi Chachnil, Barbara Carlotti, and Lio—regardless of their international appeal—have a unique charm, sophistication, and intelligence that can't be reproduced in a Chinese factory.

As a man living very near Paris myself, I sometimes need to stand back and adopt the views of a complete foreigner. Why? Because, like the man living next to Notre Dame or the Eiffel Tower, I don't want to forget how lucky I am to live around such world-class marvels. I hope I have transmitted my virus to you, and all together we will shout: *vive les filles*, and long live *la* French pop!

SELECT DISCOGRAPHY

Sixties/Seventies

Françoise Hardy
1962: *Tous Les Garçons Et Les Filles*
1963: *Le Premier Bonheur Du Jour*
1964: *Mon Amie La Rose*
1965: *L'amitié*
1966: *Françoise Hardy In English*
      La Maison Où J'ai Grandi
1967: *Ma Jeunesse Fout Le Camp…*
1968: *Comment Te Dire Adieu?*
1969: *En Anglais*
      (All on Vogue)
1970: *Soleil*
1971: *La Question*
1972: *Et Si Je M'en Vais Avant Toi*
      (All on Sonopresse)
      If You Listen (Kundalini)
1973: *Message Personnel* (WEA)

France Gall
1964: *N'écoute Pas Les Idoles*
      Mes Premières Vraies Vacances
      Sacré Charlemagne
1965: *Poupée de Cire, Poupée de Son*
1966: *Baby Pop*
      Les Sucettes
1968: *1968*
      (All on Philips)
1974: *France Gall*—an eponymous compilation of thirteen of the sixteen tracks she recorded for the indie label La Compagnie between 1969 and 1972
2012: *Made in France: France Gall's Baby Pop* (RPM/Cherry Red British compilation)

Sylvie Vartan
1962: *Sylvie*
1963: *Twiste et Chante*
1964: *A Nashville*
1965: *A Gift Wrapped From Paris*
1966: *Il Y A Deux Filles En Moi*
1967: *2'35 de bonheur*
1967: *Comme un Garçon*
1968: *La Maritza*
      (all on RCA Victor)

Jane Birkin
1969: *Jane Birkin–Serge Gainsbourg* (Mercury)
1973: *Di Doo Dah*
1975: *Lolita Go Home*
1976: *Ballade de Johnny Jane*
1977: *Yesterday Yes a Day*
1978: *Ex-Fan des Sixties*
      (All on Philips)

Brigitte Bardot
1968: *Bonnie and Clyde* (Fontana)
      Brigitte Bardot Show (AZ)

Jacqueline Taïeb
2008: *The Complete Masterworks of the French Mademoiselle* (Anthology)

Stella
2008: *Un Air de Folklore Auvergnat* (Magic Records)

Gillian Hills
2002: *Twistin' the Rock* (Barclay)

Pussy Cat
2010: *L'intégrale Sixties* (Magic Records)

Sandie Shaw
2008: *Pourvu que ça dure Chante en Français* (EMI)

Petula Clark
2010: *Une Baladine (Best of)* (Strategic Marketing)

Jeanette
1976: *Porque te Vas* (Hispavox)

Dani
1993: *N comme Never Again* (WEA)
2002: *Best of Boomerang* (EMI)
2003: *Tout Dépend du Contexte* (Trema)
2006: *L'intégrale 66-73* (Magic Records)
2009: *Laissez Moi Rire* (AZ)
2010: *Le Paris de Dani* (AZ)

Zouzou
2003: *L'intégrale* (Vogue/BMG)

Annie Philippe
2006: *L'intégrale Sixties* (Magic Records)

Véronique Sanson
1972: *Amoureuse* (Warner)

Brigitte Fontaine
1968: *Brigitte Fontaine est Folle* (Saravah)

Compilations

Beginner's Guide to French Pop
Not girls-only, but this three-CD compilation by the French DJ Kid Loco has great tracks by Alice Dona, Michèle Arnaud (with Serge Gainsbourg), Dani, Jacqueline Taïeb, Christie Laume, Charlotte Walters, and Véronique Sanson (Nascente)

C'est Chic! French Girl Singers of the 1960s
Featuring France Gall, Jacqueline Taïeb, Les Gam's, Françoise Hardy, Anna Karina, Liz Brady and Michèle Torr (Ace Records)

Femmes de Paris
Three volumes with Marie Laforêt, Ici Paris, Françoise, Eileen, Christie Laume (FGL Anthology)

French Cuts
Three volumes. Not limited to girls, featuring France Gall, Dani, Anna Karina, Brigitte Bardot, Gillian Hills, Charlotte Leslie, Jacqueline Taïeb, Stella, Delphine, Clothilde (Panatomic)

Girls in the Garage
Great vinyl compilation with Liz Brady, Stella, Caroline, Annie Philippe, Christine Pilzer (Romulan Records)

Girls in the Garage Volume 2
A great vinyl comp featuring Charlotte Walters, Annie Markan, Clothilde, Caroline (Saperlipopette Records)

La Belle Époque
EMI's French girls 1965-1968, featuring Michèle Arnaud, Ria Bartok, Alice Dona, Liz Brady, Christie Laume (EMI-Zonophone)

Pop à Paris

Five volumes. Not limited to girls, featuring France Gall, Elsa, Marie Laforêt, Stone, Anna Karina, Brigitte Bardot, Virgine, Catherine Desmarets, Violaine, Vetty, Anna St Clair, Valérie Lagrange, Chantal Kelly, Delphine, and Jacqueline Taïeb (Universal)

Sixties Girls

Five volumes with Christine Pilzer, Clothilde, Cléo, Zouzou, Liz Brady, Les Petites Souris, Elsa Leroy, Vetty, etc. (Magic Records)

Swinging Mademoiselle

Two volumes with Stella, Jacqueline Taïeb, Elizabeth, Petula Clark, Cosette, Christine Delaroche (Silva Screen)

Tres Chic! More French Girl Singers of the 1960s

Follow up to C'est Chic. Featuring Annie Philippe, Elsa, Gillian Hills, Brigitte Bardot and Liz Brady (Ace Records)

Ultra Chicks

Six volumes with Delphine, Natacha Snitkine, Minouche Barelli, Liz Brady, France Gall, Monique Thubert (hard-to-find bootleg)

Wizzz

Not girls-only, but Volume One includes Charlotte Leslie, Christie Laume, Monique Thubert, Christine Pilzer (Born Bad)

¡Chicas! Spanish Female Singers 1962–1974

Featuring Margarita Sierra, Pili Y Mili, Los Stop and Ellas (Vampi Soul)

Beat Fräuleins: Female Pop In Germany 1964–1968

Featuring Brigitt, Joy & The Hit Kids and Marion (Grosse Freiheit)

Eighties-Today

Lio

1980: *Lio*
1982: *Suite Sixtine*
1983: *Amour Toujours*
1986: *Pop Model*
1988: *Cancan*
1991: *Des Fleurs Pour Un Caméléon*
1996: *Wandatta*
　　(All reissued by ZE Records)
2000: *Chante Prévert* (M 10)
2003: *Cœur de Rubis* (live recordings of Prévert songs) (Beluga)
2006: *Dites au Prince Charmant* (Recall Records)
2009: *Phantom Featuring Lio* (Freaksville)

Marie France

1981: *39° de Fièvre* (RCA, then Anthology)
1997: *Marie France* (Last Call)
2006: *Raretés* (Edina Music/Nocturne)
2008: *Phantom featuring Marie France* (Freaksville)
2009: *Marie France Visite Bardot* (JPB Productions)
2011: *Marie France et les Fantomes: Kiss* (Freaksville)

Niagara

1986: *Encore un Dernier Baiser*
1988: *Quel Enfer*
1990: *Religion*
1992: *La Vérité*
　　(All reissued in 2010 by Polydor/Universal)

Mikado
1985: *Mikado* (Disques Vogue)
1987: "Le Fille Du Soleil" (Epic)
1998: *Mikado Forever* (Village Vert)
2005: *Oserai-je t'aimer* (Pschent)
2012: *Moyennement Amoureuse* (PB Records)

Valérie Lemercier
1996: *Chante* (Tricatel)

April March
1995: *Gainsbourgsion!* (Euro Visions)
        Chick Habit
1996: *Paris in April*
1997: *April March Sings Along with the Makers*
1998: *April March and Los Cincos*
        (Sympathy for the Record Industry)
1999: *Chrominance Decoder*
2003: *Triggers* (Tricatel)
2008: *Magic Monsters* (with Steve Hanft)
        (Martyrs of Pop)

Stereo Total
1995: *Oh Ah!*
1997: *Monokini*
1998: *Juke-Box Alarm*
1999: *My Melody*
2001: *Musique Automatique*
2005: *Do the Bambi!*
2007: *Paris-Berlin*
2010: *Baby Ouh!*
        (Most of Stereo Total's records have been
        reissued by Kill Rock Stars)
2012: *Cactus Vs. Brezel* (Staatsakt/Rough Trade)

BIBLIOGRAPHY

Magazines

Rock & Folk, Salut Les Copains, Mademoiselle Age Tendre, Formidable, Superpop Hebdo, Jukebox, and many others

Books

Daho, Etienne and Jérome Soligny. *Françoise Hardy/Superstar et Ermite.* Editions Jacques Grancher. 1986.

De Jocelyn, Noblet. *Special Pop.* Albin Michel. 1967.

Eclimont, Christian Louis. *Swinging Sixties Londres–Paris.* Flammarion. 2009.

Eudeline, Christian. *Anti-yéyé: Une Autre Histoire des Sixties.* Denoël. 2006.

Gauffre, Christian and Michel Brillé. *L'aventure Salut Les Copains.* Éditions Du Layeur. 2009.

Gaignault, Fabrice. *Égéries Sixties.* Fayard. 2006.

Goya, Chantal. *Des Poussières D'étoiles Dans les Yeux.* Flammarion. 2009.

Hardy, Françoise. *Le Désespoir des Singes et Autres Bagatelles.* Robert Laffont. 2008.

Hardy, Françoise. *Notes Secrètes: Francoise Hardy, Entretiens Avec Éric Dumont.* Albin Michel. 1991.

Lafosse Dauvergne, Geneviève. *Les Années Mlle Age Tendre.* Editions Du Layeur/Fondation Frank Ténot. 2010.

Lio. *Pop Model.* Flammarion/J'ai Lu Biographie. 2004.

Manœuvre, Philippe. *Philippe Manœuvre Présente: Rock Français, de Johnny à BB Brunes, 123 Albums Essentiels.* Hoëbeke. 2010.

Mikailoff, Pierre. *Jane Birkin: Citizen Jane.* Alphée Éditeur. 2010.

Mikailoff, Pierre. *Françoise Hardy: Tant De Belles Choses.* Éditions Alphée. 2009.

Noguerra, Helena. *Et Je Me Suis Mise À Table.* Denoël. 2004.

Noguerra, Helena. *L'ennemi Est À L'intérieur.* Denoël. 2002,

Peellaert, Guy. *The Adventures of Jodelle.* Reprinted & remastered by Fantagraphics for the first time in English in 2013.

Périer, Jean-Marie. *Françoise par Jean-Marie Périer,* Le Chêne. 2011.

Pozzuli, Alain. *Dictionnaire des Yéyés À L'usage des Fans.* Pygmalion. 2009.

Quillien, Christophe. *Nos Années 1959–1976.* Flammarion. 2009.

Rossat, Stephan. *Les Dinosaures du Rock,* Editions Mare Nostrum. 2004.

Vartan, Sylvie. *Entre L'ombre Et La Lumière.* XO Éditions. 2004.

Verlant, Gilles. *Gainsbourg: The Biography.* TamTam Books. 2012.

Zouzou. *Jusqu'à L'aube.* Flammarion. 2003.

ACKNOWLEDGMENTS

Dedicated to my sweet fairies: Helena, Fifi, Lio and Véronique!

And to my spiritual master: Jean-Pierre Dionnet and my great pal Bart Johnson!

Superthanx to Fred Fauré!

Thanks to:

Elinor Blake, Jacques Duvall, Christine Pilzer, Dani, Zouzou, Dominique Cozette, Jacqueline Taïeb, Stella Wander, Pussy Cat, Annie Philippe, Françoise Deldick, Laura Ulmer, Jil Caplan, Barbara Carlotti, Bertrand Burgalat, Filo, Jean-Louis Rancurel, François Carrière, Christian Eudeline, Clément Boulland, François (Fan de Marie France), Stéphane Loisy, Charles Berberian, Jean-Pierre Turmel, Sébastien Donati, Magali Aubert, Boyd Rice, Vincent & Anita (Walter Films) , Pierre Mikailoff, Txiki Margalef, Joëlle David, Michaël Cheron, Philippe Auclair, Jean-Marc Lederman, Bruce Marcus, Fred Somsen, Luis (Elefant), Marc (Wah Wah), Vincent Tornatore (Lion Productions), Zab & Guy Skornik, Rodolphe Lachat, Sandra Salazar, Maïven & Anne Bergeron, Mathieu Bournazel, Céline Lepage, Sandri Belmokthar, Nicolas Bellenchombre, Emma Lepers, Jean-Yves Guilleux, Patrick Fleouter, Magali Magne, Boris Bergman, Philippe Manœuvre, Marie-Agnès Hallé, Jampur Fraize, Nubia Esteban, Alix Heuer, Jacques Noël (un regard moderne), Maryline Robalo, Xavier Sanjuan, Thomas Cazals, Marie-Laure Dagoit, Coco Quefelec, Antoine Boyer, Médéric Gontier, Christophe Guillot, Eric Parent, Bernard Bacos, Arnaud Viviant, Christophe Conte, Benoit Sabatier, Emmanuel Dechancé, Cyrille Dautel, Hélène Pince, Jacky, Luis Régo, Boris Sagit, Gallien Guibert, Jon "Mojo" (Shindig), John Rovnak (Panel to Panel), Philippe Mignot, Jean-Michel Mignot, Christophe Haag, Olivier Collet & Stéphanie, Olivier Pham Ngoc Thuan, Gaël Tynevez, Satanico Nico, Jean-Marc Delacruz, Laurence Lemaire, Pascal Julou, Kim Thompson (Fantagraphics), Jacquelene Cohen (Fantagraphics), Julien Taffoureau, Maud Garmy, Lou Transat, Nadine Marteleur…My sister, parents, and sorry for those I've forgotten but you know who you are!